Makiguchi and Gandhi

Their Educational Relevance for the 21st Century

Namrata Sharma

UNIVERSITY PRESS OF AMERICA, ® INC.
Lanham • Boulder • New York • Toronto • Plymouth, UK

Copyright © 2008 by
University Press of America,® Inc.
4501 Forbes Boulevard
Suite 200
Lanham, Maryland 20706
UPA Acquisitions Department (301) 459-3366

Estover Road
Plymouth PL6 7PY
United Kingdom

Library of Congress Control Number: 2008926997
ISBN-13: 978-0-7618-4068-8 (paperback : alk. paper)
ISBN-10: 0-7618-4068-0 (paperback : alk. paper)
eISBN-13: 978-0-7618-4208-8
eISBN-10: 0-7618-4208-X

To President Daisaku Ikeda for his 80 years of selfless dedication to the contribution of world peace, and to my parents for their 40 years of love to their family.

Contents

Preface

This book is the result of my engagement with the ideas and use of Makiguchi and Gandhi for more than a decade since 1995 as a Masters student in Soka University Tokyo, a researcher working with Dayle Bethel, and as a doctoral and post-doctoral fellow at the Institute of Education, University of London. Through these years I have had the opportunity to meet and work with several Soka and Gandhian educationists across the world.

The outcome of this journey is this present study of the ideas, use and relevance of these two Asian dissidents of the early twentieth century, who have been the founders of one of the largest mass movements of their respective countries: Tsunesaburo Makiguchi (1871–1944) of Japan, and his better known contemporary Mohandas Karamchand Gandhi, alias Mahatma Gandhi (1869–1948)[1] of India. Both thinkers had made contributions to their respective countries in different ways—Makiguchi through his educational theory and Gandhi through his socio-political movement. They both possessed the will to transform their own countries, and thereby antagonised the autocratic governments, which for Makiguchi was the Japanese totalitarian monarchy and for Gandhi this meant the British colonial power.

It should be stated at the offset that Makiguchi's ideas as compared to Gandhi, were not overtly concerned with politics but education, since he had spent most of his life as a school teacher and principal. On the other hand, although Gandhi is more famous as a political leader, he was also actively involved in educating the residents of his *ashrams* or communities, and in 1937 his ideas were formally considered by the Congress under the Wardha scheme of education.

Central to both thinkers' thought and action was their notion of values and their creative use of values within their educational and political contexts. Makiguchi's main educational work was published in 1930 under the title *Soka Kyoikugaku Taikei* or 'The System of Value Creating Education.' Meanwhile, central to Gandhi's socio-political struggle was the use of two concepts: *satya* (truth) and the value of *ahimsa* (non-violence).

In my previous work *Value Creators in Education* (Sharma 1999) I had compared the educational ideas and values of Makiguchi and Gandhi. One of my findings was that both thinkers had a common understanding of truth as *dharma* or the law of the universe. Makiguchi's understanding of truth was formed through his educational research as well as through his study and practice of Buddhism. Gandhi on the other hand was influenced by his Hindu and Jain religious background. Many Asian contemporaries of Gandhi, such as Rabindranath Tagore (1861–1941) and Sri Aurobindo (1872–1950) have also been influenced by this view of truth, although, the reason I compared my chosen thinkers was that their understanding of truth was pivotal to their concept of value. (I will elaborate upon this in chapter four of this book.)

Another contemporary who shared many commonalities with Makiguchi and Gandhi, was John Dewey. In a previous study (Sharma 2002), I had compared the 'holistic' views of all three thinkers—Makiguchi, Gandhi and Dewey, and contrasted it with the 'reductionist' Newtonian-Cartesian paradigm. I had suggested that all three thinkers who were placed in the early twentieth century context had similar ideas and proposals on learning for social participation. (I will revisit this in the concluding chapter of this book.) There is however no evidence that either one of these thinkers had met each other, although, Makiguchi has mentioned Dewey several times in his educational work (as will be stated in chapter three).

The reasons for my re-engagement with Makiguchi and Gandhi in this book are the result of the questions I had accumulated in the past few years through my successive visits to educational institutions related to these thinkers. I had found that although both the thinkers had experienced different fates, within the span of the twentieth century they both became leaders of the largest mass movements of their respective countries. Gandhi, in his own lifetime (by the mid-twentieth century) had established his position as the leader of the Indian National Congress and the *Mahatma* or moral leader of the Indian masses. Makiguchi, on the other hand became well known much after his death through the post-war reconstruction of his organisation, the *Soka Kyoiku Gakkai* (Value Creating Education Society) as the *Soka Gakkai* (Value Creating Society).

In the twenty-first century Japan, Makiguchi is seldom remembered as an educationist of the Meiji (1868–1912) and Taisho era (1912–1926), and is better known as the founder of the lay Buddhist organisation, the Soka Gakkai, a civic body that currently provides political endorsement to the Komeito party, which is part of the leading coalition with the Liberal Democratic Party (LDP). In recent years Makiguchi has gained international recognition through the Soka Gakkai's growth in 190 countries and territories across the world. The Soka Gakkai in Japan has around 8,210,000 households (setai) as members. The number of votes from Soka Gakkai and their supporters for Komeito is 8,980,000 votes (hyo). In October 2005, out of the total 418 seats, Komeito has secured 31 seats.[2]

Meanwhile, before and after his death, Gandhi as a political leader has inspired several national movements across the world to fight against oppressive regimes, starting from the anti-apartheid movement in the United States. Although in India, within decades of independence there were divisions among leading Gandhians. In the 1980s, as a youth growing up in India, for me Gandhi was a national figure who I had only briefly studied in the history textbooks as part of the 'national independence struggle.' On the other hand, during my study in Soka University in Tokyo (1995–1998), I could sense the growing power of the Soka Gakkai within Japan. By the 1990s the *Gakkai* had begun to receive extensive coverage by the media, and often this was in the form of 'yellow journalism' in newspapers, as well as fabricated stories which were printed in the underground tube stations.[3]

To compare, my observations showed that although Gandhi's ideas had heavily influenced Indian politics in his own time, it was apparent that soon after his death his influence began to steadily diminish. Whereas parallel to the decline in Gandhi's influence in Indian politics, Makiguchi's ideas were able to generate an impact within Japanese society and politics within decades of his death, through the activities of the Soka Gakkai and Komeito party.

At the same time, I found that there were noticeable influences of Gandhi on certain socio-political movements that had emerged after his death, both at home and abroad. However, I was uncertain whether these two thinkers had any specific influence within the education of their respective countries. To explain briefly, since 1996 I have made several visits to the Soka Schools in Tokyo and Kansai where I have conducted observational studies. These schools are private educational institutions that regard Makiguchi as their original founder. In my visits to these schools I began to question the influence of Makiguchi's ideas and values within these institutions. His influence was not immediately apparent within the school curriculum since the schools follow the national curriculum.

Parallel to this, my investigation into the educational ideas of Gandhi lead me to visit several Gandhian institutions in India. Here, as well my observations and interviews with Gandhians made me question the use and influence of Gandhi's ideas and values within these institutions. I was aware that in all the institutions that I had visited, there was a common focus on vocational activity and rural development, which were the key components of Gandhi's socio-political movement in the early twentieth century. However, I was left with the uncertainty that whereas the impetus given by Gandhi to vocational activities had generated a social and economic impact within his own time, there was no striking evidence of the fact that his ideas were being used in any significant way for today's context. My observations and questions related to the contemporary relevance of Makiguchi and Gandhi drew this study toward consideration of the use and influence of these thinkers within their respective national educational contexts.

A word must be added here on the critical study of Soka and Gandhian institutions within this book. This constructive criticism should by no means lessen the importance of the educational work being done by the successors of Makiguchi and Gandhi today. As emphasised in the conclusion chapter, the Soka and Gandhian institutions studied in this book are models for schools in the 21st century, in terms of the sense of mission and trust that is imparted to students to better their own lives as well as their community.

To acknowledge some of the many people who have supported this work. This study would not have been possible without the numerous rigorous discussions with Professor Jagdish Gundara and Mr. Robert Ferguson of the Institute of Education, University of London, who are undoubtedly amongst the outstanding intellectuals of our time.

Many thanks to the Soka Schools in Tokyo that I have often visited during the years 1996–1998 and 2002, especially to Mr. Harima and Mr. Mizuhata whose help and advice has been indispensable for my research on Makiguchi. Also, I am grateful to Dr. Akash Ouchi of the Bharat Soka Gakkai and Dr. N. Radhakrishnan of the Ikeda Centre for Value Creation for the data on the Gandhian institution studied in this book and for their belief in the potential of young people. Last but not the least my deepest gratitude to my parents and family for their unconditional encouragement and support.

NOTES

1. The title of 'Mahatma' or 'great soul' was given to M.K. Gandhi by the Indian poet Rabindranath Tagore.
2. Information obtained from Mr. Harima Hisao, Soka Gakkai, Tokyo, by email dated 6 October 2005.
3. Amongst others, the Japanese media has tried to emphasise the Soka Gakkai's vast financial resources, and political power. Such as, articles suggesting that money is coaxed or coerced out of members. Other articles stir up suspicion against the Soka Gakkai and its political links with the Komeito political party. As I will argue later in this study, there has been no evidence to suggest that the Soka Gakkai has gained in any direct way through the political endorsement it provides to the Komeito party. Further, as Watanabe's research shows, the speculative and baseless reports by the Japanese media have often been the result of the control exercised by 'competing religious and political groups' (Watanabe 2000: 225). Also see note 10 in chapter 5 of this book.

Glossary of Japanese Terms

Bakufu: shogunate.

Bushido: samurai code of chivalry.

Fukoku kyohe: enriching the country and strengthening the army, a slogan in the Mciji government.

Juku: a cram school, after-school private course.

Kami: a comprehensive term applicable to anything high or above oneself.

Komeito: a political party in Japan organised in 1964, part of the ruling coalition, political endorsement is provided by the Soka Gakkai.

Meiji era: the time period from 1868 until 1912 (named after Emperor Meiji).

Mombusho: Ministry of Education (now MEXT: Ministry of Education, Culture, Sports, Science and Technology).

Samurai: a warrior.

Sensei: teacher, mentor.

Shihan gakko: teacher's training school or institute.

Shinto: Japanese indigenous religion.

Soka: or 'value creation' is a neology formed by Josei Toda (1900–1958) to describe Makiguchi's educational pedagogy.

Soka Gakkai: or 'Value Creating Society' is a layman's organisation of the Nichiren Shoshu sect of Mahayana Buddhism. It is successor to the organisation established by Tsunesaburo Makiguchi in 1930 known as the 'Soka Kyoiku Gakkai' (Value Creating Education Society). Josei Toda reconstructed the organisation after the Second World War. Makiguchi is considered as the first president of the Soka Gakkai, Josei Toda was the second president, and Daisaku Ikeda is the third and current president.

Tenno: emperor.

Glossary of Indian
(Mostly Hindi or Sanskrit) Terms

Ahimsa: non-injury, non-violence, harmlessness; renunciation of the will to kill and the intention to hurt; abstention from any hostile thought, word, or act; non-coercion.

Ashram: a spiritual fellowship or community.

Atman: the universal self, soul.

Brahmachari: a follower of brahmacharya, an exemplar of chastity.

Brahmacharya: fidelity, chastity; the first of the four stages of life in Hinduism.

Charkha: spinning-wheel.

Dharma: duty, righteousness, moral law; social and personal morality; natural law, natural obligation.

Guru: teacher, spiritual preceptor and guide.

Harijan: literally 'people of God', a name Gandhi gave to the untouchables.

Himsa: injury; violence.

Khadi: hand-spun and hand-woven cloth.

Kurukshetra: scene of the great war described in the Hindu epic 'Mahabharata'.

Mahatma: great soul.

Manas: mind.

Maya: appearance or only relatively real.

Panchayat: five-member village council.

Panchayati Raj: rule by Panchayat.

Raj: kingdom, rule, regime.

Ramanama: chanting the name of God Rama.

Sarvodaya: universal welfare; social good, public interest.

Satya: truth; real, existent; valid; sincere, pure; effectual.

Satyagraha: non-violent resistance; a relentless search for truth; truth-force; holding on to truth. Also, the name of Gandhi's political movement.

Satyagrahi: one who offers *satyagraha.*

Shudra (sudra): servant or menial caste, the lowest of the four Hindu *varnas* or classes.

Swabhava: non-material personality.

Swadeshi: self-sufficiency; self-reliance; patriotism.

Swaraj: freedom; self-rule; political independence.

Varnashram(a): the organisation of society into four castes and four stages.

Vasudhaiva Kutumbakam: a Sanskrit phrase meaning: the entire world is my family.

Yajna: sacred sacrifice or offering in the spirit of surrender to God.

Chapter One

Introduction

EXISTING STUDIES

This book charters into new territories in comparing the fates of two thinkers, Makiguchi and Gandhi, whose commonalities had been studied earlier in my previous book (Sharma 1999). Apart from this, Makiguchi's concept of *soka* or 'value creation' has mainly been studied by Japanese scholars, with a few exceptions from the English speaking world. There exist several debates on the understanding of his educational ideas which will be studied within this book (chapters four and six).

Meanwhile several authors have written on Gandhi, but there has been no comprehensive study on the conceptual foundations of his values. Chapter four of this book will be an exposition of the ideas and values of Makiguchi and Gandhi.

Also, no previous study has been done to examine the influence of their ideas and values within any educational institution, such as will be done within chapters six and seven of this book. The next section illustrates the documents I will use, and how I will use them within the structure of this study.

SOURCE, METHODS, AND STRUCTURE OF RESEARCH

Alan Bullock, in relation to his study of Hitler and Stalin, draws usefully upon Plutarch in order to suggest a viable approach to the comparative study of two lives. Despite the gulf between the characters and actions of Hitler and

Stalin and my chosen subjects, I would argue that the methodological core of Bullock's strategy is important for my research:

> My purpose is not to show that they were both examples of a general category but to use comparison to illuminate the individual character of each. Hence my sub-title, 'Parallel Lives,' borrowed from Plutarch: parallel lives, like parallel lines, do not meet or merge. (Bullock 1998: xxii)

In my previous work I had compared the commonality of the educational ideas and values of Makiguchi and Gandhi (Sharma 1999). In that work I had thematically categorised and compared their significant contributions made to knowledge and experience within education. In the study within this book the focus will be similar to that of Bullock, in which I will make a parallel comparison of the ideas, and use of the values of Makiguchi and Gandhi in Japan and India respectively (though at times I will make cross references).

In this comparative study, three historical readings will be given to interpret the use of both dissident thinkers. First, a history of the era and time in which they lived to provide a contextual setting (chapter two); second, the specific events and influences that shaped their personal histories and lead to the formation of their respective value systems (chapters three and four); and the third is concerned with the re-reading of Makiguchi and Gandhi, that is, the use of their values within the twenty-first century context (chapters five, six and seven).

The histories of both Japan and India from the late nineteenth century to the mid-twentieth century were periods of intense change. I will narrate these changes in chapter two and will structure the historical facts with the specific aim of discussing the two authoritarian regimes within which Makiguchi and Gandhi postulated their respective belief systems. Criticisms have been made by post-modernists, such as Keith Jenkins (1999) of the meta-narrative of historians, and the historian's subjective account of the stories that they tell. However, in writing the historical context of these thinkers I will remain close to the arguments made by R.J. Evans (1997), Eric Hobsbawm (1998) and E.H. Carr (1978) in particular who have argued that the interpretation of incidents informs their status as historical fact, that is, "History means interpretation" (Carr 1978: 18).

In the Japanese context for Makiguchi I will chronologically narrate and structure the major events of the time (see White 1980). This will include three significant changes in the Japanese society and education: (1) the opening of Japan to Western influence in the Meiji era (1868–1912); (2) the religious intervention of the state in society and education, and the dictatorial order that was eventually imposed on the citizens under the monarchy during the Taisho era (1912–1926) and the Second World War (1939–1945); and (3) the democratic conditions that resumed after 1945 under the American Occupation (1945–1952). This historical context will stand as a contrast to chapter three's personal history of Makiguchi, whose entire educational career and Buddhist life will be seen as a protest against the blind adoption of Western theories[1] and methods in education on one hand, and on the other the role played by education in the production of subjects under the dictatorial imperial rule.

Similarly, the historical context for Gandhi will narrate the growth of Indian nationalism, and Gandhi's scheme of education as a protest against the colonial education that he had received. Chapters two (the historical context) and three (the influences on both thinkers) will be narrative so as to thematically unify the diverse events and happenings in Japan and India, and in the lives of Makiguchi and Gandhi.

Chapter four will engage in a parallel comparison of their ideas and values. In this chapter a critical approach will be used towards the commentaries in secondary sources, and an interpretative approach will be taken towards the primary data in order to distinguish the thinkers' original ideas and values.

The primary literature used for this work includes both published and unpublished sources. The unpublished primary sources used consist of letters that were written by Gandhi, which I have found in the British Library at St. Pancras, London. These letters shed light on Gandhi's political strategies and understanding of non-violence that underpin it. These include:

- Correspondence between Gandhi and Sir Philip Joseph Hartog, and related papers concerning Gandhi's statement at the Royal Institute of International Affairs (20 October 1931).[2]
- Letter to Charlie from Calcutta dated 22–12–28.[3]
- Letters from Gandhi to Lord Linlithgow, Viceroy of India 1936–43.[4]

The published primary material by Gandhi that I have used mainly includes his books, autobiography, newspaper articles published in *Young India* and *Harijan*, excerpts from the *Delhi Diary*, and interviews with Gandhi. Published primary sources for Makiguchi include his extensive work in Japanese titled *Soka Kyoikugaku Taikei* (The System of Value Creating Education) and *Jinsei Chirigaku* (The Geography of Human Life). Among several methodological challenges that emerged while trying to make sense of the two dissident thinkers was one that is typical to historical researchers which as described by Kaestle is, ". . . the danger of assuming that the historical actors could have (and should have) foreseen the full consequences of their ideas and the institutions they shaped" (Kaestle 1988: 41).

Therefore, as far as possible, the thoughts and actions of Makiguchi and Gandhi will be evaluated through an open-ended argument giving weight to their time and historical context, the difficulties that faced them, and the overall complex scenario in which each one was postulating values. The secondary sources however will be useful in order to draw out the existing debates on the values of Makiguchi and Gandhi within education (these sources and their use will be elaborated upon in chapter four).

The third historical reading of the values of Makiguchi and Gandhi is placed in the twenty-first century context, and will evaluate the presence and absence of Makiguchi's and Gandhi's ideas and values in the education of Japan and India (chapters six and seven respectively). The presence and absence of these ideas and values will be evaluated within the changing values of Japan and India. These changes will provide a contextual setting in which the invocation, use and absence of the values of both thinkers can be elucidated. Chapter five therefore will be a general overview of the changing values[5] in the Japanese and Indian societies and their educational systems from the mid twentieth century till the present time. My visit to Tokyo and New Delhi in spring 2002 was useful to further my knowledge of the controversies related to history textbooks which sheds light on some pertinent issues covered by this chapter, such as, the disregard of Gandhi and his non-violent movement under the Hindu nationalists.

Moving on to chapter six on Makiguchi's values, this chapter will demonstrate that although Makiguchi is not found in any government or curricular document, there exists a discussion on his values within the narratives of the ideals and principles of Soka kindergarten, schools and university that have been founded by Daisaku Ikeda[6] who is a Japanese philosopher, educator, poet as well as the President of the Soka Gakkai.

In this chapter I will delimit my analysis to the Soka Schools in Tokyo and Kansai. This is due to a number of reasons: first, Makiguchi's educational ideas were formed during his professional career as a primary school teacher and principal; second, amongst these institutions, his ideas are implicitly invoked most clearly within the Soka School documents; and third, in the Soka Schools, unlike the university, most of the faculty, staff and students are members of the lay Buddhist organisation, the Soka Gakkai, which bears an important impact on the analysis of how, if so, the ideals of this organisation are transmitted within the schools. It must be mentioned that in spite of the link with the Buddhist organisation, religious instruction is not given in the Soka Schools that are private educational institutions from Junior to High School. The main point of distinction between these educational institutions and others is that Daisaku Ikeda has established them, and that Makiguchi is regarded as the original founder.

The following documents related to Makiguchi are analysed:

- 'The Ideal' of the Soka Schools and Soka University.
- 'The Mission Statement' of the Soka Schools and Soka University which elucidates the educational principles of Makiguchi on which the educational institutions have been established.
- The school mottos and principles in the document titled 'Soka Education: To Create a Century of Hope.'

The first document is in English and the other two are in Japanese. A content analysis of these documents (based on my translation of the Japanese documents) will be followed by a discussion centred on an investigation into key questions which these documents raise, either explicitly or implicitly, to whom they are addressed, and what is their understanding of Makiguchi.

Chapter seven will evaluate the institutionalisation of Gandhi's ideas in the Ikeda Centre for Value Creation (ICVC) in South India, and critically engage with the 'dialogue' that takes place between the ideas of Gandhi and Soka within this institution. This will be done through a study of the following documents of ICVC (in English):

- The Mission Statement of ICVC.
- The Activities of ICVC.
- The Rangaprabhat Experiment in Kerala, South India, which is a project linked to the ICVC.

In chapters six, seven and eight I will also engage with the aim of this work to evaluate the present influence of Makiguchi and Gandhi within their respective national context.

THE CENTRAL ARGUMENTS

Makiguchi and Gandhi shared many common perspectives. They were both influenced by Western thinkers, and were also inspired by their native societies and culture. Further, both were men of religion. Makiguchi was a practitioner of Nichiren Buddhism and Gandhi aimed to live his life based on the Hindu and Jain *dharma*. Most importantly however, they were both *citizens* who aspired to play an active role in their social transformation (being an Indian was more important for Gandhi, who even went against his religion and opposed the caste system). Through engaging with the thoughts and actions of Makiguchi and Gandhi, this study will demonstrate that the notion of an inclusive citizen, as exhibited by these two thinkers, is a powerful political construct that defies *exclusive* identities based solely on caste, creed, race and ethnicity. Further, through studying the present use of Makiguchi's and Gandhi's ideas, this study will revisit the task of education for citizenship in the twenty-first century.

Chapters two to four of this book will discuss their aspiration to engage with their respective societies and educational systems. I will critically engage with the different interpretations that exist for instance between Gandhi and his contemporaries like Jawaharlal Nehru and Ambedkar. Parallel to this, I will critically analyse the role and relevance of Makiguchi as an educational reformer within the Japanese educational context. I will also inquire whether or not Makiguchi, as a Buddhist leader who gave up his life for his belief had made any substantial impact within the Japanese society.

Moving on to the twenty-first century context, in chapters five to seven, this book will argue that Makiguchi's and Gandhi's aspirations for civic engagement have not diminished. Their ideas have continued to inspire sociopolitical movements within their own countries and abroad. Whereas, this study will also argue that in the case of education there are challenges posed by the tension between the thinker's aspiration for civic engagement in the community, and the socio-political structure of modern nation states in which education operates (chapter eight).

The key research questions which this study addresses are as follows:

1. What are the key contradictions and paradoxes which can be identified in a contextual and historical analysis of the value systems of Makiguchi and Gandhi?
2. How have the 'values' systems or values and beliefs of both thinkers impacted upon contemporary Japan and India?
3. Is there any way in which the findings of this analysis may have generalisable use for future research?

The exposition of contradictions and paradoxes are central to the argument of this study. In the twentieth century context there were paradoxes between the values of the dissidents and their state, as argued in chapters two, three and four. Whereas the analytical study of chapters five to eight demonstrates the changing values of the twenty-first century and the contextual use of Makiguchi and Gandhi within it.

Let me state the main arguments made in the case of Makiguchi in Japan. In the early twentieth century Japan, Makiguchi aimed at fostering critical and independent citizens. As Epp (1969) argues, in the Meiji era there was a debate on whether to produce subjects or citizens. Whereas some were of the opinion that education should produce subjects who served the *Tenno* (emperor) and *Kokka* (state), others such as Makiguchi were opposed to this view (chapter two). However, (as discussed in chapters three and four), Makiguchi's ideas and proposals were not readily accepted within his own time, although, after his death in post war democratic Japan many of his aspirations for an active citizenship were realised (even if these changes were not directly influenced by Makiguchi). At the same time, in the lineage of Makiguchi, the President of the Soka Gakkai, Daisaku Ikeda, has established educational institutions which aim to foster 'global citizens.' My critical analysis of the Soka School's documents and the socio-political role of the Soka Gakkai in Japan will demonstrate how the use of Makiguchi's ideas can end up being negotiated in the twenty-first century context (chapters five and six).

Parallel to this I will study the ideas, use and influence of Gandhi in India. The aims and policies of the nineteenth and early twentieth century Indian education were intended to provide an education based on Western lines, but Gandhi and other nationalists argued for a more indigenous system (chapter two). Gandhi in particular wanted a decentralised socio-political structure (*Panchayati Raj*) in which education was based in the local community, where he could socially and politically educate the Indian masses (chapters two to four). However, upon independence (in 1947), India adopted a centralised socio-political structure with a constitution that was framed largely on Anglo-Saxon principles. Under this new structure, Gandhi's educational proposals did not work, albeit in independent India there has been no dearth of 'Gandhians' (chapter five). My analysis of the documents of a selected Gandhian institution demonstrates that 'Gandhism' in twenty-first century India has developed a contextual meaning, that is, it can be invoked, used or disregarded according to the context (chapter seven).

Finally, in chapter eight I have argued that common to both thinkers was the normative aspect of their ideas, their reliance on truth as the law of the universe and their perceived interdependence of human life. Makiguchi's *value creating theory* and Gandhi's political philosophy aimed to develop methods by which the individual could be made socially responsible. In particular, Gandhi's ideas and values were powerful normatively and yet encouraged creative responses to particular realities. Whereas the socio-political movements in the lineage of these thinkers have exhibited political creativity and have been influenced by the normative aspects of their ideas, in education there is a need to learn from their creative modes of thought.

NOTES

1. As Bethel points out, "Makiguchi was an outspoken critic of teachers and of the educational bureaucracy, headed by the Ministry of Education with whose policies Makiguchi frequently and publicly disagreed" (Bethel 1989 ed.: xiv). In fact, Tsuke-toshi was one of the first persons who pointed out that Makiguchi's educational work was rooted in his classroom practices unlike many of his contemporary academics who blindly adopted Western theories (Makiguchi 1995: 243). My analysis of Makiguchi's works shows that Makiguchi did not refer to any specific person who he thought was 'blindly adopting Western theories,' but his concern was directed towards the Japanese teachers in general.

2. Mss Eur D551.

3. Mss Eur B. 281.

4. Mss Eur Photo Eur 087.

5. The term 'values' has been used broadly in chapter five, for example I have discussed the 'values' stated within key national policies and documents in Japan and India, such as the value of 'peace' in article nine of the Japanese constitution. However, when I refer to Makiguchi's or Gandhi's values in this book, I am specifically referring to their notion of values as studied in chapter four.

6. See (Ikeda 1981a: 281–291) for Yasuji Kirimura's brief biography of Daisaku Ikeda.

Chapter Two

The Historical Context of Tsunesaburo Makiguchi and Mahatma Gandhi

OVERVIEW

This chapter will narrate the historical context for Tsunesaburo Makiguchi (1871–1944) and Mahatma Gandhi (1869–1948). As stated in chapter one, this chapter will provide the first of the three historical readings that have been made within this study to interpret the use and influence of both dissident thinkers.

The first section of this chapter will describe the Japanese context for Makiguchi in three time phases—the opening of Japan to Western influence with the rise of nationalism in the Meiji era (1868–1912); the heightening of nationalism under the monarchy during the Taisho era (1912–1926) and the Second World War (1939–1945); and the history of Japan under the American Occupation (1945–1952). In the second section, in order to provide the Indian historical context of Gandhi, I will narrate the rise of Indian nationalism and communalism, and the subsequent downfall of the British rule in India.

At the end of each section of this chapter, I will place Makiguchi and Gandhi within their respective historical contexts. I will argue that both thinkers had positive effects within their own societies and education systems, although their actions were largely contentious. Both Makiguchi and Gandhi also demonstrated certain weaknesses that have determined their fates within present day Japan and India, respectively.

THE HISTORICAL CONTEXT OF TSUNESABURO MAKIGUCHI (1871–1944)

This section will describe the key historical developments within the Japanese society and education from the end of the nineteenth century to the mid twentieth century so as to cover the time period in which Makiguchi lived. The historical account of Japan in the Meiji (1868–1912) and Taisho (1912–1926) periods in which Makiguchi taught as a school teacher and principal, will in particular, emphasise the indoctrination of youth during the period of autocratic rule, and thereby accentuate the difference between the aims and priorities of the government, and Makiguchi's own proposals (that will be discussed in the following chapters). Such as, Makiguchi proposed that one of the major aims of education should be to enhance critical thinking and social responsibility. This was far removed from the 'nationalistic' education that was being given in Japan at that time, in which the aim of Japanese education was to prepare the youth to participate in the world wars. This section situates Makiguchi within his own historical context.

This historical study also points out that Makiguchi's aspiration for an education that fosters citizens (and not subjects) was realised after the Second World War, under the American Occupation (1945–1952).

The Ushering in of the Meiji Era and the Changes in Japanese Society and Education System

The Meiji era was preceded by the Tokugawa *Bakufu* (1603–1867) which had a rule of 'centralised feudalism' (Silberman 1993: 160). By the end of the nineteenth century, Japan was exposed to foreign threats marked by the 'Blackship Turmoil'[1] in 1853. The threat resulted in a sequence of unequal treaties[2] with the world powers—the United States, Britain, France and Russia.

From here onwards major political, social and economic changes began to take place in Japan. In 1867, the Tokugawa *Bakufu* was overthrown and the *Tenno* or emperor was enthroned. New national leaders resuscitated the sovereign power of the *Tenno* after 260 years of Tokugawa rule (Shibata 2001: 43). Political consolidation through the establishment of the central state machinery became the top priority of the Meiji government. Alongside emphasis was placed on strengthening the national economy and the military through industrialisation.

By the end of the nineteenth century, the Meiji leaders succeeded in reaching their goal of catching up with Europe and North America in the area of industry, science and technology. Japan became the first non-European nation in the world to reach parity with Europe not only in military potential but also in trade, commerce and industry. The pound and the yen became at par with each other (with 1 pound equal to 1 yen). Economically, Japan regulated capitalism, and the government had the power to intervene in the economy by way of providing guidance (Hunter 1989).

On 18 July 1871, the Ministry of Education was established, and schools were set up in many parts of the country. Government directed compulsory education was intended from the beginning to involve people with different backgrounds in the process of industrialisation and economic transformation. Every individual was given education because it was the best way of making the person useful to the nation as a whole. As the first Minister of Education Mori Arinori[3] (1847–1889) stated in January 1889, the educational work of schools was not entirely for the benefit of the pupils but also had to be in consonance with what was good for the state (Terasaki 1999: 597). This formed the core philosophy of the nation and continued to be the dominant feature of Japanese education up to the early twentieth century. Beginning in 1879, education was streamlined at all levels in order to make it more responsive to the changing political and economic needs of the nation.

In the same year a new education system was promulgated on the lines of the French educational system. However, some of the early Meiji leaders, such as Mori and Tanaka Fujimaro, the Vice Minister of Education, strongly admired the American education system and its philosophical basis in American liberalism. Mori and Tanaka attempted to adopt the principles of egalitarian education of the American common school.[4] They enacted the Ordinance of 1879, the so-called 'Liberal Educational Ordinance.' The idea of the new Ordinance was to limit state intervention in educational administration and to transfer it to the local school boards which consisted of members elected by local people (Shibata 2001: 54).[5]

The works of D.P. Page, James S. Hart, H. Spencer and James Johnot that introduced the educational practice and system of America also became popular in Japan. As a reaction to the increased influence from the West, the Meiji regime in Japan used the indigenous *Shinto*, to awaken nationalist sentiment among the people. As Shibata states:

> Originally, *Shinto* was not a dogmatic religion based on a rigid doctrine. The Meiji government politicised *Shinto* as *Kokka Shinto*, by instilling the deification of *Tenno*'s (emperor's) throne in its theology of nature—and ancestor-worship.[6] Moreover, to organise and systematise *Shinto* theology as a political device, the government embedded the ethics of Confucianism, in particular neo-Confucianism, into *Shinto*. (Shibata 2001: 49)

In 1880, the government re-emphasised Confucian learning by making *Shushin* (moral lessons) the main subject within the primary school curriculum. Further, the ideas of *Shushin* were embedded in almost every educational practice.[7] From 1881, a particularly strict policy was adopted for the control of political ideas and religious beliefs of primary school teachers.[8] In 1889, the government announced that *Kokka Shinto* was not a religion but the national ideology. This measure legitimised instruction in *Kokka Shinto* as non-religious education. On the other hand, instruction in all the other religions was ruled out in public schools in the name of freedom of religion (Shibata 2001: 55).[9]

On 30 October 1890 the Imperial Rescript on Education was drafted by Akimasa Yoshikawa (then Minister of Education), which was formulated with the main purpose of halting the 'Westernization' of Japan. The Imperial Rescript called *Kyoiku Chokugo* asserted that, the people of Japan as the subjects of the *Tenno* (emperor) ought to maintain the virtues of the state as well as filial piety to parents and benevolence to others.

Yet the influence of Western theories in education continued.[10] In the early 1900s there was a renewed interest among Japanese educators in German theories of education with the writings of Paul Bergemann holding foremost attention. In 1902 Goro Kumagai published his *Shakaiteki Kyoikugaku* (Social Theory of Education), patterned after Bergemann, which had an influence on Japanese educators for the next decade. Alongside however, nationalists such as Tetsujiro Inoue and Hiroyuki Kato, professors of Tokyo Imperial University, went ahead to champion the principles of the Imperial Rescript. Under Baron Dairoku Kikuchi, Education Minister from 1901 to 1903, the first official English version of the Rescript was published. "As Japan's entry into World War II approached," Khan notes, "the moral conduct based upon emperor-centric statism was increasingly emphasised and the Rescript was used to support prewar militaristic education" (Khan 1997: 95). *Shushin* or moral classes in schools served as the crucible in which the objectives of the Imperial Rescript were realised. In university this training was continued under the *kokumin dotoku* (literally 'national morality').

To summarise, in the first uncertain decades of the Meiji era, intense debate continued to take place among Japanese leaders and intellectuals on one hand, and the traditionalists and Confucianists on the other hand. This debate was resolved in favour of the traditionalists who argued that loyalty and obedience were primary virtues to be inculcated, and education was to produce 'good subjects.' Japan's subsequent victories over China and Russia also stimulated a sense of nationalism among the people. Some of the intellectuals (such as Mori and others mentioned above) had, however, been of the view that schooling would best serve the future by educating citizens of an independent mind. Robert Epp effectively describes the implications of this debate and its outcome for Japanese society and education when he observes that basically at issue was the question of whether the aim of education in Meiji Japan should be that of building subjects or of building citizens (Epp 1969: 72–74).

Nationalism in Japan and the Second World War (1939–1945)

Within the Meiji education system, the key role of primary education was to ensure that all the Japanese people would share the same sense of national identity, and unify within the ideological framing of the *Tenno* state (Shibata 2001: 53).

Alongside, an increased emphasis was placed on *Shushin* or moral classes. The following description of the time-table and curricula of elementary schools highlights the contents of the 'moral' lessons that were taught in the schools:

> In the ordinary elementary course, easy precepts appropriate to the age of the children, and covering such virtues as filial piety and obedience to elders, affection and friendship, frugality and industry, modesty, fidelity and courage are first given. Then emphasis is placed upon duties towards the state and society, with particular relation to the encouragement of loyalty and patriotism. These virtues are emphasized by illustrations from the lives of national heroes and by committing to memory wise sayings and proverbs. There is one set of text-books for the children, and another (set) with a teacher's manual for the teachers with one volume for each year, except that during the first year there is no book for the children, and its place is taken by a series of pictures to be shown to the whole class. In the children's books only short sentences to be read with pictures are given, but in the teacher's manual there is given first the object of each lesson; second, an outline of explanation that should be given; third, points to be attended to in the lesson, and fourth, questions that should be addressed to the children. (Keenleyside & Thomas 1937: 184–185)

Apart from the school textbook, other methods were designed to inculcate an unquestioning loyalty to the Emperor which included group visits to local shrines or historical monuments. In addition what served as an important lesson for the students was the care and reverence that was shown in the preservation of the portraits of the Emperor and Empress and the Imperial Rescript on Education. The portraits of the Emperor and Empress were distributed to most government schools, and a copy of the Imperial Rescript on Education was given to every school in the Empire without exception. There were many examples of school directors committing suicide when they were unable to save the Imperial portrait from being mutilated in any manner. On certain special holidays the teachers and pupils assembled in the school for patriotic observances. After singing the *Kimi-ga-yo* (the Japanese National Anthem) they made profound obeisance before the portraits of 'Their Imperial Majesties,' following which the principal or director of the school read aloud the Imperial Rescript on Education while wearing spotlessly white gloves. During the reading the teachers and children stood with heads bowed and bodies slightly bent (Ibid.).

As mentioned earlier, during the Meiji and Taisho periods, Japanese schools were officially declared as non-religious and teachers were forbidden to use their classrooms for the propagation of any religious creed. However, teachers and scholars alike were expected to conform to all official Shinto rites and observances. This gave rise to what was known as the 'Shrine Controversy.' That is, the government had officially declared that Shintoism (the

worship of ancestral spirits and in particular of the Imperial Family) was not
a religion, but a form of state observance and a duty of filial piety. However,
most Christians were of the view that Shinto was a religion and it was impossible for a person to worship the gods of the Shinto pantheon and the
Christian Trinity at the same time. In some schools a compromise had been
evolved by the Christian teachers and students, but in others the conflict still
continued.

Alongside, certain sentences were deleted from the *Gosho*, which are the
writings of Nichiren who was a thirteenth century Buddhist sage. Buddhist
sects in Japan were forced to accept the idol of Ama-Terasu-O-Mikami (a
ruler and religious figure of the Shamanistic type). However, there was no
reaction against this by the Buddhist authorities, except by a few such as
Tsunesaburo Makiguchi and Josei Toda who were leaders of the lay Buddhist organisation—the Soka Kyoiku Gakkai (Value Creating Education Society).

Apart from the moral indoctrination, the government also increased the
military training of youth by the end of the Taisho period. In 1925, the Department of Education, under the decision of the Imperial Government, issued
an Ordinance providing for the appointment of military officers on active
duty to give military instruction in all public normal schools, middle schools,
technical schools, special schools and higher schools. Military training of a
sort had been given in Japanese schools ever since the revision of the Educational Code in 1886, but after the first few years it had been pursued in a
somewhat inefficient and haphazard manner so that most of the early enthu-
siasm had been lost. However, after the First World War (1914–1918), it was
decided to revitalise this training and to increase its value as an element in the
preparation of the nation for whatever troubles the future might hold.

On 25 June 1943, during the Second World War, the Tojo Cabinet formally
put into force the new Students' Wartime Mobilization Law. By this Act, all
middle school and university students (aged between 15 and 22) were subject
to mobilisation for work in the war effort as factory workers, farm hands, construction labourers for defence installations or as actual members of the
armed forces. Japanese education was therefore confined primarily to train
students either as soldiers on the battlefield or as workers at home.

Meanwhile, with the rising unemployment, the increasing discontent
among Japanese youth provided a breeding ground for communism. The government set up a separate department to study and combat the communist influences:[11] however, no direct measure was taken to address the heart of the
issue, that is, the unemployment and suffering of the nation's youth. Instead
the 'Bureau of Thought Supervision' (previously known as the Bureau of Student Control) was established as part of the Department of Education (See
Keenleyside & Thomas 1937: 141–142).

However, in spite of all the physical and spiritual training, Japan was defeated in the war. Although successive victories had been achieved by Japan in China and Korea in the name of the 'Rising Sun,' with the end of the war, the emperor accepted the surrender terms and announced:

> Let the entire nation continue as one family generation to generation, ever firm in its faith in the imperishableness of its divine land, and mindful of its heavy burden or responsibilities, and the long road before it. Unite your total strength to be devoted to the construction for the future. Cultivate the ways of rectitude, nobility of spirit, and work with resolution so that you may enhance the innate glory of the Imperial State and keep pace with the progress of the world (Emperor's Surrender Broadcast of 15 August 1945). (Kase 1950: 256)

It can be argued that Japan's defeat and the denouncement of the mythical divinity of the emperor was a radical change for the people who had been indoctrinated to become obedient 'subjects' of the Imperial State, and were not educated, as pointed out earlier, to become critical and independent minded citizens like some of the intellectuals of the early Meiji era had contended for (as noted above in this chapter).

The world war had also resulted in the physical destruction of Japan, the worst of which was the bombing of Hiroshima and Nagasaki that unleashed mass destruction on civilian victims, including the unborn to which the physical disabilities would be transferred through trans-generational effects. The Great Earthquake of December 1946 followed the Second World War. Capitulation found 18,000,000 students idle, 4,000 schools destroyed, and only 20 per cent of the necessary textbooks available. The Japanese student at the end of the war was hungry, cold, often sick, and dispirited (Hartford 1959: 476). Fear, hatred, ignorance, fatigue, apprehension, guile and apathy were the feelings that the students of Japan were left with (Ibid: 22–27).

The Japanese teacher faced the same situation. At a time when one *kan* (3.75 kilograms) of sweet potatoes cost about 40 yen, the average monthly salary for a school teacher was 93 yen, and that for university professors was about 200 yen. Many were leaving the teaching profession. A waitress in an officers' mess could get a salary of about 250 yen to 400 yen per month, a place to sleep, and two meals per day of Occupation food. To add to the teacher's misery, there came the American 'purge,'[12] and as the memorandum issued by the occupation forces on 30 October 1945 stated:

> Educators who had tried to justify Japan's wartime policies, or who were involved in publications advocating those positions, or who had been employed by militaristic and ultra nationalistic organizations or government agencies responsible for those policies at anytime during the period from 7 July 1937 (the beginning of the Sino-Japanese War) to 2 September 1945, were to lose their jobs. (Khan 1997: 97)

American Occupation (1945–1952):
Reformations in Society and Education

Amongst the Allied Powers, the United States took upon itself the main responsibility of the reformation and democratisation of Japan.[13] On 17 March
1947 after a year and a half of Occupation, General of the Armies, Douglas
MacArthur granted his first formal press conference in which he described the
aims of the American Occupation in Japan. An excerpt from this speech states:

> Our occupation job here can be defined as falling roughly into three phases—
> military, political and economic.
>
> The military purpose, which is to ensure that Japan will follow the ways of
> peace and never again be a menace has been, I think, accomplished. We have
> demobilized troops, dematerialized the country, torn down military installations.
> Psychologically, I believe success has been equally propitious. Japan today un-
> derstands as thoroughly as any nation that war does not pay. Her spiritual revo-
> lution has been probably the greatest the world has ever known.
>
> The political phase is approaching such completion as is possible under oc-
> cupation. We have changed the laws, standards and ideals of this country from
> the feudalistic ideals of the past into the concept of what is the greatest thing in
> life, next to spiritual beauty—dignity of man. We have made them think nations
> exist for the welfare of those who compose them instead of the reverse. . . .
>
> . . . The process of democratization is one of continual flux. It takes years. But
> in so far as you can lay down the framework it is already accomplished. . . .
>
> The third phase is economic. Japan is still economically blockaded by the Allied
> Powers. . . .
>
> No weapon, not even the atom bomb, is as deadly in its final effect as eco-
> nomic warfare. The atom bomb kills by the thousands, starvation by the millions.
>
> . . . But this (the economic phase) is not a phase that occupation can settle. We
> can only enforce economic strangulation. (From the notes of an Associated
> Press correspondent, as reproduced in the 'New York Times' of 18 March 1947)

The Supreme Commander for the Allied Powers initiated several reforms
in the first three years, some of which were land reform, support for the
labour movement, expansion of educational opportunity, extension of the suf-
frage, the public-health programme, and re-establishment of the educational
system. Shintoism was eliminated from education because it was considered
to reside at the heart of the militarism and ultra nationalism (Beauchamp &
Vardaman 1994: 60). States Khan, "By the end of 1945, the GHQ (General
Headquarters) had issued all the directives then believed necessary for wip-
ing out the former educational system of Japan" (Khan 1997: 97). Describing
these measures Eells comments that,

> Never before in the history of the world has a nation of almost eighty million
> people undertaken such a revolutionary and far-reaching reorganization of its

educational structure as has Japan. The structure and operation of her schools was changed almost completely after the Second World War. (Eells 1957: 113)

In September 1945, a new education policy was formulated that covered eleven different areas: educational structure, textbooks, measures regarding teachers and other educators, students, science education, social education, youth organisations, religion, athletics, and organisational reform of the Ministry of Education. In the spring of 1946, MacArthur invited the first Education Mission from the United States to offer 'advice' for the new educational system. Before its return to the United States, the mission reported its opinions in detail which included proposals for the overall scheme of the new educational system, its content, and the method of education. In 1947, the United Nations Far Eastern Commission also issued directives regarding the Japanese educational system, with the intentions similar to the policy of the GHQ.

To impose the educational structure proposed by the US Education Mission, the Japanese government established an Educational Reform Committee (*Kyoiku sasshin iinkai*) in August 1946. Based upon the advice of the mission, this committee considered various ways to implement the reform. This committee changed its name to the Education Reform Deliberation in 1949, and performed its official duties under that title until it changed to the Central Educational Deliberation Committee in 1952. Although there were many twists and turns, the government faithfully carried out the proposals offered by the Occupation (see Khan 1997: 98).

The relationship between the new Education Ministry and the Education Committee that emerged was no longer 'vertical' as it had been in prewar years, but 'horizontal' and 'equal.' The multiple track system was abolished and a 6.3.3 System with 9 years of free and compulsory education in co-educational schools was adopted. With this new system, a higher education system was also adopted of 2 years junior college, 4 years university including teacher education, and a graduate system. Within this structure, the power of the Ministry was weakened, and efforts were made to strengthen the autonomy of prefecture and regional communities in the administration of educational affairs. Members of the prefecture and community boards of education were elected by direct public vote of the inhabitants. The duties of the boards were to prepare and administer the local education programme. The directors of education were to be appointed by the members of the board from among specialists. A supervisor was assigned for actual orientation and advisory services. Thus, the direct and centralised control of the Ministry of Education ceased to exist and only general guidance and advice were to be given by the Ministry to the local boards of education.

Such a decentralisation policy was executed not only at the administration level, but also in the actual education programme of each school. The Ministry of Education provided the national standards for the subjects and their contents by issuing the 'Guide for Courses of Study.' The board of education for each prefecture referred to it and made the course suitable to their prefecture, taking into consideration the specific conditions of the region. Each school in the prefecture likewise planned their own curriculum. This trend lasted till the 1950s, when decentralisation of education gave way to centralisation.

Apart from the change in the socio-educational structures of Japan, the terms of the historic Potsdam Proclamation, made public on 26 July 1945 also laid down the aim of the American Occupation to establish democracy in every other aspect of Japanese society. Such as, in the tenth article it is written that the Japanese Government shall remove all obstacles to the revival and strengthening of democratic tendencies among the Japanese people, and freedom of speech, of religion, and of thought, as well as respect for the fundamental human rights shall be established. The twelfth article states that the occupying forces of the Allies shall be withdrawn from Japan as soon as these objectives have been accomplished and there has been established in accordance with the freely expressed will of the Japanese people a peacefully inclined and responsible government.

There emerged, however, several impediments towards democracy, such as, some people noted that the advisors in the military government teams could be more dictatorial than democratic and that it would be better to have no advisor at all than to have one whose activities and attitudes defeat the basic purpose of both the new constitution of Japan and Occupation policy, namely, growth toward the democratisation of Japan (Hartford 1959: 478). Also, there still existed the long term effects of the trend towards nationalism which could be seen in widespread prejudice by the Japanese against the Korean and Chinese minorities in Japan and in reduced opportunities for various groups enrolling in the Japanese education system or applying for employment as teachers. At the same time, what seems to have been the main obstacle to democracy was not really understood by many Americans and Japanese who were involved in the task of rebuilding Japan, which, as some have argued, was the failure to fully understand the Japanese culture and society since the measures taken towards democracy were done in a hurry (Kamijo 1985: 231).

As Kamijo argues, after roughly 2,600 years a foreign enemy had occupied Japan which was a nation that had developed a culture which was peculiar to her—a culture based on Confucian loyalty and filial piety, and the 'success' of the Imperial Rescript had been in the art of using these virtues in the world war. Even in occupied Japan the notion that the Rescript was the basis of Japanese education persisted in some measure until the Fundamental Law of Education was adopted in 1947, which was drafted by the Civil Information and Education Section (CI&E) in order to replace the Imperial Rescript on Education. The Fundamental Law declared that the aim of education should be the realisation of representative democracy.[14] In June 1947 the ministry notified the schools to return to it the certified copies of the Rescript, finally marking the end of this significant era in Japanese education. However, some such as Khan (1997) argue that even today within the Japanese education there is an emphasis on virtues such as loyalty and filial piety, in spite of the change in moral education from *shushin* to *dotoku kyoiku*. The changes in values in Japanese society and education since its democratisation will be further studied in chapter five. For now let us turn our attention to Makiguchi within this historical setting.

A Narrative Critique of Makiguchi within His History

To recapitulate, the period from the Meiji era to the American Occupation had been one of intense changes and extreme conditions. During the First World War (1914–1918) Japanese society and education had been highly influenced by Europe, France and America, which were its 'Allies' as part of the 'Entente power.' However, during the Second World War (1939–1945), due to Japan's coalition with Germany as part of the 'Axis power' there was an increased influence in Japan of German theories in education. Along with this the Japanese government exercised 'thought control' on the people, and made use of '*shushin*' (moral education) promulgated by the Imperial Rescript to further nationalistic sentiments. In the early twentieth century there was a pendulum shift in the Japanese nation and its classrooms from liberalism to nationalism. Youth, who had been exposed to foreign ways of thinking, were now trained to participate in Japan's victory in her barbaric wars with Korea, China and America. In August 1945, Japan came under American Occupation, and the nation moved from extreme nationalism and militarism towards democracy and pacifism.

In this period Tsunesaburo Makiguchi (1871–1944) grew from a student to a teacher and an educational reformer as will be discussed more in further chapters. The values that shaped Makiguchi and his theory of education known as 'The System of Value Creating Education' (*Soka Kyoikugaku Taikei*) will be evaluated in light of this historical background in chapter four since Makiguchi's entire educational career was a protest against the production of subjects.

Although Makiguchi made several proposals for the 'revitalisation of Japanese education,[15] it can be argued that since he was 'just a school teacher' in the extremely hierarchical Japanese society, his ideas were only acknowledged by some of his acquaintances within the academic circle such as Kumezo Tsuboi, professor of history at Tokyo University; and Shigetaka Shiga, a widely recognised geographer; both of whom had encouraged Makiguchi to publish his first book *Jinsei Chirigaku* or 'The Geography of Human Life.' This book was published in 1903 and was well received and considered by some scholars as a milestone in the development of the study of geography in Japan.[16] It was even recognised by the government and became the standard reference in geography for students preparing to take the government examination for teachers. Furthermore, the publication of this book brought Makiguchi into contact with scholars whom he otherwise might not have had the opportunity to meet, such as Kunio Yanagida and Inazo Nitobe.

At the same time as Bethel notes, "it did not serve to increase materially either his social standing or his financial resources" (Bethel 1973: 36–37). Coupled with this was the birth of his fifth child in 1907 and his increased financial straits. There may have also been an indelible impact on Makiguchi of the 'ivory tower' in which academics placed themselves to which his entry as a school teacher seemed forbidden. Consequently Makiguchi's experiments in education were only conducted by him in his classrooms, and later by Josei Toda, a fellow school teacher, in the Jishu Gakkan. As a school teacher and principal Makiguchi was transferred from one school to another by the educational authorities (as explored in the next chapter). This was not because of the creative educational ideas and proposals (that he had painstakingly developed), but because of his refusal to favour the children of certain elites.

To summarise, this section locates Makiguchi as a capable and an ambitious educator, who unfortunately had ended up being imprisoned by the authoritarians of his time due to his objection to the violation of religious rights by the militaristic government (as noted above). Makiguchi's educational proposals were not given a fair trial within his own time. It is likely that if Makiguchi's life did not end in prison on 18 November 1944, and he had lived to see the new democratic Japan that emerged shortly after his death, some of his ideas would have been accepted within the new educational context.

THE HISTORICAL CONTEXT OF M.K. GANDHI (1869–1948)

This section will give an account of the educational, socio-political and economic developments in India under the East India Company[17] and British Empire, before and during Gandhi's life. In particular, this section will focus on the changes within formal education in India under the British Raj or rule, and show how education had been used to further the socio-political and religious goals of the colonisers, as well as the elite members of the Indian society. Further, this section will point out the indigenous nationalistic aspirations that were rising within India during this time, and within it locate Gandhi's political and educational work. This section will conclude with a critical evaluation of some of the key influences Gandhi had within India in his own time.

Indian Education under the British Rule

Analysing the educational influence of the British colonisers in India, Aparna Basu states that:

> In countries under colonial rule, the metropolitan power shaped and guided the educational policy and the educational institutions promoted the needs of the coloniser, ignoring for the most part the aspirations of the colonised. (Basu 1982: 60)

This was especially true in the case of Indian education. Throughout the nineteenth century, while in Burma and Ceylon (also a part of India till 1935) primary education made widespread progress under the indigenous Buddhist system of education and the network of monastic schools, education in the rest of the country was lagging behind. Though there had been universities in ancient India, such as in Nalanda, by the nineteenth century education was being imparted in an unstructured way under the indigenous schools of Hindus (*Pathshala*) and Muslims (*Madrasa*).

During the nineteenth century the above 'oriental education' was challenged by the Utilitarians, Evangelicals, and Liberals. Championing the cause of the utilitarians was James Mill. Meanwhile, Charles Grant who had been associated with the East India Company's administration in London and Calcutta voiced his opinion that the Hindus erred because they were ignorant and this darkness could be dispelled by the introduction of Christianity and the art and sciences of Europe (see Embree 1962). Grant's treatise[18] was the beginning of Evangelical pressure on the East India Company to adopt a more positive education policy in India. While Grant and other members of the Clapham sect urged the Company to introduce English education as a means of propagating Christianity, there was also an undertone in their writings that religious reformation would bring about an economic and political regeneration in India as it had done in the West.

Meanwhile, liberals like Lord Macaulay (1800–1859) were convinced of the superiority of 'Western Education.' An important document of the nineteenth century Indian education was Lord Macaulay's Act of 1835. Macaulay had come to India as a law member of the council of Governor General on 13 June 1834. He was later appointed chairman of the society of Public Instructions of Bengal. The impact of Macaulay's Act on Indian education, as Gandhi noted in his work *Basic Education* (1951) was that it had enslaved the Indians. Macaulay's prejudice is clearly revealed in his statement that, "a single shelf of a good European literature was worth the whole native literature of India and Arabia" (Aggarwal and Bhatt 1969: 2).[19] His proposed educational policies were not secular in practice, and he is known to have stated that,

> There is no Hindu who may keep real faith in his religion after studying English. I have full confidence that if our educational policy succeeds, then no idolater will be left. . . . All this will be done without any religious preaching and interference. (Rai 1993: 109)

In addition Macaulay also played an important role in carrying forward the 'Downward Filtration Theory.' This theory had the intention of carrying a class of persons, "Indian in blood and colour but English in tastes, in opinions, in morals and in intellect" (Aggarwal and Bhatt 1969: 3). This class was to be the connection between the British government and the native Indians.

This 'theory' was succeeded by Lord Harding, and under his direction, from 1844 preference was given to English school graduates for government services. However, this theory was not immediately successful because of the highly stratified nature of the Indian society. Most of the educated people who usually came from the higher castes got comfortable jobs and became absorbed in bettering their own prospects rather than sharing their learning with the masses. Woods Despatch (known after the President of the Board, Sir Charles Wood) of 1854 rejected the 'Downward Filtration Theory.' It laid emphasis on primary education for all, and practically suggested a pattern from primary level to the university level. This Despatch was said to be the corner stone of Indian education. However, people educated on 'Western lines' still continued to receive preference and a new problem emerged under this system. An excessive emphasis was now laid on cramming information and passing examinations, which was similar to the elementary schools in Britain (Curtis 1967), and this was further perpetuated by the industrialisation of India.

The Government of India Resolution of 23 October 1884 stated that every variety of study should be encouraged, which may serve to direct the attention of native youth to industrial and commercial pursuits. The subject was taken up by Lord Dufferin at whose instance in July 1886, MacDonnell, then Home Secretary, prepared an elaborate memorandum setting forth the history of technical education in India, the actual conditions and the lines of future development (see Basu 1982: 40). Suggestions were put forward to teach science and drawing at the primary school stage. Alongside, many reports, committees and commissions were appointed for technical education in India, but despite this, till the 1920s the progress was very slow.

During this period religious teaching occupied a large place in the course of instruction provided in the indigenous schools. Christian missionaries such as Francis Xavier tried to impart Christianity by setting up schools and colleges in the first half of the sixteenth century and this practice continued for the next three centuries. Criticising such efforts of the missionaries in the nineteenth century Whitehead comments:

> It is, however, too often assumed, as though it were an obvious truth, that the moral tone of missionary schools and colleges must be higher than that of Government schools and colleges, simply because religious instruction is given in the former and not in the latter. It is certainly true that the Government attitude of strict religious neutrality in education cuts off one important instrument for the training of character, especially in a country like India where religion has been for three thousand years closely interwoven with the daily life of the people. But it is also true that the missionary colleges have not been able to give their Hindu and Muhammadan students a really Christian education. Christian teaching is given in missionary institutions to Hindus and Muhammadans in an atmosphere of antagonism or indifference which goes far to discount its moral influence. A lad's character is affected by the religious truth that he sincerely believes and assimilates and not by what he hears and rejects. It needs to be remembered that the large majority, indeed all but a very small minority, of the students in missionary colleges have the claims of Christ put before them week after week and either reject them, or are indifferent to them, or are afraid to accept them. Whichever attitude they adopt, the influence on their characters is not wholly for good. (Whitehead 1924: 184)

In the Despatch of 1854 the government, following a policy of strict religious neutrality, declared that the system of grants-in-aid should be based on an entire abstinence from interference with the religious instruction conveyed in the school assisted (Johnston 1884: 38). Though in England the grant-in-aid system was applied only to the Church and Dissenting Schools, in India it was applied to all schools of religion. Religious and moral education was not directly taught in public schools, but it was agreed that if the students wanted, they could be given religious education before or after school. Some such as Johnston found the religious neutrality of the Despatch of 1854 highly questionable:

> But wherein does neutrality consist? Does it mean that the Government will not in any way interfere with the religious beliefs of the natives of India, then I unhesitatingly maintain that in the matter of direct teaching in the higher departments, the principle of neutrality is violated in the most practical and important manner. It is true the Government professors do not *directly* attack the heathen systems of religion in class hours, nor do they teach Christianity. But they do what is far worse—they undermine the religion of the Hindus, and offer no substitute in its place. I admit it is not intentional, but it is not the less true and effectual. It is impossible to teach European science and literature without destroying belief in the gods and religions of India. I will not waste time in showing how it is that such is the effect. It is well known that their false religions are so

interwoven with the most erroneous systems of geography, history, astronomy, and science, that the mere teaching of the truth in these departments of a higher education necessarily destroys religious belief. (Johnston 1884: 37–38)

During this time the Christian Vernacular Education Society published many papers, including that of Hickleton's that was hard-hitting on the Hindu religion, referring to it as 'despotic' and the Hindus as people who needed moral courage (The Christian Vernacular Education Society 1889: v). Among the Indians there emerged voices that called for a separation of religion and state. The Indian poet and educator Rabindranath Tagore (1861–1941) held the view that religion was not a fractional thing that could be doled out in fixed weekly or daily measures as one among various subjects in the school syllabus. Echoing the same concern Gandhi remarked that education in India should be separated from religion because religions as they were taught and practiced during that time lead to conflict rather than unity (Gandhi 1938a: 57–58).

Rising Nationalistic Aspirations and the Impact on Mainstream Education

As McCully notes, the British rule in India was not entirely successful for the colonisers:

> Schooled in a foreign culture, speaking a foreign tongue when occasion demanded, indoctrinated with foreign political, social and economic concepts, the native intelligentsia developed individual and collective aspirations very different from those once expected. Instead of being the staunch ally of the Anglo-Indian administration as Grant and Trevelyan had prophesied, educated natives became vigorous competitors of the bureaucracy. Instead of serving as a buttress of British imperialism, they had turned into its bitterest critics. Instead of dwelling with loving appreciation upon the benevolence of their rulers, they found constant fault with those in authority against whom they raised the cry of "Indian for the Indians." Finding their aspirations blocked by the opposition of bureaucrats and resident non-official Europeans, they denounced the racial prejudices of their foes and turned to the task of building their own political organizations. (McCully 1966: 396)

India in the beginning of the twentieth century constituted a fairly complex society with contending aspirations of Utilitarian, Evangelicals, and Liberals from the West, and the rising concerns of nationalists for home rule. Even though the Indian nationalists had gained strength at least twenty years or more after the Sepoy Mutiny in 1857, there remained a comparative dearth of works giving expression to it, which suggests how extremely feeble was the growth of such sentiment in the popular mind until some time after the turn of the century. Ali argues that two distinct strands appear in the fabric of early Indian nationalist theories. One school of thought, deeply imbued with English political and economic doctrines, drew its chief inspiration from contemporary European nationalism. The other school, alarmed by the steady penetration of foreign civilisation throughout the peninsula, advocated a revival of ancient Hindu culture in order to check the threatened Europeanization of their country (Ali 1919: 313).

Explaining this Pradhan states, "If ancient Hindu culture is synonymous with religious and philosophical idealism, modern Western culture is synonymous with nationalism, the spirit of patriotism, the love of freedom" (Pradhan 1930: 1–17). Ironically however, these two lines of thought were often expounded by the same persons. As McCully points out,

> This paradox reflected the inner conflict which practically every educated native experienced at some time or the other in the course of his (or her) life. Many members of the educated class never succeeded in resolving the conflict. To the end of their days some of them, like Keshub Chundra [sic] Sen and his cousin Norendranath Sen, the editor of the *Indian Mirror*, vacillated between these two poles of nationalist thought. Later dissensions in the Congress Party as well are traceable to the differences represented by the two opposing theories. (McCully 1966: 39)

During this time the First World War further strengthened nationalistic aspirations through the contact of Indian troops with English and British Empire soldiers, which Kale argues made the Indians aware of their inferiority and in this way revealed the need for a radical political, economic and social reform in India (Kale 1915: 87–90). Another factor that contributed to the rise in nationalistic sentiments, as Mukerjee (1923) states, was the association of Indians with other Asians during the war. Both Indians and Japanese fought to secure the liberties of Europe and raised the demand for the recognition of equality between white and Asiatic races to the forefront of world-politics. Rawat notes the impact of this on Indian education,

> The sequel of the warfare between Russia and Japan has evidently proved that Asiatic civilisation still commanded some position in the world. It gave much inspiration to the national sentiments of the Indian people. The natural result of it was that a keen curiosity was engendered in the hearts of the Indians to make a close study of the Japanese system of education. A Government report on (the) Japanese system of education was published and many Indian scholars went to Japan for the sake of education. (Rawat 1965: 290)

By the beginning of the twentieth century, there emerged a non-violent and non-co-operation movement fanned by Gandhi, Tagore, Ashutosh Banerjee and others. Part of their struggle for freedom was the boycott of British goods in favour of *Swadeshi* or indigenous products. This was the *Swadeshi*[20] Movement that had started in 1906. This movement gained further strength during the First World War. The Indians had supported the British war efforts with the hope that they would be given self-government. However, contrary to their expectations, in March 1919, the British government in India issued the Rowlatt Bills as measures to combat political violence and curtail civil liberties. Although all the leaders of various Indian political parties voted against this bill, it was passed as law. An intensive campaign was launched as a result, in which Gandhi took a prominent share as a leader of the Congress Party.

A part of the national struggle was the withdrawal of children from the Government schools, and thousands of students from all over the country left their schools and colleges (Sharma 1999: 32). Alongside this, the Congress and other parties established numerous national schools and colleges, chief among which were the Bihar Vidyapith at Patna, the Kashi Vidyapith in Benares, the Gujarat Vidyapith in Ahmedabad, and Jamia Millia Islamia in New Delhi (Ibid.).

During this period the Montague-Chelmsford Report, which was given shape in the Government of India Act of 1919, lead to the opening of a number of national schools and universities (*vidyapith*) in the country. However, the number of students in the Government schools, or those recognised and aided by the State, dwindled considerably. In 1921, the percentage of decrease in attendance for the whole country was 8.6 in colleges, 5.1 in high schools, and 8.1 in middle schools. This involved, moreover, financial loss to the British government owing to decrease in income through tuition fees and examination fees. With the enforcement of the Government of India Act of 1935, the Provincial Governments were given full autonomous powers, and consequently the representative Indian ministers took the administrative reins in their own hands. In 1937, out of eleven provinces, the Congress Ministries had six. The Congress had supported Mahatma Gandhi, and thus, when Gandhi announced his new scheme of education,[21] the Congress lent its support for the discussion and implementation of his educational proposals.

Following this, in 1939 several Congress Ministers tendered their resignations as a protest against the Government's policy to compel India to participate in the Second World War. Succeeding this, in 1942 the famous 'Quit India' movement broke out in the country and a majority of the Indian political leaders were imprisoned as a result of the movement. The rise in Indian nationalism and the weakening of England's position after the war were amongst the several major factors that lead to the independence of India on 15 August 1947.

Independent Indian Society and Education System

At the time of independence the challenges faced by the Congress party and the first Prime Minister Jawaharlal Nehru were not just the task of governing the world's largest democracy, but also the complexities posed by the nation's colonial past, diversity, and over population, most of whom were living below the poverty line. In education the most significant problems before the national government were the expansion of facilities for mass compulsory education, reform of the secondary and university educational systems, development of vocational and technical education, enhancement of women's education, along with the reorganisation of the structure of educational administration. To add to this was the problem of unemployment that had risen considerably during the Great Depression, World Wars and internal communal strife.

The disparate Indian society had been alienated by class bifurcations that had been perpetuated by factors such as the Downward Filtration Theory and the contention for an English education and lifestyle over the indigenous one. The nationalistic movement of Gandhi and the Congress had a strong spiritualistic intonation to it.[22] However, as the Indian constitution framed in November 1949 specified, India was to maintain secularity in all its affairs.[23]

However, after independence, several commissions had recommended the need for religious values in education, but nothing had been done yet, due the frequent communal violence that was taking place in the country. This will be further explored in chapter five. In that chapter I will also analyse the change in Indian political structure and values, and how that has determined to a large extent the fate of Gandhi in twenty-first century India.

A Narrative Critique of Gandhi within his History

In the early twentieth century India Gandhi wielded one of the largest influences within the key decisions of the national struggle. For the wider purposes of this study, in this section I will situate Gandhi within the above historical context so as to set the ground to critically evaluate the development of Gandhi's ideas in relation to the context in which he was formulating his political and educational ideas.

During most of the first half of the twentieth century Gandhi largely remained the undisputed leader of the Congress, although, gradually his influence on Indian leaders and statesmen had begun to decline by the time India gained its independence. The roots of departure lay as much in the whirlpool of political events as in the different interpretations between Gandhi and his contemporaries like Nehru and Ambedkar. The leading political changes—nationally as well as internationally—that largely determined the fate of the Indian nationalistic movement and Gandhi from the early twentieth century society were the Khilafat movement, the demands of the Hindu Mahasabha, the contention for a separate state of Pakistan, and the negotiations of the Congressmen with the British Raj. This section will take a critical overview of Gandhi's political maneuvers, his success and failures, within each of these political and personal conflicts.

It may not be an exaggeration to say that the most challenging political decision for Gandhi was to win the support of the Muslim community during the Khilafat movement. To give a brief background, at the end of the nineteenth century a Pan-Islamic movement had gained momentum for the restoration of the deposed Sultan of Turkey to the Caliphate—the supreme head of the Islamic world. With the victory of Great Britain in the First World War and defeat of Germany and Turkey, the Sultan lost his throne and his territory, the Turkish Empire was dismembered and Mustafa Kamal Pasha, known as Kamal Ata-turk, became the secular head of the State. He abolished the Caliphate and constituted the liberated Turkey on the model of a modernised European State, with Ankara, as its new capital. The movement for restoration of the Caliphate known as the Khilafat Movement in India was supported by almost all sections of Muslims in the country, and the lead was taken by Maulana Muhammad Ali and his brother Shaukat Ali, of Uttar Pradesh.

The resentment of the Muslims in India was also due to an associated factor. The Muslim merchants of Bombay and Gujarat had long established business connections with the Middle East, then a part of the Turkish Sultanate. Many of these merchants had been going on annual pilgrimage to Mecca for centuries, and were profoundly stirred by the abolition of the Caliphate—which meant complete disruption of Islam to them (Lahiry 1976).

Gandhi's link with the above Muslim community had already been established through his association with the Anjuman Islamia during his stay in England.[24] For Gandhi the support of the Muslim community was crucial for his struggle against the British, as well as for the fact that Gandhi had realised through his tours of India that the Muslim community, unlike the Hindu one, was politically organised (see Lahiry 1976: 6). Also, the unity of Hindus and Muslims towards a common goal was a prerequisite for the success of a stable nation. Thus two parallel movements against the British Raj were planned—one, by the Congress under Gandhi's leadership, and the other by the Muslim leaders of the Khilafat front for the liberation of India, with the help of king Amanulla of Afghanistan, in which Gandhi served as a consenting link between the two (Ibid.: 7).

However, soon Gandhi ended up alienating himself from the Muslim community. It can be argued that the chief reason for this was Gandhi's inability to retain the confidence of the Muslims. Even though from the offset of his involvement Gandhi had tried to maintain a strict code of religious neutrality in all the meetings held by the Hindus and Muslims, unable to control the dissension between the minds of the elites of both communities, Gandhi had absented himself from some of the most important political sessions of 1926–27 which resulted in alienating him from the Muslims. Further, as Chakravartty finds, during the nationalistic movement, the Congress was becoming financially dependent on the Hindu Mahasabha, and perhaps it was therefore no coincidence that Gandhi began advocating Cow Protection Conferences during this critical phase, although he knew that the question of the cow was a sore point for millions of Muslims (see Chakravartty 1987).

Further, even though Gandhi had tried to be an exponent of secular nationalism, the expression of his personal religious beliefs was seen as his bias towards Hinduism. Within public speeches he frequently used Hindu terminology and considered the spiritual text, the *Bhagvad Gita* as his "only dictionary of reference" and "the only infallible guide."[25] In his article, "Why I am a Hindu", which he wrote in the same year, he said "being born in a Hindu family, I have remained a Hindu Indian."[26]

Also, as Chakravartty argues, Gandhi's strong religious bent of mind was the cause of the prominent differences between Gandhi and Jawaharlal Nehru. With Nehru's entry into Indian politics a secular atmosphere was introduced for the first time in socio-political life. Nehru realised the necessities of economic struggle to provide a check to communalism (Chakravartty 1987: 219–220).[27] However, it will be argued through the conceptual analysis of Gandhi's values in chapter four, that for a detailed critical analysis it is necessary to first gain an understanding of the reasons behind Gandhi's obsessive invocation of religious notions and his political experiments with his notion of truth. At present it can be stated that the result of the conflicting political ideologies lead to the disastrous communal violence during the partition in 1947.

Not only were there differences in interpretations between Gandhi and Nehru, but also between Gandhi and Ambedkar, such as Ambedkar's antipathy to Gandhi and the latter's stance towards the removal of untouchability. For Gandhi untouchability was a problem of adjustment and understanding amongst the members of the four varnas or classes. On the other hand Ambedkar and Savarkar had condemned the caste system, being from the lowest rung of Shudras or untouchables, and were therefore hostile to Gandhi's intent of the purification of the caste system, rather than its total removal. As I will argue in chapter four, Gandhi's reason for not taking a drastic step to remove the caste system was so that he did not alienate the Hindus.

Chatterjee (1984) argues that as a result of their differences, when Ambedkar formed the new constitution of independent India, Gandhi's desires found partial and limited expression in the articles for Fundamental Rights and the Directive Principles of the Indian Constitution.[28] Further, as I will argue later, the new constitution was based on a centralised form of governance rather than the decentralised form of *Panchayati Raj* or rule by the five-member village council, as had been advocated by Gandhi. I will analyse the implications of this later within this study (chapters five and eight).

It can further be argued that the differences in political judgements between Gandhi and Nehru as well lead to the rejection of many of Gandhi's key proposals in independent India. The gap between Gandhi's and Nehru's ideals had widened especially after the Calcutta Congress in December 1928, in which, speaking as a champion of the peasants and urban workers, Nehru called for basic social and economic changes and criticised the theory of trusteeship advocated by Gandhi.[29]

Also, Nehru did not always understand the need for Gandhi's fasts. Gandhi's 'inner voice'[30] was vague to Nehru who judged issues on practical grounds. Most importantly, Gandhi's views on industrialisation as expressed in the *Hind Swaraj* or Indian Home Rule (Gandhi 1958) did not appeal to Nehru. In the Second Five Year Plan after independence Nehru insisted that more importance should be given to industry. After the Third Plan was launched, the election manifesto of the Congress for the Third General Elections held in 1962 was issued. This manifesto approvingly referred to the Industrial Policy Resolution of 1956. This policy emphasised that the public sector would increasingly expand and play a dominant role for accelerating the industrialisation of the country.

The above factors and the later factions between Gandhi's successors under Jayaprakash Narayan and Vinoba Bhave has consequently lead to the marginalisation of Gandhi—the man and his movement in modern day India (see chapter five). Within education as well, factors such as the impact of the policies on industrial and technological growth has not allowed for any significant influence of Gandhi's Basic Education or New Education, in which he sought to weave the entire process of education through a craft (see chapter five, last section). It is only within certain Gandhian institutions that Gandhi's educational ideas have been experimented on within present day India, such as the one selected in chapter seven of this book.

In conclusion it can be said that Gandhi's entry into politics had been at a strategic time to unite the myriad contending forces and lead the nation towards independence. However, factors such as the different interpretations between Gandhi and other political leaders have resulted in India's alienation from the Father of the Nation. In spite of this, I will argue through this study that a detailed exposition of Ghandhi's ideas is necessary to evalute his use and influence in the twenty-first century India.

NOTES

1. This was the historical incident in 1853 when the American Commodore Perry came to Japan in the 'Black Ship' at Uraga to demand Japan's opening.

2. For instance, the treatise of 1858 deprived Japan of its tariff autonomy and commercial rights (Hunter 1989).

3. Mori Arinori was the Minister of Education from 1885–1889.

4. For Mori's statements see (Okubo 1972 ed.: 344–346).

5. This idea was stated in Article 11 of the Educational Ordinance of 1879.

6. Ross 1965: 132–133.

7. Passin 1965: 154.

8. The Ordinance of the Ministry of Education No. 19 regarding the Attitude of Primary School Teachers of 1881 (Ministry of Education of Japan 1972: 172).

9. Article 28 of the Meiji Constitution.

10. As mentioned in chapter 1, note 1, Makiguchi protested against the 'blind adoption' of Western theories in education. His own work shows that he was prepared to learn from both Eastern and Western educationists, but spun his own indigenous theory of education based on the needs of the children in his classroom (as will be argued in chapter four).

11. Such departments and special regulations were made from 1913 and revised from time to time up to 1934 (see Keenleyside & Thomas 1937: 136–143).

12. Altogether about 210,000 Japanese were removed from their positions (Masuda 1995: 110).

13. The Far Eastern Advisory Commission, founded in August 1945 proved to be unworkable. On 26 December 1945, the eleven Allied countries finally agreed to form the Far Eastern Commission (FEC) as an official policy-making body for the Occupation in Japan. Some such as Shibata have argued that the power distribution within the FEC was unequal:

> Following the agreement of Roosevelt, Churchill and Chiang Kai Shek in Cairo, the United States, the United Kingdom and China identified themselves as the Three Great Allies in the war against Japan. After the agreement at Yalta in February 1945, the Soviet Union joined the Three Great Allies. These four countries formed the Allied Council for Japan (ACJ) in December 1945. They were exclusively in charge of the political settlement after the War in Japan. (Shibata 2001: 147–148)

14. Article 8 emphasises that political knowledge is valuable for intelligent citizenship.

15. See Bethel 1989 ed.: 91–161.

16. See Bethel 1973: 35–38.

17. The East India Company (a group of merchants) had come to India on 31 December 1600 and from then onwards the Company began its economic and later political expansion, until it was dissolved in 1858, after which the administration of India became the responsibility of the Crown.

18. See Charles 1813: 82–87.

19. These words of Macaulay have been quoted in every Indian education book, but the original citation has not been stated anywhere.

20. See glossary.

21. See chapter five, last section, for further information on Gandhi's education.

22. See note 7, chapter 3.

23. Article 28(1), 28(2) and 28(3) of the Indian Constitution are related to the separation of religion and state.

24. Gandhi was a student in England from 1888 to 1891.

25. Gandhi to G.L. Nanda, 28 May 1927, Collected Works of Mahatma Gandhi, Vol. 33, p. 384.

26. Young India, 20 October 1927.

27. "We must . . . begin to think of and act on common economic issues. If we do so, the myth of communalism will automatically disappear. Conflict there may be, but it will be between different classes and not different religions" (Presidential Address at Punjab Provincial Conference by Jawaharlal Nehru on 11 April 1928) (Gopal 1972–1979 ed.: 226).

28. Article 17 declares that untouchability is abolished and its practice in any form is forbidden. Article 14 assures equal protection of the laws; Article 15(1) prohibits the State to discriminate against any citizen on grounds of religion, caste, sex, place of birth, or any of them. Article 15(2) assures all citizens access to public places. Article 16 on matters of employment. Articles 23 and 24 guarantee right against exploitation. Article 46 declares that the State shall promote with special care the educational and economic interests of the weaker sections of the people, and, in particular, of the Scheduled Castes and the Scheduled Tribes, and shall protect them from social injustice and all forms of exploitation (Chatterjee 1984: 9–10).

29. According to Gandhi the rich were to act as the trustees for the poor.

30. Gandhi referred to the 'inner voice' in some of his writings including a letter written on 25 May 1932 to Bhuskute (Iyer 1991 ed.: 213). Here Gandhi calls it the 'voice of one's heart,' and elsewhere refers to it as the 'voice of conscience'. He chose to be guided by it, as he explained: "For me the reasoned course of action is held in check subject to the sanction of the inner voice. I do not know if others would call it the mysterious power or whatsoever . . . I have faith, and knowledge, too, that a Power exists beyond reasoning" (Ibid).

Chapter Three

An Evaluation of Makiguchi's and Gandhi's Personal Histories

OVERVIEW

Makiguchi's and Gandhi's values were formed mainly by their religious, political and educational associations and experiences. The following sections on Makiguchi and Gandhi are a brief account of their personal history, in which I will note only the key people and events that were the decisive factors in nurturing their respective notions of value. Following this, I will critically evaluate their choice of influence from the broad raft of events that were taking place within their respective historical contexts.

There are notable differences between Makiguchi's and Gandhi's personal histories and societal contexts. Gandhi started in a better financial position as the son of a middle-class Jain family who was educated in Britain through the support of his family. However, like Makiguchi, Gandhi as well was subject to discrimination. Makiguchi had faced the elitism in the Japanese academia, while Gandhi was ostracised by his own community in India upon his return from England, and later he was subject to discrimination in South Africa by the British colonisers. Unlike Makiguchi however, events in the life of Gandhi lead to the creation of a niche for him in Indian politics and society as the leader of the Congress, where he gained the reputation of a great soul or *mahatma*.

Although they both experienced tumultuous events in their lives and were imprisoned, Gandhi's life did not end in prison like Makiguchi. Two main reasons can be given. First, the 'authorities' that they both faced were different in nature. The British were political occupiers of India, unlike the Japanese nationalistic government that was dictatorial in nature and therefore ruthless in its conduct to both the citizens as well as their enemies in the Second

World War. Second, Gandhi unlike Makiguchi was a force to reckon with for three important reasons. First, he was spearheading the Indian National Congress; second, he had established his position as the moral leader of the Indian masses, and lastly, because of the efficacy of his movement.

Transcending these differences what Makiguchi and Gandhi held in common was that both were heavily influenced by their religious beliefs—Makiguchi by Nichiren Buddhism, and Gandhi by Hinduism. They were both professionals as well—Makiguchi was a teacher and educator, and Gandhi was a lawyer (coincidentally they began their career from the same year 1893).

THE PERSONAL HISTORY OF MAKIGUCHI

This section will provide a brief personal history of Makiguchi and the people and events that had influenced him and his ideas on *value creation*.

The Life of Makiguchi

Here I will briefly describe Makiguchi's life in three stages: his childhood; youth as a teacher and principal; and adult age as a Buddhist leader.

Makiguchi was born on 6 June 1871. Describing his childhood Ikeda states that

> Makiguchi's empathy and support, particularly for the downtrodden, can probably be traced to the sufferings of his youth. The process by which Japan transformed itself, in the last decades of the nineteenth century, from a feudal, largely agrarian society into a modern industrial power was accompanied by large-scale dislocation and disruption. Niigata Prefecture, where Makiguchi was born in 1871, felt these changes deeply. The supplanting of Japan Sea trading routes sent once prospering communities into decline. Amidst extreme poverty, Makiguchi's father abandoned him at age three. His mother felt unable to care for him, and he was entrusted to relatives. (Ikeda 2001c: 2–3)

Later the relatives could not afford to send Makiguchi to school, and so he obtained a job with the Otaru police department as an errand boy. The seriousness and dependability that he exhibited on his job impressed the chief of police so much that when he moved to Sapporo, he invited Makiguchi to come along with him and enroll in Hokkaido Normal School. Makiguchi accepted the invitation, and two years later after moving to Sapporo in 1891, he entered the normal school as a third-year student.

In March 1893 he entered the teaching profession. Kumagaya notes that Makiguchi may have chosen teaching as a career due to the fact that at his time education and living expenses were free at the teacher training institutions and for Makiguchi, who though capable, was financially poor and therefore enrolling in a teachers institution would have been an ideal situation (see Kumagaya 1994a).

These trying circumstances in childhood gave Makiguchi an opportunity to develop a penetrating insight into reality and his beliefs about it. The substance of his character thus formed can be attributed to the strength he showed in his protest against the fascism that his nation was going to face in the coming years (Ikeda 2001).

Makiguchi was an educator by profession and so his life and educational philosophy were shaped considerably by the educational environment of his time. Although he does not note this anywhere, as a student of the teacher training institute Makiguchi must have gone through the regular drills of military and spiritual indoctrination in the moral education classes. Even later, as a teacher and school principal, he must have been a witness to the inculcation of the virtues advocated by the Imperial Rescript in the nation's classrooms. However, a reading of his educational work shows that notwithstanding the nationalism of his time, Makiguchi held utmost respect for the rights and beliefs of the individual, as expressed by him in the following statement: "the freedom and rights of the individual are sacred and inviolable" (Makiguchi 1980: 5).

Even as a school teacher Makiguchi did not blindly follow the dictates of his time. Such as, in the highly stratified Japanese society it was not unusual for teachers to give special favour to the children of elite people. However, Makiguchi did not support this view, and consequently he was transferred from one school to another, until in 1929 in a subtle way he was forced to resign from active school work. This was done by transferring him to a school in 1928 that was scheduled to be closed the following year (see Bethel 1973: 40–41). In spite of this, each time that he was transferred, many parents and teachers of the school rallied to Makiguchi's defence (see Sharma 1999: 14).

This was not the only discrimination that Makiguchi had to confront in his academic career. The fact that Makiguchi did not graduate from a prestigious national university was one impediment to the acceptance of his ideas within the Japanese educational establishment, which then—as now—placed foremost emphasis on higher education (see Ikeda 2001c: 3). However, as noted in the previous chapter, Makiguchi's work was supported by some colleagues and certain elite members of the Japanese society. Chief among these was Inazo Nitobe, a Japanese diplomat and League of Nations Undersecretary, who had encouraged Makiguchi's independent scholarship and wrote the foreword to Makiguchi's work 'The System of Value Creating Education' (Ibid.: 10).

During John Dewey's visit to Japan in 1919, Nitobe had played host to Dewey, and here is an indirect point of contact between Dewey and Makiguchi (Ibid.). Dewey was one of the educationists whose writings had influenced Makiguchi. As Ikeda states, "Makiguchi's interest in geography, in particular the interaction between and impact of geographical features and human activities, finds a parallel in Dewey's own thought" (Ikeda 1996b: 4). Also, the background of Japan's opening to the outside world may have served to initiate Makiguchi's own interest in geography (Kumagaya 1994b: 37).

Later however, Makiguchi moved on from research on geography to a study of 'The Geography of Human Life.' It was an attempt to grasp the relationship between human life and natural phenomena as a manifestation of the cause and effect relationship. That is, how the land and people who live in it are mutually related. As Makiguchi's research on this aspect deepened, he extricated the key term called 'value.'

Value was a popular concept in education from the Taisho period (1912–1926) through the Showa period (1926–1989). The term 'value' had been used since the eighteenth century in the area of economics by Adam Smith in his book *Wealth of Nations* and since the mid nineteenth century in philosophy by neo-Kantianism. Though the term 'value' was highly popularised in the field of education, it was only Makiguchi who linked value with happiness. For Makiguchi, a life of happiness was one in which value that is useful for life is created (Sharma 1999: 18). His resulting work, the 'The System of Value Creating Education,' was later published in 1930 under the title *Soka Kyoikugaku Taikei* (details of this work are in the next chapter).

Due to social problems, such as unemployment, that existed in the Meiji era (1868–1912) sociology emerged as an important subject of the day. Makiguchi too had a keen interest in sociology and intensely read the work of sociologists such as Durkheim, Spencer, and Lester Ward. He realised that in order to implement his educational proposals society had to be changed since the existing social and political circumstances of his time were not conducive to his ideas. A turning point for Makiguchi came through his encounter with the Nichiren Shoshu School of Buddhism. As Ikeda states,

> In 1928 Makiguchi encountered Buddhism. Buddhism, in that it recognizes and seeks to develop the wisdom inherent in all human beings, can be considered a philosophy of popular education. Makiguchi felt that in Buddhism he had found the means by which to realize the ideals he had pursued throughout his life—a movement for social reform through education. Makiguchi was already 57 when he embraced Buddhism—an event that commences the dramatic final development of his life. (Ikeda 1996b: 4)

Together with a fellow school teacher Josei Toda (1900–1958) and some other lay fellow Buddhists Makiguchi established the *Soka Kyoiku Gakkai* or 'Value Creating Education Society' in November 1930. The *gakkai* held its first general meeting in 1939, the year that the Second World War began with the Nazi invasion of Poland. After its establishment, this organisation held more than 240 small discussion meetings where Makiguchi openly expressed his religious and moral convictions and continued to criticise military fascism. Often his speech would be cut short by the police who stood there inspecting the meeting (Ikeda 2001c).

Consequently in July 1943, Makiguchi and Toda were arrested by militarist Japan's equivalent of the Gestapo. They were charged with violation of the notorious 'Peace Preservation Act' and with *less majesty*, disrespect for the emperor. One of the charges listed in the indictment against him at the time of his arrest in 1943 was his assertion that the Emperor should not demand loyalty, the chief virtue advocated by the Imperial Rescript (see Ikeda 2001c: 4). On 18 November 1944, Makiguchi passed away in prison, suffering from age and malnutrition.

A Critical Analysis of Makiguchi's Choice of Influence

In his educational works Makiguchi has extensively quoted educators, philosophers and thinkers such as Kant, Maslow, Mori Koichi, Pestalozzi, Plato, Socrates, and Aristotle. Makiguchi's work will be evaluated in the next chapter, however here I will argue that his conversion to Buddhism in 1928 has been the most significant determinant in analysing his use and influence today (this will be further examined in this study).

On the one hand some scholars such as Bethel (1973) and Brannen (1964) consider Makiguchi's conversion to Buddhism as his turning towards religion due to the frustrations he met within his personal life and educational career. In considering his educational ideas and proposals they have separated the influence of religion, since they claim that Makiguchi's conversion took place after he had written the major part of his value creating pedagogy. On the other hand, members of the Soka Gakkai[1] and those that are sympathetic to their view have stressed the commonality between the educational values of Makiguchi and the philosophy of the Nichiren School of Buddhism (see appendix III and IV).

Both sides of the debates will be considered in the next chapter, however, it must be pointed out that whatever side of the debate one might take, it was for certain that both before and after accepting faith in Nichiren Buddhism, Makiguchi chose to be influenced by notions of justice and equality—as a school teacher and principal, and later as a religious leader.

Makiguchi's indignation at the injustice and inequality within his society is expressed by Ikeda, president of the Soka Gakkai, in one of his recent organisational speeches on the 20 January 2004:

> Whenever my mentor, second Soka Gakkai president Josei Toda, talked of how his mentor and predecessor Tsunesaburo Makiguchi died in prison, he wept bitter tears and shook with anger. Shortly after the end of the war, Mr. Toda wrote:

> Looking back, I recall the following words by Suketoshi Tanabe, a former lecturer of Nihon University, when President Makiguchi first made public his theory of value: "When a French elementary school principal by the name of Jean Henri Fabre (1823–1915) wrote his *Souvenirs entomologiques* (Entomological Souvenirs),[2] the French education minister visited him on behalf of France, a country known for its culture, and personally expressed his appreciation. Now, in Japan, a primary school principal named Tsunesaburo Makiguchi has announced his theory of value—a great theory of world importance. How will Japan repay him?" However, the Japanese nation repaid President Makiguchi by sending him to his death in prison.[3] (Ikeda 2004: 5–6)

Later in this speech Makiguchi is referred to as a 'martyr' who died for his beliefs. However, as I will argue through this study, this is a perspective of the Soka Gakkai, whereas a more critical assessment of Makiguchi's life is required. As stated in the introduction to this chapter, Makiguchi was in no way a threat to the existing educational or political world in which he existed. Unfortunately, his martyrdom had no meaning for Japan. It is only several decades after his death that through the re-establishment of the Soka Gakkai under Toda and Ikeda, and the power holding that it has gained, that Makiguchi's struggle is given a meaning and relevance for those within this community, and the broader network of people that support the Gakkai.

To conclude it can be argued that one of the 'real' influences that Makiguchi did have within his own time was within the narrow confines of his classrooms where he gained popularity among students and parents for his humanistic actions. As explored in my previous study,

> At an age when it was unthinkable for students to even enter the principal's room, Makiguchi gave personal attention to his students. As an elementary school teacher in Hokkaido he would go out to meet the students walking to school when it was snowing, and he would take them home after school. When he did so, he tried to make sure that the students who were in poor health did not fall behind the others, carrying them on his back or leading them by the hand if necessary. He would always have some hot water ready in which to gently soak the children's hands.

> Even at Tosei primary school, where the students belonged to poor families, Makiguchi took the initiative of buying stationary at reduced prices from wholesalers for his students.

At Mikasa elementary school Makiguchi used his personal resources to prepare lunch for the children whose parents could not afford to send them one (this was more than ten years before lunches were supplied in schools throughout Japan). He would do this even though he had eight members of his own family to feed. He was also considerate enough to place the prepared lunches in the janitor's room where the needy children could have an access to them easily without having to feel ashamed or embarrassed. Due to the continued efforts of Makiguchi and Toda, the cases of juvenile delinquents and children with skin diseases reduced in the school considerably.[4] (Sharma 1999: 14–15)

THE PERSONAL HISTORY OF GANDHI

This section consists of three sub-sections: a brief description of Gandhi's life events;[5] the people that Gandhi himself acknowledged being influenced by; and a critical analysis of Gandhi's choice of influence.

In the following sub-section, I will briefly narrate the significant influences, of people and events on Gandhi's life in four stages: his childhood in India from 1869 to 1888, his life as a student in England from 1888 to 1891, his transformation towards greatness in South Africa from 1893 to 1914, and finally his return to India in 1914 till his death on 30 January 1948.

Formation of the Mahatma

Gandhi was born on 2 October 1869 to the chief minister of Porbander in Western India. Gandhi describes his father Karamchand Gandhi, as "a lover of his clan, truthful, brave and generous" (Gandhi 1982: 19). Referring to his mother, Putlibai, he states,

> The outstanding impression my mother has left on my memory is that of saintliness. She was deeply religious. She would not think of taking her meals without her daily prayers. . . . She would take the hardest vows and keep them without flinching. Illness was no excuse for relaxing them. (Ibid: 20)

In 1885 Gandhi's father died, and three years later, in wanting to succeed his father as a Prime Minister, Gandhi went to London in order to qualify at the bar. His stay was to last for 2 years and 8 months. Impressed by the foreign country and culture, Gandhi went on to imitate the British life-style and in due course he realised the necessity of frugality as a student, more-so-ever due to his financial dependence on his generous elder brother in India. Reflecting on this, Gandhi writes, ". . . the change harmonised my inward and outward life. It was also more in keeping with the means of my family. My life was certainly more truthful and my soul knew no bounds of joy" (Gandhi 1982: 66).

Gandhi's life as a student in England gave him an opportunity to gain many experiences that proved to be useful for his future political career in South Africa and India. For instance, apart from pursuing his studies, Gandhi set up a vegetarian club in London. He notes in his autobiography that, "Vegetarianism was then a new cult in England, and likewise for me . . ." (Gandhi 1982: 69). Describing his management of the club, he states that ". . . this brief and modest experience gave me some little training in organizing and conducting institutions" (Ibid.).

Apart from vegetarianism, Gandhi became interested in religion during his stay in England. Though he was born to a staunch Jain family, Gandhi had gradually turned towards atheism, but here, in England, under the influence of friends, he crossed the 'Sahara of atheism' by reading and pondering on the Gita and Sermon on the Mount (Gandhi 1982: 78). By the time Gandhi left England he had already begun to develop his views on morality and religion that in the coming years had an indelible impact on the strategies he used to fight the racial discrimination in South Africa.

On returning to India in 1891 after completing his studies in England, Gandhi found himself quite a disaster at practicing law and within two years he ventured out to South Africa as he wanted to run away from the intrigues of Kathaiwad (Gandhi 1982: 155).[6] His stay in South Africa was to be the crucible in which his personal and political life would largely be shaped. Louis Fischer succinctly describes Gandhi's transformation in South Africa as follows:

> . . . the contrast between the mediocre, unimpressive, handicapped, floundering M.K. Gandhi, barrister-at-law, who left England in 1891, and the Mahatma leader of the millions is so great as to suggest that until public service tapped his enormous reserves of intuition, will power, energy and self-confidence, his true personality lay dormant. To be sure, he fed it unconsciously; his loyalty to the vow of no meat, no wine, no women, was a youthful exercise in will and devotion which later flowered into a way of life. But only when it was touched by the magic wand of action in South Africa did the personality of Gandhi burgeon. (Fischer 1990: 34–35)

In May 1893, Gandhi landed in Durban, Natal. During this time the South African society was sharply divided by colour, class, religion and profession. Indians were called 'coolies' or 'samis' that was a way to label them as manual labourers. The Parsis who had come from India thus tried to evade being ridiculed and chose to introduce themselves as Persians or Arabs. Gandhi's first personal confrontation with the racial prejudice is the well-known incident of his ejection in Maritzburg, the capital of Natal, from the first class compartment of the train bound from Durban to Pretoria, the capital of Transvaal. As Fischer finds, "Many years later, in India, Dr. John R. Mott, a Christian missionary, asked Gandhi, 'What have been the most creative experiences in your life?' In reply, Gandhi told the story of the night in the Maritzburg station" (Fischer 1998: 50). The struggle initiated by Gandhi later grew into the non-violent resistance of *Satyagraha* or truth force which gained popularity among the Indians in South Africa. By the time Gandhi returned to India in 1914, he was already a familiar figure for the Indian nationalist leaders.

India at the advent of the twentieth century had on one hand, Hindu revivalists, such as Rabindranath Tagore, who had emerged in the Indian politico-religious scenario to liberate the country as well as the individual self.[7] Fairly recently the country had also witnessed the nonviolent struggle of Abdul Ghaffar Khan and his movement based on Islamic ethics. During the same time political parties, such as the Congress under the leadership of Gokhale and Surendranath, and the Muslim League were emerging as prominent political powers seeking national independence. Gandhi's return to India from South Africa in 1914 was timely, given his own political philosophy that he had developed in South Africa, which, as Nanda notes, would now help him to "forge a new technique of social and political agitation, which was destined to play a great part in Indian politics in the next thirty years" (Nanda 1958: 125). I will discuss this in the next chapter.

Three Moderns and Gandhi's Impression

In his autobiography Gandhi mentions, "Three moderns have left a deep impress on my life, and captivated me: Raychandbhai by his living contact; Tolstoy by his book, *The Kingdom of God is Within You*; and Ruskin by his *Unto This Last*. But of these more in their proper place" (Gandhi 1982: 93). Here onwards I will discuss the nature and extent of these influences on Gandhi.

My study shows that the main influence that Raychand had on Gandhi was that Raychand encouraged Gandhi to read and learn more about Hinduism, which proved to be a useful exercise for Gandhi to consolidate his views on notions of truth and morality. The influence of Tolstoy and Ruskin, on the other hand, was that they inspired Gandhi to take action based on such moral views. Such as, under the influence of Tolstoy, Gandhi established the Tolstoy Farm in South Africa, which was the first settlement of people that had come together to boycott the government. Later in India as well Gandhi similarly established *ashrams* or communities, which, it can be argued, became part of Gandhi's socio-political strategy. In these communities Gandhi educated the settlers to fight against the colonial powers, but more importantly these spaces provided the necessary forum where Gandhi could tackle key social issues within the Indian society, such as caste and untouchability (see chapter four).

From the beginning of Gandhi's stay in South Africa enthusiastic Christian friends went all out to convert him to Christianity by inviting him for prayer meetings and sharing with him literature on this subject. He appreciated and admired the faith of others but felt that he found no need to convert. Later in India, Gandhi remembered his friends with gratitude saying, "Though I took a path my Christian friends had not intended for me, I have remained for ever indebted to them for the religious quest that they awakened in me" (Gandhi 1982: 137). Sometimes, however, Gandhi would be in an awkward situation with his Christian friends when he tried to resist being converted to Christianity. In these moments he turned to Raychandbhai, a poet and friend in India. From South Africa he wrote letters to Raychandbhai expressing his difficulties, who in reply asked Gandhi to be patient and study Hinduism more deeply.

Gandhi had met Raychand or Raichandra in India after his return from England. *Bhai* is the suffix for brother, and Gandhi fondly referred to Raychand as Raychandbhai. Gandhi notes that, ". . . his (Raychand's) wide knowledge of the scriptures, his spotless character, and his burning passion for self-realisation had cast its spell over him" (Gandhi 1982: 92) and was "his refuge in moments of spiritual crises" (Ibid: 93).

Gandhi had first read the Hindu text, the Bhagavad Gita, or simply known as Gita, in Sir Edwin Arnold's translation as a second-year law student in London. Gita is amongst the two most notable Hindu spiritual texts, the other being the Ramayana. Subsequently, Gandhi read the original Sanskrit version of the Gita and later even went on to translate it into Gujarati (his mother tongue). The Gita is part of the Mahabharata, the greatest Indian epic and the world's longest poem, seven times as long as the Iliad and Odyssey combined (see Fischer 1998: 35–45). This sacred book of the Hindus advocates the *karma* philosophy, and it can be argued that it was his adherence to the action or *karma* philosophy that later enthused Gandhi to take action as a leader of the masses. Gandhi wrote in the 6 August 1925 issue of *Young India*,

> When doubts haunt me, when disappointments stare me in the face, and I see not one ray of light on the horizon, I turn to the *Bhagavad Gita*, and find a verse to comfort me; and I immediately begin to smile in the midst of overwhelming sorrow. My life has been full of external tragedies and if they have not left any visible or invisible effect on me, I owe it to the teaching of the *Bhagavad Gita* . . . I regard it today as the book *par excellence* for the knowledge of Truth. (Gandhi 1982: 76)

As I will argue in chapter four, Gandhi's understanding of 'truth' or *satya* in turn informed his understanding of the value of *ahimsa* or non-violence. Also, the next chapter will argue that Gandhi's values were strongly influenced by his view of morality that originated from his religious beliefs. As Gandhi himself stated,

> . . . One thing took deep root in me—the conviction that morality is the basis of all things, and that truth is the substance of morality. Truth became my sole objective. It began to grow in magnitude every day, and my definition of it also has been ever widening. (Gandhi 1982: 47)

Apart from the Gita, the other religious book that influenced Gandhi as a child was the Ramayana, which is a story of the life of the God Rama. As a child Gandhi deeply feared ghosts and thieves, and his maid Rambha, would ask him to chant the name of Rama (*Ramanama*) to cast off his fears. Although several biographers of Gandhi such as Nanda (1958) and Fischer (1998) have elaborated on the influence of Hinduism on Gandhi, I will argue in this work that Gandhi was not only influenced by Hindu texts, but other religious beliefs and values as well, and when deemed necessary he would cite his association to a particular community or group (the last section of this chapter argues this).

Moving on to the influence Tolstoy had on Gandhi, in his autobiography Gandhi states that the Russian novelist Leo Tolstoy (1828–1910) had a major influence on him through his book *The Kingdom of God is within You* (1893), which he read while he was staying in South Africa (Gandhi 1982: 93). According to Nanda, Tolstoy became Gandhi's favourite author: "Tolstoy's emphasis on the necessity of an accord between moral principles and daily life confirmed his own strivings for self-improvement" (Nanda 1958: 123). As Gandhi had stated, "What has appealed to me most in Tolstoy's life is that he practiced what he preached and reckoned no cost too great in his pursuit of truth" (Gandhi 1959: 175). Martin Green comments that

> They were great men by virtue of their achievements in these two areas (Tolstoy in art and Gandhi in nation building), before or besides becoming men of religion; which in Tolstoy's case came later, in Gandhi's ran alongside in uneasy tandem. But their religion, their cult of peace, and their attack upon empire, all had their roots in their other experience. (Green 1983: 5)

In 1910 as the first step of the *Satyagraha* movement in South Africa, in order to boycott the Transvaal government, Gandhi established a settlement of Indians in a farm 20 miles from Johannesburg and named it the Tolstoy Farm.

Whilst in South Africa, his journalist friend, Polak, had given Gandhi Ruskin's *Unto This Last*, which influenced him considerably. Nanda (Nanda 1958: 77) attributes a greater effect of this book on Gandhi than Fischer (Fischer 1998: 86) who mentions that Gandhi in 1932 said that he 'was content to revolutionise his mind' by the book but that it lacked the strength to change his life. Nanda comments,

> Ruskin had denounced classical economists for not conceiving economics in terms of human welfare, and condemned poverty and the injustice which industrialism had brought or intensified; these and other ideas were to ferment in Gandhi's mind and to colour his outlook. (Nanda 1958: 77)

Fischer points out three lessons that Gandhi learnt from this book:

> The first was that economy is good which contains the good of all. The second lesson, which he had 'dimly realised,' was that 'a lawyer's work has the same value as the barber's, inasmuch as all have the same right of earning their livelihood for their work.' Gandhi derived this interpretation from one sentence in Ruskin's book: 'A labourer serves his country with his spade, just as a man in the middle rank of life serves it with the sword, the pen, or the lancet.' But as Ruskin did not say, as Gandhi did, that work of all 'has the same value.' On the contrary, Ruskin stressed, more than anything else, 'the impossibility of equality' between men. He merely contended that the underprivileged must find protection in the morality of the fortunate. Ruskin hoped to alleviate the hardships of inequality by an appeal to the conscience of the devout.
> The third lesson of *Unto This Last*—'that the life of labour, that is, the life of the tiller of the soil and the handicraftsman, is the life worth living'—was completely new to Gandhi. But these are Gandhi's words; the teaching, though not alien to Ruskin, is scarcely to be found in the four essays. Ruskin merely suggested, in a footnote, that the rich would be healthier with 'lighter dinner and more work' while the poor could do with more dinner and lighter work. (Fischer 1998: 85–86)

After reading *Unto This Last* Gandhi went on with his family and associates to live in a farm near Phoenix, a town fourteen miles from Durban. In addition to this, under the impress of Tolstoy and Ruskin, he wrote the *Hind Swaraj* or Indian Home Rule in 1908 during a return voyage from London to South Africa. States Nanda,

> . . . *Hind Swaraj* is a compendious political manifesto. It ranges over a wide field; it discusses 'Home Rule,' the main-springs of the British authority in India, and of the nationalist discontent, the balance sheet of British rule in India, the nature of parliamentary system of government, the curse of industrial and materialistic civilisation of the West, the Hindu-Muslim problem, and the comparative efficiency of 'brute force' and passive resistance.[8] (Nanda 1958: 124)

A Critical Analysis of Gandhi's Choice of Influence

Biographies on Gandhi by Nanda and Fischer (that have been used above) provide an account of the people and events that influenced him. The main aim of this section has been two-fold—to provide a brief description of Gandhi's life, but also, to critically analyse Gandhi's choice of influence. I will argue here that as and when required, Gandhi made use of his interaction with people and places to cite his allegiance to a particular group or community. Some of the influences stated in the above sub-section are considered here onwards, bearing in mind that Gandhi was a key protagonist in the Indian national struggle, and therefore as a political leader he made deliberate choices from the wide raft of events that had surrounded him.

Gandhi's political career in India began in 1914, and he was inducted into the country's public life by Gokhale and C.F. Andrews at around the time that the First World War broke out. He spent around four years touring the country, studying the political and social conditions of the people and developing contacts with the Indian leaders primarily due to Gokhale's suggestion. Through his tours, Gandhi would have realised the immense diversity of the Indian populace whom he had the responsibility to involve in the common cause of *swaraj* or independence. It was crucial, also, that Gandhi as a leader should try and make these diverse communities and people able to identify with him.

For instance, Spodek critically examines Gandhi's selectivity in emphasising some aspects of his Gujarati bania[9] tradition and his rejection of others in the formation of his political methodology (Spodek 1971). The author emphasises the keen *political* sense behind Gandhi's adaptation of the Gujarati bania role and indicates not only the successes it enabled him to win, but also the contradictions to which it exposed him. States Spodek,

> In choosing Ahmedabad (as his new home after South Africa), Gandhi chose to exploit a wholly new aspect of the Gujarati bania heritage, the economic side, in order to support his drive for political leadership of the entire subcontinent. Ahmedabad, and especially its bania community, provided Gandhi with necessary financial backing as well as a long tradition of political self-assertiveness and of social service. (Ibid: 365)

This is interesting, because instead of choosing Kathiawad, where he was raised, he chose Ahmedabad, which was a dynamic urban centre in his own region of Gujarat that provided him the financial backing. Spodek notes the shift in Gandhi's own stance towards industrialisation and modernisation through the need of this economic support:

> As businessmen supported Gandhi, so Gandhi began to appreciate the significance of industry to the nation. His much-publicised anti-business views began to mellow shortly after his arrival in Ahmedabad. Compare his later respect for industry with negative attitudes he had earlier expressed in *Hind Swaraj* in 1908 before he had had direct, intimate contact with Indian industry. *Hind Swaraj* had argued, "Moneyed men support British rule; their interest is bound up with its

stability."[10] In fragmented, princely Kathiawad that was true; Ahmedabad's textile industrialists, however, chafed under British rule. At a meeting of local businessmen in 1917, Gandhi paid tribute to the Ahmedabad banias: "It is my view that until the business community takes charge of all public movements in India, no good can be done to the country. . . . If businessmen elsewhere start taking livelier interest in political agitation as you of Ahmedabad are doing, India is sure to achieve her aim."[11] (Ibid.)

Spodek's analysis of Gandhi is not that he was a freedom fighter or a religious saint, but someone who is economically astute:

Then in 1930, Gandhi reintensified his efforts to gain independence. By marching from Ahmedabad to the sea at Dandi 200 miles to the south and by making salt from seawater, he broke the law prohibiting the private manufacture of salt and captured the imagination of India and the world. In launching this civil disobedience campaign, Gandhi reemphasised the economic component of his programme. Together with rapidly rising tariffs, this *swadeshi* programme reduced imports of cotton piece goods to 890 million yards in 1930–31 and further to 776 million yards in 1931–32. Indian mill production, conversely, rose to 2561 million yards in 1930–31 and 2990 in 1931–32.[12] (Spodek 1971: 367)

In Spodek's account Gandhi can be viewed as a person who had forged his political identity with careful eclecticism. However, Spodek's assessment of Gandhi is limited to viewing him only like a *neta* or politician, but misses the point that Gandhi was also trying to give shape to his moral understandings within the given political reality. As argued earlier, the normative aspect of Gandhi's values and understanding of truth and morality were formed in his childhood and youth through his religious upbringing, the influence of his parents from whom he learnt the qualities of justice and loyalty, and through his interaction with other philosophers and people like Tolstoy and Ruskin, whom Gandhi has mentioned in his *autobiography* as noted above.

I will argue in this study that there was a continuous conflict between Gandhi's moral values and the political reality in which he was placed. For instance, as a youth in Britain Gandhi's allegiance to Britain manifested in his actions to imitate the British lifestyle, study Christianity, and even sing patriotically to the national anthem. However, during his political struggle in South Africa he was forced to withdraw his loyalty to the British Raj.

The conflicts between Gandhi's aspirations and the political reality often lead to his isolation from his political contemporaries. Gandhi's suggestions for trusteeship, *Panchayati Raj*, and basic education, all makes sense when we get to the crux of what was at the basis of his ideas and values which lead to his strategies for action. The next chapter explores this.

NOTES

1. The *Soka Kyoiku Gakkai* or 'Value Creating Education Society' established by Makiguchi in 1930 was disbanded during the Second World War and was later reconstructed by his successor, Josei Toda, under the new name of *Soka Gakkai* or Value Creating Society, and encompassed not only the academic community but non-academics as well. Today this 'society' is a lay Buddhist organisation, internationally known as the 'Soka Gakkai International' (SGI) that is registered with the United Nations as a Non Government Organisation (NGO), and aims to promote peace, culture and education.

2. A translation of this book by the renowned French entomologist Jean Henri Fabre—a pioneering work detailing the behavior and anatomy of insects written in layperson's terms—gained wide popularity in Japan.

3. Toda 1992: 320.

4. See Kumagaya 1994a.

5. For a complete biography of Mohandas Karamchand Gandhi see Fischer 1998 and Nanda 1958.

6. In the state of Gujarat, India.

7. As the next chapter argues, Gandhi's understandings of the human nature lead him to believe that an effective social change could only be brought about by a change in each individual. It is not an exaggeration to say that Tagore subscribed to a similar view.

8. Gandhi himself later used the term *Satyagraha* instead of passive resistance.

9. Literarily meaning businessman, or a person who does business as an occupation. It is associated with the Vaishya caste that is the third in line of the four castes—Brahmin, Kshatriya, Vaishya and Shudra.

10. Gandhi 1938b: 95.

11. Gandhi 1958–1994: 510.

12. Report of the India Tariff Board 1932: 27. Also see Report of the India Tariff Board 1936: 32, 37.

Chapter Four

A Critique of Makiguchi's and Gandhi's Values

OVERVIEW

This chapter is an exposition of the values of Makiguchi and Gandhi, that is, Makiguchi's concept of *value creation* and Gandhi's understandings of *ahimsa* or non-violence. A critical approach will be adopted towards the commentaries in secondary sources, and an interpretative approach will be taken towards the primary data in order to distinguish the thinkers' values. In this study I will focus on the polemic that exists on Gandhi's primary value of *ahimsa*. I will argue that whereas most scholars are of the view that Gandhi's use of non-violence was absolute, my study shows that it was not, and that Gandhi's usage of non-violence varied within his experiments with *satya* or truth.

In the case of Makiguchi there is no huge controversy regarding his work except that there exists a tension between academics, some of whom see Makiguchi's educational work as being independent of his religious beliefs that they argue was already well formulated before his religious conversion. On the other hand there are some who, sympathetic to the view of the Soka Gakkai, agree that Makiguchi accepted Nichiren Buddhism as it was philosophically close to the notions of truth and value creation that were generated within his educational theory. Noting both sides of the debate, but relying on the analysis of primary data, in this chapter I will analyse the conceptual foundations of Makiguchi's values.

According to my findings, a feature common to both the thinkers was that their notion of values was dependent on their concept of truth. Both Makiguchi's and Gandhi's understanding of truth was in turn informed by their respective religious and cultural philosophies. The notion of truth that was formulated by Makiguchi and Gandhi was different from the socially constructed notion of truth that had emerged in post-enlightenment industrial societies. Whereas Makiguchi and Gandhi conceptualised truth as the law of the universe, their respective societies had begun to move towards a more mechanistic concept of human beings and the universe.[1]

At the same time, the impetus given to rationalism over spiritualism by their respective societies had also some influence on Makiguchi's and Gandhi's notion of values. Although (due to their religious views) they perceived the universe within a spiritual dimension of inter-relatedness of all phenomena, they were also forced to grapple with and respond to the sociological and educational changes that were taking place within their post-enlightenment societies.

Through the exposition of Makiguchi's and Gandhi's values I will argue that both thinkers developed their unique socio-political and educational theories. At the same time, my critical study of their values has exposed the limitations in Makiguchi's work, and the contradictions in which Gandhi placed himself due to the philosophical positions adopted by him.

MAKIGUCHI'S NOTION OF VALUES— HIS EDUCATIONAL AND POLITICAL ASPIRATIONS

This section is an exposition of the values of Makiguchi. In comparison to Gandhi, who was a national figure, Makiguchi was less well known in Japanese society and education. In the last few decades of the twentieth century, however, a steady flow of literature has emerged on the values of Makiguchi and their relevance for the educational systems of not only Japan, but other countries as well, such as America, Brazil and India (see Bethel 1973; Dobbelaere & Wilson 1994; Harima 1997; Ikeda 2001a, 2001b, 2001c; Kumagaya 1994a, 1994b, 2000; Metraux 1994; Murao 1998; and Sharma 1999). In practice, the Soka Schools and Universities[2] (founded by Daisaku Ikeda) have been established in various parts of the world, and in several educational centres[3] research has been taking place on the application of Makiguchi's ideas.

The main educational work of Makiguchi, the *Soka Kyoikugaku Taikei* or 'The System of Value Creating Education' had gained some recognition in the educational circle of 1930s, but was cast aside under the ultra nationalism of the early twentieth century. In the past few decades there has been a renewed interest in the values and ideas that were proposed in this pedagogy. Research on the educational values of Makiguchi can be classified as shown in the following:[4]

- Individual teachers have been applying Makiguchi's ideas in their classroom.
- Such experiments of some teachers have been adopted by the public schools and non-government organizations.
- Some schools have been established, the underlying philosophy of which is Makiguchi's educational values and principles (see Sharma 1999).

In order to delimit this section to an exposition of Makiguchi's values, in the following sub-section I will analyse the core concepts that informed his values, and in doing this I will review some of the existing diverse interpretations of his values. Based on my analysis, in the concluding sub-section I will critically evaluate the limitations that exist in Makiguchi's own work.

The Conceptual Foundations of Makiguchi's Values

The primary ideas and proposals of Makiguchi were published in two of his most important educational works, *Jinsei Chirigaku* or 'The Geography of Human Life,' and *Soka Kyoikugaku Taikei*, or 'The System of Value Creating Education' (henceforth referred to as the Value Creating Pedagogy). In the Value Creating Pedagogy, that had emerged from Makiguchi's experiments carried out in the classrooms, he arrived at his original conception of 'value' which is stated in the 'Theory of Value Creation' (*kachitaikei* or *kachiron*) in volume two, section three of the *Soka Kyoikugaku Taikei*.[5] The term *Soka* (value creation) is taken from two words, *so* from *sozo* (creation) and *ka* from *kachi* (value). As Bethel explains, for Makiguchi this formed a key word and a key concept:

> Creation of value is part and parcel of what it means to be a human being. Human beings do not have the ability to create material; but they can create value, and it is in the creation of value that the unique meaning of human life lies. (Bethel 1973: 49)

Though Eastern and Western thinkers influenced Makiguchi, and several confluences of thought can be found between the Value Creating Pedagogy and other philosophies (noted in the following sub-section), Makiguchi's ideas did not depend on any one particular individual or philosophy. As Ikeda states, his educational ideas developed "from perusing various published works, from reading newspapers and magazines, from listening to the conversation of businessmen, from nature, from observing people, in other words, in response to necessity and according to feeling and experience" (Ikeda 1969: 42). The main bulk of his ideas originated from his thirty years of teaching which was a departure from what Makiguchi states was the usual procedure adopted by educationists of the Meiji (1868–1912) and Taisho era (1912–1916) to blindly adopt theories from the West.[6] Makiguchi's compilation of 'notes' can be classified under the following sub-topics: the purpose of education, the fundamentals of value, role of the teacher and teacher education, the revitalisation of education, educational methodology and teaching materials.

Value was one of the three main principles of Makiguchi's theory, the others being experience and economics, as he suggested: "Start education from experience. Take value as the aim. Take economics as the principle" (Makiguchi 1982: 27) (see Kumagaya 1994b: 67). The term value itself was a familiar term in the start of the twentieth century Japan, being commonly used in philosophy (mostly in association with neo-Kantianism), and in economics (through Adam Smith's 'Wealth of Nations'). Kumagaya, one of Makiguchi's Japanese biographers, finds that though the term value was popular in the Taisho period (1912–1926) until the Showa period (1926–1989), it was not thought of as deeply in relation to education as Makiguchi did (Kumagaya 1994b: 106). The following pages discuss the concept of value that was original, as well as central to Makiguchi's educational ideas.

An understanding of Makiguchi's concept of value, must begin from the distinction he makes between truth and value in questioning the age-old debate carried out since the time of Socrates, of whether Truth is a value or not. The answer to this for Makiguchi is in the negative, that is, according to Makiguchi truth is not a value. He defines truth as an expression of things as they are, which unlike value cannot be created, but has to be discovered (Bethel 1989 ed.: 61). Acknowledging that a study of human history shows the uncertainty of truth as constant, such as is in the case of the Copernican revolution, Makiguchi holds that certain truths or facts are constant (see Toda 1964: 9, 22) which he categorises as 'spatial concepts' and 'temporal laws' (see table 4.1).

Value, on the other hand, for Makiguchi is variable and changes according to the relationship of the person or subject, and the object of evaluation. Citing the example given by Brannen to explain the relation between truth and value: truth says: 'here is a horse,' whereas value states: 'this horse is beautiful' (Brannen 1964). The above can be stated as an example of truth as a spatial concept. An example of truth as a temporal law can be the fact that water boils at 100 degrees centigrade. In this case value is in the use hot water is put to. Further, according to the Value Creating Theory, value is different for each

Table 4.1. Makiguchi's Summary of His Discussions on Truth and Value (Bethel 1989 ed.: 63)

1. Truth	Spatial concepts		Recognition of the intrinsic nature of form, substance, and reality
	Temporal laws		Recognition of the intrinsic nature of change and permanence
2. Value	Aesthetics		Judgments on beauty
	Advantage	Private gain	Judgments on benefit
		Public gain	Judgments on good

person. Makiguchi classifies values into three broad categories: value of beauty, benefit and good.

To explain further, the creation of values takes place as in 'the relationship between the evaluating subject and the object of evaluation' in which the evaluating subject is the individual, or, as Makiguchi puts it, the 'life' (*seimei*) of the individual (see Bethel 1989 ed.: 61).[7] The kind of value that is created depends on the bearing that the object has on the life of the individual (which could be positive as well as negative). To explain this concept let us take a simple example. Suppose there is a glass of water. The process of creating value would first demand that we objectively cognise the water, and then move on to subjectively evaluating it. Subjective evaluation can proceed as follows. When someone sells the water and thereby gains a profit, it results in the creation of the value of benefit. When the water is given to a drought victim the value of good is created. The water may appeal to someone's aesthetic sensibility, thereby resulting in the creation of the value of benefit.

Makiguchi also stresses the importance of distinguishing between cognition and evaluation. Giving an example he states,

> Suppose a student asks his teacher, "What does this mean?" and the teacher snaps back the reprimand, "What do you mean? Don't you understand that yet?" The teacher obviously confuses evaluation with cognition. The student did not ask for an evaluation of his ability; he was asking for information or for instruction on a point he did not understand. . . . Regrettably, similar leaps of judgement past the facts are encountered at every level of society—in government, in business, and in the home. (Bethel 1989 ed.: 62–63)

Bethel comments that, "the accuracy of Makiguchi's insights in this regard and his grasp of the learning process are being verified today by competent educators" (Bethel 1973: 54; see Bethel 1973: 54–57).

The Theory of Value Creation is therefore a 'life-centred' concept, in which creating value adds to the life of the individual and society. Similarly the creation of anti-values[8] is detrimental to life. To explain further, elucidating the three kinds of values, Bethel states:

> . . . beauty is perceived to be an emotional and temporary value, derived through one or more of the five senses, that concerns only a part of man's life. Gain is an individual value that is related to the whole of man's life. It has to do with the relationship between an individual and an object that contributes to the maintenance and development of his life. Goodness, however, is a social value related to the life of the group. It refers to the personal conduct of an individual that intentionally contributes to the formation and development of a unified society. Goodness is a public gain. (Bethel 1973: 51, see Toda 1964: 92–93)

Makiguchi's concept of value creation can be summarised by his following statement:

> Only those relationships whereby the influence of some object tends to reinforce or diminish, prolong or shorten, our vital being[9] can be considered beneficial or detrimental, good or bad. We first become cognizant of the existence of such relationships, and then we access their significance for human life. Moreover, the evaluation may proceed on a number of bases, which we may call the scales of economic, moral and aesthetic value. (Bethel 1989 ed.: 71–72)

The aim of value creating education is therefore to enable individuals to create value. Defining his educational theory Makiguchi states,

> Value Creating Education Theory is the system of knowledge of the method by which to cultivate people of talent who can create value, which is, the aim of life. (Makiguchi 1982: 13)

In order to arrive at the conceptual foundations of Makiguchi's values, I will engage with the following lines of thought that I will argue are central to Makiguchi's work:[10]

1. The relation between the learner's geographical environment and the process of value creation.
2. The view of happiness of the individual as an aim of value creating education.
3. The recognition of the sociological dimensions of education for value creation.
4. A pragmatic education—creating value through the use of experience and scientific method.
5. Relative value in education and absolute value of religious experience.

1. The Relation between the Learner's Geographical Environment and the Process of Value Creation

In 1903 Makiguchi published his first major work 'The Geography of Human Life' (henceforth referred to as *geography*). This work was an attempt to grasp the relationship between human life and natural phenomena as a manifestation of the cause and effect relationship, that is, how the land and the people who live in it are mutually inter-related. As Makiguchi's research on this aspect deepened, he extricated the key term called 'value,' which he found to have a great bearing on the relationship of cause and effect. After writing the *geography*, Makiguchi came across the value philosophy of neo-Kantianism through the works of Kiichirou Seyuda. Though Makiguchi's theory of value is different from Seyuda's in many respects, as Kumagaya notes, some influence of Seyuda can be traced in Makiguchi's theory (Kumagaya 1994b: 113, see appendix I).

Through his work on *kyodoka* or Community as a Learning Centre, Makiguchi had developed a keen interest in sociology, and like some sociologists he thought deeply of the impact of the land that surrounds the individual learner. In fact, as noted by Nazzaro, Makiguchi makes a landmark in geographic scholarship in the way in which he considers geography not just as learning maps but as the impact of the land on the development of the individual and society living in it (Makiguchi 2002: 305).

Another vital aspect of the *geography* is the description of the shifts over time in modes of national competition: from the military, to the political, to the economic—which Makiguchi saw becoming, at the turn of the twentieth century, the predominant mode of competition. Ikeda states that in the *geography*, "moving on from the descriptive to the predictive, he set out a vision of what he termed "humanitarian competition"—where he saw the future of his country and of humankind to lie" (Ikeda 2001c: 6). Ikeda specifies that,

> What Makiguchi described as humanitarian competition is not merely a locational or methodological shift in the competitive arena and modes. It represents a profound qualitative transformation in the very nature of competition, toward one that is based on the recognition of the interrelatedness and interdependence of human communities and that emphasizes the cooperative aspects of living. (Ikeda 2001c: 6–7)

In Makiguchi's own words, the ideal state of 'humanitarian competition' was one in which "all other forms of competition—military, political, economic—must be conducted within a humanitarian framework" (Makiguchi 1981: 399). In defining 'humanitarian competition' he states, "I would describe it as the endeavor to achieve individual and social goals through invisible moral influence rather than military force or naked economic power" (Makiguchi 2002: 285–286). Makiguchi clarifies that though it may seem unrealistic to apply such an approach to the real world, he was optimistic that a 'humanitarian approach' is possible, given the importance of

> . . . setting a goal of well being and protection of all people, including oneself but not at the increase of self-interest alone. In other words, the aim is the betterment of others in doing so, one chooses ways that yield personal benefit as well as benefit to others. It is a conscious effort to create a more harmonious community life. (Makiguchi 2002: 286)

Makiguchi acknowledged that it will take time for humankind to achieve this goal. The contributive aspect of the *geography* can be noted in its shift from the usual learning of the topography of the earth in geography classes, to studying the relation of the human being to his/her natural environment, such as, the effect of a natural setting on the human mind and body. In essence this work looks beyond a sociological or anthropological study of geography to a study of 'the geography of human life.'

2. The View of Happiness of the Individual as an Aim of Value Creating Education

The aim of education, for Makiguchi, was to be derived from the aim of life, which as he found, was that everyone ultimately desires to lead a happy life. In his words, "The purpose of education should be derived from the purpose of life itself; and the purpose of life is deduced and recognized by the general public from their own lives as they live them, not by philosophers and theoreticians" (Bethel 1989 ed.: 22). Several scholars have distinguished the term 'happiness' as understood by Makiguchi from the lesser aim of 'pleasure' (see Norton in Bethel 1989 ed.: 207–208, and Kumagaya 1994b: 69–74). That is, they argue that whereas pleasure is the gratification of individual desires (unrelated to any social concern), according to the Value Creating Pedagogy happiness of the individual is a state in which one creates value for the benefit of the individual as well as the good of society.

Meanwhile Kumagaya identifies the influence of utilitarianism, in particular the utilitarian philosophy of J. Bentham (1748–1832) on the aim of happiness as the goal of Makiguchi's value creating philosophy (see Kumagaya 1994b: 114–119). However, arguably, even though Makiguchi may have been influenced to an extent by utilitarianism, value creation was not a utilitarian concept, but a life-centred approach (Bethel 1989 ed.: 72), in which the happiness of the individual could take place in its full form in a social life. As shown earlier, his value creating theory itself was life-centred. Therefore, according to Makiguchi's line of thought, a life of happiness is a life in which to create the capacity to find meaning, to enhance one's own existence and contribute to the well being of others, and true happiness can only come through sharing in the trials and successes of other persons of our community. Hence it was essential according to Makiguchi for any true conception of happiness to contain the promise of full commitment to the life of society (see Ikeda 2001: 97–109).

Makiguchi states that the reason why Kant and his followers objected to taking the students' own happiness as the goal of education is that, "Kant's objection stemmed primarily from traditional thinking that the purpose of education must be established by philosophers and scholars and partially from narrow interpretations of the concept of happiness in his day" (Bethel 1989 ed.: 22). He also notes that Kant's concept of happiness did not include a societal element, because "Prior to the development of sociology by Auguste Comte, society was not an object of cognition and hence was not taken into consideration by Kant" (Bethel 1989 ed.: 24).

3. The Recognition of the Sociological Dimensions of Education for Value Creation

H. Spencer, F.H. Giddings, E. Durkheim and L. Ward were sociologists who Makiguchi has cited in his educational pedagogy. In my work, *Value Creators in Education*, I analysed the four ways in which the relation between society and education was central to Makiguchi's work, and the influence of sociologists, primarily that of E. Durkheim (see Sharma 1999: 21–23).[11] The four interlinks between society and education for Makiguchi were: society as the content and method of education; education as a basic function of continuing society; society as the environment for education; and education for social transformation. As this study is delimited to an engagement with Makiguchi's value, here I will analyse the implication of Makiguchi's interest in sociology for value creation.

Apart from the personal value of benefit and the social value of good, Makiguchi also mentions the term 'character value' in his pedagogy.[12] Furukawa states that character value, for Makiguchi was the value found in living a social life (Furukawa 2001: 159). This value had two aspects for Makiguchi according to Furukawa. Firstly, character value was found in the aim of the happiness of self and others. Secondly, character value could be created in harmonising the thought, word and action of the individual. The core theme of life according to Makiguchi was to create a happy life in which a person's existence centres in creating value that enhances to the fullest both personal life and the network of interdependent relationships that constitutes the individual's communal life. Therefore, Makiguchi concludes that,

> Creating value is, in fact, our very humanity. When we praise persons for their 'strength of character,' we are really acknowledging their superior ability to create value. (Makiguchi 1972: 25)

There is an underlying assumption by Makiguchi, when considering the aim of education and the role of society in education, that personal and social goals and values can be harmonised. According to Makiguchi, the means to cultivate character value were primarily through the influence of the teacher (see Bethel 1989 ed.: 98 and Sharma 1999: 60). Within the curriculum one of the methods of inculcating character value for Makiguchi was "by studying the success stories of persons who embody the value-creation life-style, analysing them in light of psychology, and by reviewing the hard-won victories of incisive mastery, rather than mulling over mediocre accomplishments, although such comparisons can prove instructive also" (Bethel 1989 ed.: 90).[13]

4. A Pragmatic Education—Creating Value through the Use of Experience and Scientific Method

Bethel (1973) and Ikeda (2001b, 2001c) find confluence of thought between the American pragmatist John Dewey and Makiguchi. Makiguchi's concept of value had a pragmatic orientation in the sense that the creation of value could be possible through experiential learning and a scientific method that allows such learning to take place. In Makiguchi's words,

> Education consists of finding value within the living environment, thereby discovering physical and psychological principles that govern our lives and eventually applying these newfound principles in real life to create new value. In sum, it is the guided acquisition of skills of observation, comprehension, and application. (Bethel 1989 ed.: 168)

Therefore, whereas teachers in the early nineteenth century were cramming knowledge in classrooms, Makiguchi was positing his idea, developed through his thirty years of experience, that instead of force-feeding vast amount of knowledge into the 'empty vessels,' students should be enabled to possess "the keys to unlock the vault of knowledge, (so that) it becomes possible to obtain for oneself all the learning one will ever need in life without having to memorize endless volumes of scholarship" (Ibid.). He further states that "implicit in the pragmatic orientation of education "for living, of living, and by living" is the understanding of both living and learning as *process*" (Bethel 1989 ed.: 23). In the broader context, contrary to the existing aim of education for the accumulation of wealth, social position or similar gains, the aim of education by Makiguchi was not in "a fixed mark to be achieved, but as a sense of *becoming*", that takes place through the "dynamic, growthful nature of happiness" (Ibid.).

The pragmatic goal of experiential learning is a cornerstone in value creating education. Makiguchi's proposal of the half-day school system is a method of learning through half day at school and a part of the day learning apprenticeship in society. In his words,

> To sum up the fundamental idea of the half-day school system, study is not seen as a preparation for living, but rather study takes place while living, and living

takes place in the midst of study. Study and actual living are seen as more than parallels; they inform one another intercontextually, study-in-living and living-in-study, throughout one's whole life. In this sense, it is not the better economic budgeting of school programmes but the instilling of joy and appreciation for work that becomes the main focus of the proposed changes. (Bethel 1989 ed.: 156)

The relevance of actual experience for teachers was to devise their own research in education, so that education was not carried out by the "philosopher's method of abstract thinking" (as Makiguchi found happening in Japan during his time) but was conducted through "the scientist's method of inducting findings from actual experience" (Bethel 1989 ed.: 8).

It can be pointed out here that Makiguchi had read the works of J.F. Herbart who had been introduced in Japan in 1895 by Tomeri Tanimoto, a professor in Advanced Teachers Training College or *Koutou Shihan Gakko*. However, Makiguchi's scientific education was different from Herbart's. For Herbart scientific education was to be based on ethics and psychology that Makiguchi argued was incorrect and should be based on sociology as noted above (see Makiguchi 1982: 12; Kumagaya 1994b: 60–61). It must also be mentioned here that, though Makiguchi was impressed by Western pragmatism, he objected to what he saw as the confusion between truth and value. The understanding of truth as a value by pragmatists, according to Makiguchi, was based on the false assumption that if a thing is true it is beneficial. To the contrary Makiguchi argued that experience shows that there are some things have no usefulness to human life, but are true (see Makiguchi 1964: 20–21; Bethel 1973: 56). This serves as another example of Makiguchi's critical thinking and his ability to draw upon the various educational debates of his time, both within Japan and outside, and postulate his own ideas based on his teaching experience.

5. Relative Value in Education and Absolute Value of Religious Experience

It can be argued that there are two primary debates in relation to Makiguchi's acceptance of Nichiren Shoshu Buddhism within the varied researches that have been conducted in understanding his concept of value. To state the first debate, one group of researchers (such as Kumagaya 1994b; Furukawa 2001) share the view that the educational theory of value creation discusses relative values, but after joining Buddhism Makiguchi advocated absolute values. Another group has argued that, "during his career as an educator he consistently rejected the idea of absolute values" and therefore do not consider any significant influence of Buddhism on Makiguchi's concept of values (Bethel 1973: 51; also see Brannen 1964). The second debate that emerges from this is that, the second group, unlike the first, regard Makiguchi's turning to religion as the result of the 'failures' he encountered in his educational career.

First this section clarifies the discrepancies in understanding Makiguchi's value as being relative or absolute. The Value Creating Theory that developed within the educational career of Makiguchi describes value as a variable factor that changes according to the effect of the object on the subject (as noted above). Makiguchi states that when he encountered Buddhism in 1928 he found a resonance of his educational ideas in those of Nichiren and his theory was 'revitalized' by this influence (Makiguchi 1987: 146) (see Ikeda 2001c; Kumagaya 1994b; Furukawa 2001). Among the several commonalities between the two philosophies—held by Makiguchi and that within Buddhism—was that absolute value was placed on life itself. As Nichiren states, "Life itself is the most precious of all treasures. Even the treasures of the entire universe cannot equal the value of a single human life" (Hori 1952 ed.: 1569). This clearly resonates with Makiguchi's own views: "The only value in the true sense is that of life itself. All other values arise solely within the context of interaction with life" (Makiguchi 1982: 232).

It is quite possible that this philosophical view inspired Makiguchi to openly condemn the authoritarian regime in Japan.[14] As Ikeda notes, "Both Buddhism and Makiguchi's philosophy contain a powerful critique of the prevailing militarist ideology that saw the lives of individual citizens and soldiers subservient to—and expendable in—the overriding interests of the state" (Ikeda 2001c: 27–28).

Some authors such as Kumagaya and Furukawa have stated that in according absolute value to life, Makiguchi went on to propose that a life of absolute good was only possible through the practice of Nichiren Buddhism. However, it must be argued that Makiguchi did not imply that this was the only way to create value of absolute good. In his pedagogy Makiguchi classified the 'value of good' (*zen no kachi*) into small (*sho*), medium (*chu*) and great (*dai*) and found that the greatest value was to uphold, sanctify, and preserve life (Makiguchi 1984: 61). This was also the basis of Nichiren Buddhism which Makiguchi adopted, and he later formed the *Soka Kyoiku Gakkai* (Value Creating Education Society) as a lay movement dedicated to realising a 'life of good' through the practice of Buddhism.

Another factor, associated with the 'value of great good' is, as Furukawa notes, that creating the value of great good could also be done by actively opposing great evil (understood as anything that is destructive to life). Furukawa further moves on to analyse that Makiguchi's entire life exemplifies this— earlier in his life as an educator who was persecuted by authorities for not currying favours with influential parents, and later as a Buddhist leader in being indignant towards the imperial and militaristic state.

To re-state my claim based on the above discussions, both absolute and relative values for Makiguchi were 'life-centred' concepts. Makiguchi's concept of good and evil is removed from the common understanding of these terms, that is, both good and evil do not exist in the person or place, but in their bearing on life in which 'good' is that which sustains life and 'evil' that which destroys it. However, it must also be specified that Makiguchi did not postulate any specific religious values. Contradicting Winderband's suggestion for a 'sanctity' value he states that, "the beauty-benefit-good value system we have set forth thus far can accommodate the entire range of values possible without need to generate a separate sacred value" (Bethel 1989 ed.: 84).

Let us now move on to the second debate, that is, whether or not Makiguchi had turned from a rationalist to an irrational religious adherent. Dayle Bethel, one of Makiguchi's biographers, and Brannen, one of the first writers on Makiguchi, conclude that even though the Soka Gakkai draws confluence between the 'pragmatic values of Makiguchi' and the religious tenets of Nichiren Buddhism, the conceptual foundations of Makiguchi's values were laid before his conversion (see Bethel 1973; Brannen 1964). Bethel adds that for Makiguchi "it was primarily a sense of frustration and futility, which accompanied this recognition of powerlessness to bring about a change in Japanese society through educational means that led him eventually to see religion rather than education as the most strategic means for effecting societal change" (Bethel 1973: 91).

Arguably, Bethel takes a biographical view of Makiguchi based on an introspection into the challenging events that took place within Makiguchi's life, such as the abrupt end of his career as an educator and the death of his two sons and a daughter, all of which may seem to indicate that his religious faith would have given him some form of encouragement. Bethel and Brannen in particular base their critique on Makiguchi's "unquestioning absolute faith in an Object of Worship" (Bethel 1973: 92) which in their writings insinuate his turning to a deity for finding solutions to his problems in secular life. However, their study does not probe into the 'Object of Worship' in question, and thereby unfairly judges Makiguchi as turning away from reason.

The *Gohonzon* or 'Object of Worship' which Makiguchi revered after accepting faith in Nichiren Buddhism depicts the universal law or principle (*dharma* or *dhamma*) rather than a deity. This law was not only pertinent for Buddhists, but as Makiguchi had earlier found in his educational pedagogy, it was an "underlying order" (Bethel 1989 ed.: 85), a "law of causality" which presides over humanity (Makiguchi 1984: 63) and therefore extends to science as well, as he notes that "Such awareness of law and of an order inherent in human life is, likewise, the essential foundation on which science rests" (Bethel 1989 ed.: 84).

Arguably, even Darwin's theory of evolution which is one of the tenets upon which modern rational sensibility rests (which Makiguchi (1997:127) notes in his work), underlines the function of a moral order[15] in the universe. In his theory of the survival of the fittest, Darwin came across the complexities with which species adapt to their environment in order to survive. It has been recently presented that Darwin's theory insinuates that in the process of evolution with the growth of the human brain, human beings developed the ability to survive through their ability to create.[16] This resonates with Makiguchi's basic assumption that human beings are essentially creative, and the purpose of life is therefore to sustain and enhance life through creating value in our environment. Here we get an insight into Makiguchi's suggestion that even though competition is an integral part of humankind's natural and social life as noted in the *geography*, the essential nature of human life is also to create value.[17]

The effect of this discussion on Makiguchi's relative and absolute values for education can be deduced as follows: 1) Value Creating Education is a method to create value, which is relative to the individual, but is aimed towards the greater purpose of the happiness of the individual and society; and 2) This theory accords absolute value to life as a fundamental of education. These implications of Makiguchi's values, along with its pragmatic, environmental and sociological dispositions are valid in theory, but posed certain challenges in practice during his own time.

The Limitations in Makiguchi's Work

Several reasons can be given for the inapplicability of Makiguchi's ideas and values during his own time, the most prominent amongst which was the ultra nationalism in Japan, the forceful postulation of the values of loyalty and filial piety towards the emperor and state, and the negative use of these values in education. Apart from this was the academic elitism within which Makiguchi, who lacked academic qualification as a researcher, found it increasingly difficult to put forward his own theory of education which was a departure from the values and ideologies of his time. To summarise, two aspects of Makiguchi's work that stood in contradiction to that time were: 1) it was a pragmatic theory of education developed through practical classroom experience, and 2) the happiness of the individual learner was the central purpose of education.

While the ministry of education and the Society of Educational Critics (*Kyoiku Hyoronka Kyokai*) were reworking the curricula, elevating the level of teaching, and extending the term of schooling, Makiguchi considered these reforms to be scarcely useful in improving education, and suggested an overhauling of the present system—such as—a renewed focus on the purpose of education as value creation; for education to be reoriented to more practical ends and thereby the shortening of the term of study; and for education to include the home and community. As Bethel states, Makiguchi may have been "too naïve to think that society and power structures could allow individuals to express creativity" (Bethel 1989 ed.: 14).

Notwithstanding this, it can, however, be argued that Makiguchi's value creating education may have been experimented with by other scholars under the democratic conditions that followed, given his undertaking the following corrective measure. The main bulk of his work itself remained a rather unsystematic compilation of notes lacking the use of clear research methods such that it becomes challenging to understand and analyse the way in which he arrives at the specific principles and proposals outlined in his theory.

It can therefore be argued that even though recent scholars have been interested in Makiguchi's educational ideas, their research on these values has been carried out within a comparative framework. In spite of the originality of Makiguchi's ideas and proposals, his theory has been re-interpreted for today's education. Bethel's (2000) and Norton's (Bethel 1989 ed.) analysis of the value creating theory therefore borrows from the philosophy of eudemonism. Kumagaya (1994b) interprets these values in comparison with sociologists such as Emile Durkheim. Harima (1997) and Furukawa (2001) look at the commonalities between and influence of Nichiren Buddhism on Makiguchi's values. Ikeda (2001c) draws confluences between the ideas of Makiguchi and John Dewey. My previous researches as well (Sharma 1999, 2002) have been a comparative study of the values of Makiguchi, Gandhi and John Dewey.

Arguably, today as well there are factors that have made it difficult to apply Makiguchi's ideas within the classroom. Chapter six will further explore this through a study of the documents of the Soka Schools.

GANDHI'S NOTION OF VALUES—
HIS EDUCATIONAL AND POLITICAL ASPIRATIONS

Within the movement of *Satyagraha* (truth-force) the values of non-violence, tolerance, love for humanity and other such values were associated with Gandhi—the man, his personality, symbols, and the entire movement. These values cannot be attributed solitarily to Gandhi, for they were the religious, cultural, social and humanitarian values that already existed in the Indian society. However, amongst all these values the value of *ahimsa* or non-violence was expounded extensively through Gandhi's life and movement. *Ahimsa* was the primary value for Gandhi as expressed by him in his speech on 'Ashram Vows' at the YMCA, in Madras on 16 February 1916: "Ahimsa does not displace the practice of other virtues, but renders their practice impera- tively necessary before it can be practiced even in its rudiments" (Gandhi 1964b: 297). Other values such as *tapascharya*[18] (meditation and austerity) and *brahmacharya*[19] (fidelity or chastity) were essential to the attainment of *ahimsa* or non-violence.

Gandhi himself has written on the value of *ahimsa* in most of his speeches and writings in the *Collected Works* published by the Ministry of Information and Broadcasting, Government of India; in the book *All Men are Brothers* (Gandhi 1959); and in several correspondences he had with world figures such as Bart de Ligt (Bartolf 2000 ed.). Several authors—both Indian as well as foreign—have written on Gandhi's concept of *ahimsa* including Bhikhu Parekh (1989b, 1997), Blanche Watson (1989), B.R. Nanda (1995), Dennis Dalton (1993), Devdutt (1994), D.S. Sarma (1949), Eknath Easwaran (1989), J.T.F. Jordens (1998), Mary King (1999), Mohit Chakrabarti (1992), Ragha- van Iyer, (1994), Ratan Das (2002), S.R. Bakshi (1988), Stephen R. Covey (1994) and V.P. Gaur (1977). Most of the work done on Gandhi's values has been a hagiography on the relevance of *ahimsa* as a value that Gandhi bor- rowed from traditional Hindu thinking.

There needs to be a thorough analysis of the conceptual foundations of Gandhi's values as Iyer points out, "Despite the vast and fast accumulating literature on Gandhi, scant justice has been done to the solid conceptual foun- dations of his thought" (Iyer 1986 ed.: i). This section analyses Gandhi's con- cept of truth and value and his notion of human nature that informed these concepts. Based on an analysis of the conceptual foundation of Gandhi's val- ues, this section finds a rationale for many of the seemingly self-contradictory and extreme statements and actions of Gandhi. This does not mean that this section aims to provide a justification for Gandhi. Rather, the discussion in- corporates the society and politics in which Gandhi was placed and evaluates his response to it. It will be argued that even though his ideas were norma- tively powerful, at times they simply ended up skirting the surface of the events that took place within his time.

The Conceptual Foundations of Gandhi's Values

The compilation of concepts that were basic as well as essential to Gandhi's life and mission have been successfully arranged by Raghavan Iyer in the ed- ited three volume series—The Moral and Political Writings of Mahatma Gandhi—of which volumes two (Iyer 1986 ed.) and three (Iyer 1987 ed.) deal specifically with truth and non-violence. Bhikhu Parekh has undertaken a co- herent analysis of the conceptual foundations of Gandhi's thoughts and val- ues in his work *Gandhi* (Parekh 1997).

In this section I will borrow from Parekh's analysis of the conceptual foundation of Gandhi's values, and incorporate certain dimensions that need to be analysed in order to understand and evaluate Gandhi's values. In this section I will also review Gandhi's notion of *ahimsa* or non-violence in the light of his concept of a 'moral law.' I will argue that *ahimsa* was not a fixed value, but something that was derived from and worked inseparably with Gandhi's concept of a 'moral law.' I will also inquire into Gandhi's notion of human nature and argue that it was informed by his belief in the existence of a universal law. I will also argue that his understanding of human nature in turn influenced the concept of *ahimsa*.

According to Gandhi, a 'moral law' applied to all peoples, nations, religions, cultures and civilisations. Elaborating on this 'moral law' Gandhi stated,

> This mysterious moral law brings prosperity to the man who observes it, sustains the family who obeys it, and the community which lives by it ever flourishes. Freedom, peace and happiness are the lot of the nation that lets itself be ruled by this highest law. (Gandhi 1961b: 300)

Stressing the transcendental applicability of this law he stated,

> There is no reason to believe that there is one law for families and another for nations. History, then, is a record of an interruption of the course of nature. Soul-force, being natural, is not noted in history. (Gandhi 1959: 139)

Gandhi was of the view that transcending the differences between societies, religions, cultures and civilisations, there was a common understanding of the principles of truth and non-violence.[20] The moral realm for Gandhi was one that was informed by a broader raft of things than just the moral precepts of religion. According to Gandhi, "Anyone who observed the laws of morality for their own sake and not for any selfish end can be regarded as religious" (Gandhi 1961e: 280). Even in the secular world Gandhi argued that a civilisation would eventually perish if it began to morally degenerate. To substantiate his argument Gandhi insisted that Darwin also had spoken of the validity of the existence of a law of morality. Gandhi must have knowingly chosen to cite Darwin since the latter's well-known theory of evolution itself had been a major force in challenging the distinction made by the Church between human beings and other animals by virtue of human beings only having a 'soul.' What Gandhi may be refuting here is that unlike what some scholars may suggest, Darwin's theory does not imply that human beings, like animals, are 'soul-less' and therefore free from any causal retribution and from abiding by any sense of morality.[21]

Here it is worth pondering for a moment on the above critique of history made by Gandhi, that history has ignored the achievements of 'soul-force.'

History for Gandhi had been a notation and record of all that is tangible, visible and rational. Therefore what Gandhi may be arguing here is that although history would be able to account for his political strategies, there were no methods by which one could record the use of 'soul force' within his political struggle. Gandhi must have found it extremely difficult to give a 'scientific' explanation to his belief in a moral law. As Wybergh[22] himself had admitted to Gandhi that, although he believed in the value of 'soul-force,' he had "grave scruples about employing 'soul-force' for the attainment of physical or political objects . . . " (Gandhi 1997: 141).

Gandhi's understanding of the 'moral law' formed the basis of his concept of human nature, community and society. His identification with the moral law gave him a sense of identity and perception of the human community expanding beyond the national boundaries.

Bhikhu Parekh has traced the germination of Gandhi's ideas on man, society[23] and the universe to the Hindu tradition in which the world is envisaged as being Cosmo centric, interdependent and interrelated. The nature of the human being within the Hindu tradition is inherently good[24] but is often clouded by *maya* or appearance that makes human beings commit acts of evil (Parekh 1997: 36). It is a common saying in India that the legendary battle of *kurukshetra*[25] that was fought between two armies—good and evil—was a depiction of the battle between good and evil that takes place within the life of a human being. The battle of *kurukshetra* is part of the Gita, the Hindu epic that Gandhi was influenced by (as noted in chapter three). According to Parekh's analysis, Gandhi found human beings to possess fundamental characteristics:

> First, they were an integral part of the cosmos. Second, they were necessarily interdependent and developed and fell together. And third, they were four-dimensional beings made up of the body, the *manas* (mind), the *atman* (soul), and the *swabhava*[26] (non-material personality), whose interplay explained their behaviour and formed the basis of morality. (Parekh 1997: 38)

Among these the radical difference between classical Indian traditions and Gandhi's thinking was in his understanding of *atman* which Gandhi recognised as spiritual energy "and argued that, while mankind had long recognised and explored ways of mobilizing the former, it had neglected spiritual energy which, if tapped, could work wonders . . . his method of *satyagraha* was intended to do this" (Ibid.: 44). Explaining Gandhi's Cosmo centric view Parekh states,

> Unlike almost all the major traditions of Western thought, which neatly separate human beings and animals and assign the former a supremely privileged position on earth, Gandhi followed Indian traditions in taking a Cosmo centric view of

man. The cosmos was a well coordinated whole whose various parts were linked in a system of *yajna*, or interdependence and mutual service. It consisted of different orders of being ranging from the material to the human, each governed by its own laws and standing in a complex relationship with the rest. Human beings were an integral part of the cosmos, and tied to it by the deepest bonds. In Gandhi's favourite metaphor, the cosmos was not a pyramid of which the material world was the base and human beings the apex, but a series of ever-widening circles encompassing human kind, the sentient world, the material world, and the all-including cosmos. Since the cosmic spirit pervaded or infused the universe and was not outside it, the so-called natural world was not natural or material, terms he generally avoided, but spiritual or divine in nature. (Parekh 1997: 38)

In Gandhi's own words,

> . . . the ocean has no existence, if the drop has not, i.e., no individuality. They are beautifully interdependent. And if this is true of the physical, how much more so of the spiritual world! (Gandhi 1991: 174)

Parekh states: "That human beings were necessarily interdependent and formed an organic whole was another 'basic' truth about them according to Gandhi" (Parekh 1997: 39–40). Further Parekh adds that since human beings were necessarily interdependent, they "could not degrade or brutalise others without also degrading and brutalizing themselves, or inflict psychic and moral damage on others without inflicting it on themselves as well" (Ibid.: 41). Thus, Parekh notes that,

> Gandhi's concept of indivisible humanity formed the basis of his critique of systems of oppression and exploitation. Such dominant groups as the whites in South Africa, the colonial governments in India and elsewhere, and the rich and powerful in every society believed that their society's exploitation and degradation of their respective victims did not in any way damage them as well. In fact it degraded and dehumanised them as much as their victims, and sometimes even more. (Ibid.)

Gandhi, according to Parekh, challenged the definition of man as understood in the Western tradition. In exposing the unity between human life with other human and natural life, he gave meanings to the concepts of rights, duties, claims, interests and obligations. As Parekh points out, Gandhi's original thesis in political philosophy was that not only was the individual, his political community and humankind ontologically and morally inseparable, but going beyond most political philosophers Gandhi maintained that no political community can ignore the claims of those 'outside' its boundaries and still call itself moral. Although territorially outside it, they are very much inside it by virtue of a shared moral nature and ontological and cultural interdependence (Parekh 1989b: 197–199).

Two points need to be emphasised which Parekh has not done. The first is that although the doctrine of *ahimsa* was a contribution of Hinduism, the conceptual basis of Gandhi's values was not necessarily restricted to being produced within the fold of Hinduism. For instance, according to Gandhi the equality of human life was Islam's "distinctive contribution" (Iyer 1991 ed.: 152),[27] Gandhi's quotes on morality were often associated with Jesus (Ibid: 93–101),[28] and as Ikeda argues, his understanding of interdependence is similar to the Buddhist concept of dependent origination (Ikeda 1995: 119).

Secondly, moving beyond Parekh's analysis, I will argue in the next section that Gandhi's concept of *ahimsa* or non-violence must be understood in relation to his notion of a moral law. This will allow us to analyse the contradictions in Gandhi's ideas and strategies.

The Contradictions in Gandhi's Values

Analysing Gandhi's notion of values, in particular the value of *ahimsa* is problematic due to the contradictions that besiege Gandhi's writings and actions. These include Gandhi's abstinence from applying nonviolent means, for example, his consent for India's participation in the Second World War as part of the British allied force, the advice he gave to women to protect themselves in case of abuse, and his reluctant yet agreed support to maintain an Indian military force after independence. These were amongst many such seemingly hypocritical stances taken by someone who was renowned as an absolute pacifist. This is a difficulty that arises if one is to try and understand Gandhi's concept of *ahimsa* as a fixed value that must be applied irrespective of the time, place or situation.

In my book *Value Creators in Education* I mentioned that within education Gandhi had laid emphasis on the values of the head, heart and the hand, which necessitated the creation of a pattern of living based on *satya* (truth) and *ahimsa* (non-violence) (Sharma 1999: 43–44). I argued that although Gandhi regarded truth as the universal law which was constant, his concept of values, and in particular that of *ahimsa* was variable. Here, I would like to go a step further and analyse Gandhi's concept of value as originating in the relation between truth and value. In order to do this one needs to look at the inextricable link that Gandhi drew between truth and non-violence. *Ahimsa* (non-violence) was interlinked with the concept of *satya* (truth) according to Gandhi. For him, "*Ahimsa* is the means; truth is the end. Means to be means must always be within our reach, and so *Ahimsa* is our supreme duty" (Gandhi 1994: 18). Gandhi's notion of truth defined the universe in constant laws and a life that was ruled by the law of truth was one of greatest moral value. In Gandhi's words, "But truth, as it is conceived here, means that we have to rule our life by this law of truth at any cost" (Gandhi 1951: 40).

In spite of this several thinkers such as Raghavan Iyer (1994: 139) and Dennis Dalton (1993) have regarded the concept of *satya* or truth as a value. Gandhi described the universe as a set of laws according to which natural and human life was governed, and breaking away from these laws of life resulted in moral and hence physical destruction. It can therefore be argued that for Gandhi, value was found in living a life in rhythm with the law and therefore a moral life was a life that was spent in contributing to the betterment of humanity. This necessitated the use of tolerance, self-discipline and empathy. Gandhi's talisman was an embodiment of a life aspiring towards this.[29]

Gandhi's notion of good was also informed by his notion of human nature. Describing Gandhi's concept of 'good,' Parekh notes that Gandhi's theory of man "bypassed the traditional Western debate on whether human beings were naturally good and evil. . . . Since human beings had souls and were spiritual in nature, they had a deep *tendency* towards good" (Parekh 1997: 49). Gandhi understood that in spite of man's basic tendency towards good, they were often misled by appearance. In his words,

> Men are good. But they are poor victims making themselves miserable under the false belief that they are doing good. I am aware that there is a fallacy underneath this. I who claim to examine what is around me may be a deluded fool. This risk all of us have to take.[30] (Iyer 1991 ed.: 165)

In spite of the prevailing factor of appearance, Gandhi's belief in the tendency of human beings towards good was absolute. This was not necessarily the case with his stance on non-violence as seen in the following statement made by him:

> Even the seeming endorsement of violent action by my participation on the side of Britain in the Boer War and Zulu Revolt was recognition, in the interest of non-violence, of an inevitable situation. That the participation may nevertheless have been due to my weakness or ignorance of the working of the universal law of non-violence is quite possible. Only I had no conviction then, nor have any now, of such weaknesses of ignorance.
>
> A non-violent man will instinctively prefer direct participation to indirect, in a system which is based on violence and to which he has to belong without any choice left to him. I belong to a world which is partly based on violence. If I have only a choice between paying for the army of soldiers to kill my neighbours or to be a soldier myself, I would, as I must, consistently with my creed, enlist as a soldier in the hope of controlling the forces of violence and even of converting my comrades. (Bartolf 2000 ed.: 61)

In the 'violent world' Gandhi was postulating values according to the given situations in which he was placed. What was absolute was not his usage of non-violence, but his belief in the tendency of human beings towards good, which drew from his belief in the moral law of life. This shift in understanding Gandhi's concept of value clarifies to a large extent the changes in his stance towards *ahimsa*. At the same time, one cannot ignore the extremity of Gandhi's statements on *ahimsa* for which he has been severely criticised. For example during the Second World War Gandhi argued that even Hitler could be won over by non-violence. He had even planned to visit Germany, though his trip did not materialise.

Through such instances Gandhi leaves himself open to criticism. A sympathetic view of Gandhi would be to interpret him as an obstinate moralist who would challenge even Hitler to prove the efficacy of *soul-force*. One might even argue that Gandhi was apprehensive of the effect of fascism and the nuclear holocaust and therefore considered it his moral duty to condemn these, but since he was engaged in the struggle for Indian independence, it made it impossible for him to take any concrete action. Also perhaps the Nazi regime could not cope with or understand Gandhi. Or alternatively, Gandhi could not understand the real political issues of a Nazi state. In any case, Gandhi's belief in the 'good' of human nature has relevance for his political theory as Thomas Pantham states,

> Gandhi rejected a central assumption of modern political theory, namely, that as men originally belonged to a state of 'nature,' they are bound to remain, even in a civil or political society, tied to the law of 'brute force,' and that therefore a *natural-scientific* theory of politics, rather than any conception which 'fused' morality or spirituality with politics, was appropriate to the enlightened circumstances of modernity. Gandhi . . . explicitly rejected the modernist political theories of Herbert Spencer, Adam Smith, etc., who, he felt, merely extended the Galilean and Newtonian laws of the physical world and the Darwinian law of the animal world to human/social life. In a departure from these theories, Gandhi maintained that non-violence is, 'the law of our species as violence is the law of the brute.' (Pantham 1995: 115)

One can question whether Gandhi should be interpreted as a rationalist who would consider the pros and cons of the situation before taking action, or should he be seen as a moralist who advocated absolute values. Perhaps Gandhi can be understood as a relativist with a strong notion of morality and the rationality to gauge the situation that confronted him (though later in his political career his decisions were based more on his 'inner voice').[31] For example, though he had a profound belief in the good of all human beings, he was clear that one must not confuse rascality with saintliness (Iyer 1991 ed.: 387–388).[32] Gandhi had strong moral influences in his childhood and youth, as considered earlier in this study, while arguably at the same time he also developed a rational thinking in his years of training and practice as a lawyer.

Let us consider here the example of Gandhi's engagement with the issue of untouchability. Untouchables were the lowest class in the four-*varna* or caste system of the Hindu tradition. Under the direction of Gandhi, the untouchables, or *Harijans*[33] as Gandhi called them, were welcome in his *ashrams* and the Congress strove for the removal of untouchability through its programmes. However, Gandhi did not launch a direct attack on the Hindu tradition of the caste-system, but portrayed untouchability as a social evil. He remarked that the fourfold division of caste was a law of nature or law of heredity (Iyer 1986 ed.: 22) which meant that one is born into a family because of one's past deeds. He added that the individual's will to change one's occupation must be duly considered (something that was not allowed by the caste-system).

In Parekh's analysis, Gandhi "acknowledges the existence and legitimacy of the dominant strand within Hindu religious tradition. He does not explicitly reject it; rather he marginalises it . . . " (Parekh 1986: 23). Nanda too makes a similar comment that "Gandhi's reluctance to make a frontal assault on the caste system in the early years may have been a matter of tactics" (Nanda 1985: 26). He states that in a conversation with the Hungarian journalist, Tibor Mende, in 1956, Jawaharlal Nehru recalled:

> I spoke to Gandhi repeatedly: why don't you hit out at the caste system directly? He said that he did not believe in the caste system except in some idealised form of occupations and all that; but that the present caste system is thoroughly bad and must go. 'I am undermining it completely,' he said, 'by tackling untouchability.'
>
> You see . . . he had a way of seizing one thing and concentrating on it. 'If untouchability goes,' he said, 'the caste system goes.' (Ibid.)

Arguably, Gandhi can be described as a political strategist who was sensible in not provoking the Hindu orthodox.[34] At the same time, it must be pointed out that the political strategies that Gandhi adopted were not just the means towards the end of *swaraj* or independence, but were the end in itself.[35] Herein lay the difference between Gandhi and the Congress,[36] which was the main organ in his movement called the *Satyagraha*[37] movement.

To explain, under the Constructive Programme of their movement, the Congress carried forward Gandhi's directives out to the Indian populace. This programme focused on individual and social transformation through the removal of untouchability, boycott of British goods and so on (see Singh 1991). Other organs that transmitted Gandhi's movement included the *ashrams* or communities established by Gandhi, the newspapers such as *Young India* and *Harijan*, and Gandhi's speeches such as those recorded in the *Delhi Diary*.

In addition to this Gandhi extensively travelled through the length and breadth of India. The efficacy and complexities of Gandhi's *Satyagraha* has been analysed by several scholars who include Anthony Parel (1995), Bhikhu Parekh (1986: 14–30; 1989a; 1989b), Blanche Watson (1989), David Arnold (2001), Dennis Dalton (1993) and N. Radhakrishnan (1992 ed.). An in-depth analysis of the same is beyond the scope of this section. However, it must be clarified again that within Gandhi's experiments with truth, the use of a non-violent strategy was not just a means, but an end in itself. The strategies for the removal of untouchability, spinning of the *charkha* (wheel), wearing handmade *khadi* cloth,[38] protecting the cow from being slaughtered, and other social reforms were to transform the minds of the Indians and educate the populace in a life of values that contributed to both the individual and social welfare.

To the Congress this was an effective policy but for Gandhi it was his creed which stemmed from his commitment to *ahimsa* which he hoped would allow the Indians to see "the universal and all-pervading Spirit of Truth leading to 'identification with everything that lives'" (Gandhi 1957: 504). Unlike the Congress, Gandhi saw his movement as an educational one, in which the educator (himself in this case) was also a role model. Through his own experiments in non-violence Gandhi hoped to lead people to understand and practice a life of truth and non-violence (this will be further discussed in the conclusion chapter).

It can be argued that the Congress and the Indian polity in general failed to understand Gandhi's powerful construct of an inclusive citizen, and were not able to override their contention for ethnic and religious differences, and continued to engage themselves in communal conflicts. As Gandhi remarked in retrospect, the non-violence displayed during the freedom struggle had only been the 'non-violence of the weak.'[39]

At the same time it can also be argued that one of the difficulties in following Gandhi has been that he had declared that there was nothing known as 'Gandhism' or 'Gandhian,' which was understandable given the religious fundamentalism and fascism that existed in India. However, at the same time Gandhi did not even lay down a way by which people might comprehend the philosophical basis and rational means by which he sought to carry out his experiments in India. To the contrary one finds contradictions in Gandhi's conduct as a *satyagrahi*.[40] For instance Gandhi considered it a necessity for a *satyagrahi* to be aware of all facts. Admonishing the other *Satyagrahis* he wrote in 1916,

Experience shows that although people talk of non-violence, many are mentally so lazy that they do not even take the trouble of familiarizing themselves with the facts. Take an example. India is a poor country. We wish to do away with poverty. But how many people have made a study of how this poverty came about, what its implications are, how it can be removed, etc.? A devotee of non-violence should be full of such knowledge.[41] (Iyer 1991 ed.: 384)

In spite of this in 1938 in an instructive lecture in Muir Central College Economic Society he stated:

> . . . a civilian friend deluged me with a series of questions on my crankisms. As he proceeded in his cross-examination, I being a willing victim, he found no dif-ficulty in discovering my gross ignorance of the matters . . . To his horror, and even indignation, I suppose, he found that I had not even read books on eco-nomics by such well-known authorities as Mill, Marshall, Adam Smith and a host of such other authors. In despair, he ended by advising me to read these works before experimenting in matters economic at the expense of the public. He little knew that I was a sinner past redemption.
>
> My experiments continue at the expense of trusting friends. For, there come to us moments in life when about some things we need no proof from without. A little voice within us tells us, 'You are on the right track, move neither to your left nor right, but keep to the straight and narrow way.' With such help we march forward slowly indeed, but surely and steadily. That is my position. It may be satisfactory enough for me, but it can in no way answer the requirements of a society such as yours. (Iyer 1991 ed.: 93)

Gandhi had remarked that in case of discrepancies found in his statements, one should refer to the latest one, as his experiments in life would allow him to change his mind. This would have posed to be a difficult proposition for those who wanted to follow Gandhi. As the next chapter explores, this and other related factors have lead to Gandhi being marginalised within the changing values of twenty-first century India.

NOTES

1. By this I am referring to the Newtonian-Cartesian paradigm that I have written on in my earlier work and termed as a 'reductionist view' (Sharma 2002). As com-pared to this, Makiguchi, Gandhi and even Dewey had a more 'holistic' perspective of human nature and society. I will explore this further on in this chapter.

2. For details on the application of the values of Makiguchi in Soka University see Bethel 1973: 122–123. Details of Soka University in Japan and America can be found at http://www.soka.ac.jp/en/ and http://www.soka.edu/ respectively.

3. One of the leading institutions is the Soka Research Centre (see Harima 1997: 242).

4. For further details see paper tilted 'Brilliance in Experiments—Value Creators in Education' in Sharma 1999: appendix I.

5. The works of Makiguchi have been compiled in 10 volumes by Daisanbunmei-sha under the title *Makiguchi Tsunesaburo Zenshu* [The Complete Works of Tsunesaburo Makiguchi].

6. See note 1, chapter 1.

7. Based on my investigation of Makiguchi's work, the use of the word 'judgment' in table 4.1 in this translation (from Bethel 1989 ed.: 63) should be seen as 'evaluation.'

8. Specifically, according to Makiguchi, the negative or anti-thesis of each of the positive values of beauty, benefit and good are ugliness, loss and evil respectively.

9. Life or *seimei*.

10. Bethel states that "If one considers the mixture of these three lines of thought—the importance of the learner's geographic environment to the educational process, the emphasis on experience and the scientific method stemming from the pragmatic orientation, and the recognition of education's sociological dimensions—all within the particular context in which Makiguchi worked, it is possible to discern the broad outlines of the educational philosophy and pedagogy that issued from his thought and work" (Bethel 1973: 45). Bethel does not thematically proceed to undertake this in his book. Also, there are other influences and thoughts that should be taken into account, which are stated in my analysis in this chapter.

11. See appendix II.

12. See third section, chapter six of Makiguchi 1981.

13. This thought is both contributive as well as problematic, as will be discussed in the last section of this chapter and in the conclusion chapter eight.

14. See appendixes III and IV.

15. Gandhi as well makes a similar argument as noted later in this chapter.

16. From the Channel Five Television programme titled 'The Big Question,' series title: 'Why are we here?' presented on Monday, 5 January 2004.

17. Also, in light of this perhaps Makiguchi may be slightly misjudged as being too naïve to imagine that it can be possible to harmonise individual and social values.

18. Gandhi defined it as 'voluntary suffering' with the use of compassion and intelligence; and also in *Navajivan* dated 4 October 1925 he describes it as self-purification, knowledge of the *atman* (soul) and its realisation (Collected Works, Vol. 33, 25 September 1925–10 February 1926).

19. It is the first of the four stages of life in Hinduism. Gandhi often used it as 'self-discipline.' In a letter to Mirabehn dated 27 April 1933 he stated that, "It means not suppression of one or more senses but complete mastery over them all" (Collected Works, Vol. 61, 27 April 1933 to 7 October 1933).

20. See Gandhi 1959, chapter II.

21. There are many questions related to this that I will not go into the details of, but as Wiker points out, "An important part of the current controversy over the theoretical status of evolutionary theory concerns its moral implications. Does evolutionary theory undermine traditional morality, or does it support it? Does it suggest that infanticide is natural (as Steven Pinker asserts) or is it a bulwark against liberal relativism (as Francis Fukuyama argues)? Does it rest on a universe devoid of good and evil (as Richard Dawkins has bluntly stated) or can it be used to provide a new foundation for natural law reasoning (as Larry Arnhart contends)" (Wiker 2001)?

22. W.J. Wybergh was a theosophist and a member of the Transvaal legislature.

23. For details on Gandhi's concept of a 'good society' see chapter six of the book *Gandhi* (Parekh 1997).

24. 'Good,' as used here can be explained as the human disposition to contribute to the betterment of self and society. Neither Parekh nor Gandhi have specifically defined the terms 'good' and 'evil,' but since the use of these terms is important to my analysis of Gandhi's values, I have accordingly quoted Parekh and Gandhi in this chapter.

25. In the Bhagavad Gita (which is part of the ancient Hindu epic the Mahabharata), it states that a battle was fought on the grounds of the place known as *Kurukshetra* in India, between two cousins—the Pandavas and Kauravas—who stood on the side of good and evil respectively.

26. Parekh describes *manas* as mind, *atman* as soul, and *swabhava* as non-material personality (Parekh 1997: 46).

27. In an interview with Dr. John Mott dated 1 March 1929, *Young India*, 21 March 1929.

28. Speech at Muir College Economic Society, Allahabad on 22 December 1916 (*The Leader*, 25 December 1916).

29. The talisman reads: "Whenever you are in doubt, or when the self becomes too much with you, apply the following test. Recall the face of the poorest and the weakest man who you may have seen, and ask yourself if the step you contemplate is going to be of any use to *him*. Will he gain anything by it? Will it restore him . . . Then you will find your doubts and . . . self melting away" (Fischer 1983: 316).

30. Letter to A.H. West dated 12 January 1910, Collected Works of Mahatma Gandhi (1958–1994), p. 4413.

31. Refer to note 30, chapter 2.

32. In a letter written dated 16 March 1932, Gandhi stated, "It is possible and necessary to treat human beings on terms of equality, but this can never apply to their morals. One would be affectionate and attentive to a rascal and to a saint; but one cannot and must not put saintliness and rascality on the same footing" (Iyer 1991 ed.: 387–388, from The Diary of Mahadev Desai, Vol. 1, p. 15).

33. See glossary.

34. Gandhi's work on the removal of untouchability has been debatable, such as, on one hand it had impressed even his staunch critic, Sir Winston Churchill, but on the other it, it was rebuked by B.R. Ambedkar who was from the scheduled caste.

35. For instance, in a letter written to M. Asaf Ali dated 26 June 1933, Gandhi states, "Non-violence for me is not a mere experiment. It is part of my life and the whole of the creed of *satyagraha*, non-co-operation, civil disobedience, and the like are necessary deductions from the fundamental proposition that non-violence is the law of life for human beings. For me it is both a means and an end . . . " (Iyer 1994 ed.: 244). Also see Gandhi 1959, chapter III.

36. For Gandhi's own account of the disagreements between Gandhi and the Congress on this issue see for instance, Gandhi's article in *Harijan* on 29 June 1940 (Iyer 1994 ed.: 248–252).

37. See glossary.

38. The economic component of Gandhi's movement included activities such as manufacturing salt from the sea, and spinning the wheel to make the khadi cloth. These activities were directed to boycott British goods and were an important part of the Indian national struggle for freedom.

39. In an interview to Deputation from Quetta dated 8 July 1947 in the Collected Works, Vol. 96, 7 July 1947 to 26 September 1947. Also see *Harijan* dated 26 March 1938, 4 November 1939.

40. A person who carries out *satyagraha*.

41. 'What is Sarvodaya?' (H.) GN 7680 written in Segaon on 21 July 1938.

Chapter Five

An Exposition of Changing Values in Japan and India

OVERVIEW

The deaths of Makiguchi (1944) and Gandhi (1948) came at a time in which the world was on the brink of one of the greatest political changes it had ever witnessed. America and Russia were emerging as two superpowers; Japan had adopted a peace-loving constitution; India, Korea, and China, among others, had emerged as independent nation states; decolonisation in Asia and Africa was a major development; and international agencies such as the United Nations were given power to provide stability in the world affairs.

Alongside such political movements another great world-wide impact was being created by the increase in economic and technological development. The impact of the scientific, industrial civilisation had transformed the values and structures of most societies and their education with a speed such as the world had never witnessed before. This lead to new forms of unions, new bilateral agreements between nations, new forms of dominance by those countries that had quickly climbed the ladder of economic supremacy, new forms of family structures, changed food habits, and the impact of these on education. If in the last half of the twentieth century Japan was at the top of the economic ladder, India was at the lower bottom half. However, since the 1990s changes in both countries have occurred on an unprecedented scale, with Japan moving down from its position as No. 1, and India slowly strengthening its economic and technological role in the world market.

This chapter will highlight some of these changes that have taken place from the twentieth to the twenty-first centuries in Japan and India. It will focus on the interplay of power-holding by the educational authorities, military, and politicians that, to a great extent, have given shape to the leading values[1] in society and education. Within the changes of the twenty-first century, this chapter will analyse the fates of both Makiguchi and Gandhi in the twenty-first century.

MAKIGUCHI AND THE CHANGING VALUES
IN JAPAN 50 YEARS ONWARDS

Changing Values in Japanese Society

The transformation of Japan that took place under the American occupation is perhaps one of the greatest changes in the shortest period that history has ever witnessed. The Americans were swift in providing adequate measures to transform the nation that had a strong imperial hold into a newly independent democratic state with a new constitution, new political party and well-informed public. The Japanese cooperated and seized every opportunity for political, economic and social advance. Virtues of loyalty and filial piety towards the emperor had motivated the Japanese for several years, but in the new democratic state, the aims of the nation turned towards 'of the people,' 'for the people' and 'by the people.' In 1952, the US decision not to prosecute Emperor Hirohito for war crimes was controversial as allies and leftists in Japan believed that he should be held accountable for the excesses committed by the Imperial armed forces. In spite of such pressures, no action was taken against the emperor.

As Jeffrey Kingston remarks, "The Americans believed that Hirohito was more valuable to their reform efforts alive and free than dead or incarcerated and feared creating a martyr for the nationalist movement" (Kingston 2001: 15). This fear of the Americans was not misplaced. When Prime Minister Hideki Tojo hanged himself after the proceedings of the Tokyo War Crimes Tribunal, the popular press and right-wing writers began to portray the Japanese defendants solely as victims of biased legal proceedings. Perhaps for similar reasons American occupiers let the Japanese Constitution, which was drafted in 1947 have in Article 1 mention that the emperor was the symbol of Japan. The same was mentioned in the first page of the Fundamental Law of Education in spite of it being a replacement of the Imperial Rescript on Education.

After the Americans left, the challenges that faced Japan as a nation were less to do with imperialism and more with the domination of power under the Liberal Democratic Party (LDP), the political party that has sustained itself until now in Japanese politics. A nexus of power gradually developed involving politicians, bureaucrats, big business and the *yakuza* or organised crime syndicates. Political scandals have been a regular feature of press news and even then few are convicted of the crimes. For instance, in the Recruit Scandal of 1988 which involved a real estate affiliate called Recruit Cosmos, among the bureaucrats that made efforts to rig the system, only one government official was convicted for his part in the scandal and that was also not until 1999. Another famous example is that of the *Minamata byo* or Minamata sickness, also known as *itai-itai byo* or the painful sickness, in which mercury poisoning caused by local chemical plant lead to numerous sufferers and severe birth defects.

The 'iron triangle' of big business, bureaucracy and the LDP has been one of the main influences on Japanese society and education, and any talk of values cannot be undertaken without taking a look at the shape and meaning that has been given to public affairs by this group. The three have grown along with each other through Japan's economic development. The economic development of Japan or the economic miracle has been attributed by Chalmers Johnson (1982) to the not-so-invisible hands of state-sponsored development, and the Ministry of International Trade and Industry (MITI) which played a main role in orchestrating economic growth by channeling low-cost loans and extending other benefits to targeted sectors of the economy. Japan, as noted by some, had already witnessed technological growth and modernisation even before the Second World War, but after the large-scale damage created by the war, through the contribution of SCAP (Supreme Command of the Allied Powers)[2] favourable conditions was created for Japan's unprecedented growth.

Along with this, another reason for the economic progress of Japan has been attributed to America's war with Korea. Describing this, Kingston notes,

> The war procurements of the American military during the Korean War (1950–53) are often credited with pulling Japan out of a dire postwar recession and putting the economy on a steep growth trajectory. Prime Minister Yoshida referred to this estimated $3 billion windfall as a 'gift from the gods' because austerity measures imposed by the US in 1949 had drastically shrunk domestic demand and threatened to stifle recovery. War on the peninsula provided a much-needed stimulus. Unhindered access to the US market and technology also played a key role in Japan's growth spurt. . . . The war devastation proved an opportunity as Japan had to rebuild most of its industrial plant and equipment from scratch. Thus, Japanese industrial plants were, on average, more modern and had more advanced technology than was the case in the US where there was no urgency in renovating or replacing aging facilities or production lines. The war thus inadvertently played a key role in modernizing Japan's factories. (Kingston 2001: 38)

Added to this was the increasing demand for Japanese consumer goods abroad, migration of youth to cities, high rate of savings, good employment system, that is, lifetime employment, seniority wages and enterprise unions, which lead to a spectacular economic growth. The LDP at this stage provided all the necessary support for the growth of Japanese business. Under the LDP Japan adopted a role as a liberator of Asian countries from Western rule, the basic intent being to stabilise its own economy. In 1977 Prime Minister Fukuda committed Japan to assist ASEAN (The Association of Southeast Asian Nations) in large-scale industrialisation projects and Official Development Assistance (ODA) to Asian recipients was increased. Japan also renounced military intentions and worked hard to broker a resolution to the post-Vietnam War problems engulfing Indo-China. This continued emphasis on forging political, economic and cultural relations in Asia, as was hoped, worked to mutual advantage.

However, for a long time in its international relations Japan avoided an apology and compensation for the war victims in Korea and China. Though countries like Germany, which had a similar history as Japan, had quickly settled its relations with its neighbours, Japan was hesitant till the 1990s. Selden and Hein (2000) claim that whereas Germany considered it as an advantage to be a part of Europe, Japan felt no such pressures on its stability and growth. This discrimination could also be found within Japan, with the Korean ethnic minority, which is the largest ethnic minority in Japan, facing the main brunt of it.[3] War compensations that were later settled in the San Francisco Peace Treaty have only settled state-to-state claims, and claims of most individual sufferers have been avoided. The apology given by the government since 1990s has resulted in the growth of a reactionary force amongst the Japanese. This force of ultranationalists has already initiated a strong movement which seeks to revive in the Japanese a sense of identity and belongingness to their own culture. Books written by the leaders of this movement such as the *Shin Nihongo Kyokasho* or New Language Textbook by Nobukatsu Fujioka, professor of Tokyo University, has even gone on to become the best-seller in the year 2001.

The support this group has received from the larger society brings one to wonder whether the Japanese actually find themselves lacking a sense of identity and values that they seemingly had during the war. It is true that in the Meiji era and under America's influence during occupation, Japan had looked outwards for values. Japanese education in particular had ushered in theories from abroad without much concern given to the cultural context in which the realities of the children were shaped.[4]

Added to this has been the predominance of capitalistic values in an economically progressing Japan. The self-constructed image of Japan as a nation of subjects bound together with the Emperor which existed during the Second World War may well have been replaced by an image of Japan as No. 1 in world economy (Vogel 1979). The bursting of the economic bubble after 1980s therefore seems to have been a greater blow than expected to the sense of identity of the people of Japan. For half a century the average Japanese had given their life to their place of work. For their loyal services the employees were compensated with lifetime employment and seniority wages. However, the bursting of the bubble and economic recession resulted in 1999 in the number of suicides reaching an all-time high of 33,000, with 20 per cent of those deaths being attributed to debts or job losses, which is nearly double the corresponding figure for 1998. In Tokyo especially even now one can find a growing cardboard-box community of homeless men gathered in train stations.[5] The crash has affected corporate Japan, but weighed more heavily on small and medium sized business. Meanwhile political scandals continue to be a regular feature. Arguably, such events have proved to be an opportune time for the ultranationalists to voice their concern about the lack of sense of identity and values amongst the Japanese.

If on the one hand the Japanese had identified themselves as an economic force to reckon with, on the other hand they have boasted of being the only nation that has a constitution which refrains from maintaining a military base. States Kingston,

> Article Nine of the Constitution bans the development of military forces and eliminates Japan's sovereign right to wage war. This article is unique in the world and is the reason the Japanese Constitution is often referred to as the Peace Constitution. As the only nation to have experienced the devastation of atomic bombs, Japan has assumed a unique role in global efforts to halt nuclear proliferation and eliminate nuclear weapons. It has embraced three principles that have served as the basis of its nuclear policy: (1) no development of nuclear weapons; (2) no possession of nuclear weapons; and (3) no introduction of nuclear weapons on Japanese soil. (Kingston 2001: 65)

This peace-loving image of Japan has also been, to borrow Benedict Anderson's words, "merged with a correspondingly wide variety of political and ideological constellations" (Anderson 1991: 4). This constitutional constraint imposed by the US has been regretted by it ever since its enactment. MacArthur's demand that Japan establish military forces for its own defence were parried by Prime Minister Yoshida, who was worried that Japan might be called into a combat role on the Korean peninsula. At this time Japan did create a small armed force that evolved into the SDF (Self Defence Forces),[6] but did so in a minimalist way, reflecting strong national reservations about remilitarisation. Japan had over the years steadfastly refused to participate in collective defence, maintaining that the constitution only permitted the right of individual rational self-defence. President Nixon renewed US pressure in

1969 when he requested Japan to assume a greater role in ensuring the stability of East Asia. Within this context the Japanese government has used and ignored article nine as felt appropriate.

Till the end of the 1960s Japan used Article Nine to safeguard its economy and Asian relations and refused to participate directly in America's wars. While using it as an excuse not to join American wars, it has simultaneously built its infrastructure through catering for America's war with Korea. While pretending to be a peace-loving country, it chose to remain silent on the US deployment of nuclear weapons in Iwo Jima till the end of 1959, Chichi Jima until 1965, and Okinawa till 1972. In 1998 when faced with the nuclear threat from North Korea the Japanese government for the first time agreed to US requests to clarify and expand its posture on collective security and developed a system for Theater Missile Defence (TMD). Synopsising this bilateral alliance Kingston writes,

> The brutal rape of a twelve-year-old girl in 1995 by US marines brought anti-base resentments to a head and since then the US and Japan have accelerated negotiations over reducing and relocating US bases. On the other hand, the US security presence is unobtrusive to most Japanese and appreciated by many who oppose a remilitarization of Japan. Many Japanese remain haunted by the ghosts of militarism and see the US military presence as a safeguard against a return to the past. In addition, the bilateral alliance reassures Japan's neighbors in Asia, easing concerns that still linger about Japanese militarism and signaling that the US will remain engaged in the region. Other Japanese across the political spectrum worry, however, that the US security presence might involve Japan in some conflict against its wishes and that it symbolizes a diminution of Japanese sovereignty. (Kingston 2001: 59)

Recently, in America's war with terrorism following the incident on 11 September 2001, Japan went against the constitution to support the Iraq war. The Asahi Shimbun (newspaper) on 19 December 2002 reports that the Japan-US Security talks have developed positively since Japan agreed to send the Maritime Self-Defence Force Aegis destroyer Kirishima to the Indian Ocean to provide support in the US led fight against terrorism. Present day Japan continues to maintain a large military force and defence budget in spite of the continued existence of article nine.

The moorings of Japan have altered through these power-dominated relations that have constructed in the last five decades image, identity and values for the nation as deemed appropriate for them to sustain their continued existence. The educational agenda of political parties, economic aims of the nation, international pressures, and other such factors have continued to affect the values of the education system as well.

Changing Values in Japanese Education

Education in Japan, as elsewhere, is influenced by a myriad of factors within which perhaps one of the most significant is the aims of the government. Here I will explore some of the important government decisions, aims and ideologies that have exerted their influence on values in education, both conspicuously and inconspicuously.

Since the American occupation there has continued to be a vacillating control between the *Nikkyoso* (Japan Teachers' Union) and the *Mombusho* (Ministry of Education) within which the former has often exerted a powerful force in education related matters, and has also expanded the scope of its activities to raise issues that are social or political in nature. For instance, the teachers union has pointed out flaws in the Japan-US Security Treaty, expressed concern about the nuclear rearmament of Japan, and asked for the return of Okinawa from American control, asking at the same time to intensify the People's Movement for Peace (Nikkyoso May 1966: 1).

At the same time, in spite of a strong Teachers' Union, some scholars find the educational agenda of the Liberal Democratic Party (LDP) to have a greater impact on the values in education. Yoshimitsu Khan in his book *Japanese Moral Education Past and Present* (Khan 1997) argues that the LDP has used moral education as an instrument for nation building since the 1960s, and that the state-controlled moral education contradicts the shared intention of the Japanese Constitution and the Fundamental Law of Education. For instance, the contents of the 'Image of an Ideal Japanese' (Ministry of Education 1966) postulated by the Ministry of Education in 1966 portrays the ideal Japanese as conscious of himself/herself as an individual, a family man, a part of society, and as a citizen. Analysing this Khan notes that,

> At first glance each section represents an appropriate area of concern. But, when seen in the context of other government tactics, such as control of the content of education, the establishment of political neutrality of schools, the Act of Education Council Appointment System, and the enforcement of textbook authorization, the draft report sheds a bright light on LDP's agenda: through control of education, the government will control the populace. The real aim of the interim draft for the "Ideal Image of Human Beings" also explains that to respect the emperor is equivalent to loving Japan. Here we come full circle to the same cultural root that informed and justified Japan's belief system for ages. (Khan 1997: 115)

It should be mentioned here that the 'Image of Ideal Japanese' as constituted in 1972 by the Teachers Union (Nikkyoso 1972) does not mention the emperor, but instead highlights the values of the Constitution and the Fundamental Law of Education. However, the aim of the 'Image of the Ideal Japanese' are too general, that is, it does not specify any concrete way in which the 'values' stated in this document can be realised in the classroom.

Returning to the educational agenda of the LDP, during the time in which the above document, the 'Image of an Ideal Japanese,' was being used in schools, the history textbook controversy of Ienaga Saburo versus the Ministry of Education had started revealing the government's intention to hide the historical facts of Japanese atrocities committed in Korea and China during World War II. It was not until the 1990s that under international pressure the LDP finally began to acknowledge these historical facts. One can however argue that the change in stance by the LDP was a government tactic to woo foreign investors and international help in its economic crises. The result of this is that history textbooks which a few decades ago were 'protecting the children' from the horrors of Japan's past, now reveal an extreme picture of Japan as a barbaric nation.

My analysis of history textbooks collected in 2002 suggests that illustrations such as the picture of the painting of a Japanese soldier cutting off the breasts of his Chinese captive (ISEI 1994: 320) is one such example, which, as the Textbook Reform Society has proven, is based on lack of historical evidence (Reform 1998: 5). I must clarify here that the Textbook Reform Society on its own fits my above description of 'ultranationalists' in present day Japan, and I am in no way defending their aims or ideals.

Along with the above agenda (of hiding, revealing or misrepresenting historical facts when it suits them), the LDP and the *Mombusho* have also aggressively pursued economic growth since 1960s through the enrichment of science and technology in education. One of the key documents that elaborate on this aim is the Economic Investigation Council of Tokyo (1963). Another important document that puts stress on Japan's economic growth through education is the white paper of 1962 by the Ministry of Education titled, 'Japan's Growth and Education: Educational Development in Relation to Socio-Economic Growth.' Above all this paper advocates the importance of meritocracy. It can be argued that the high rate of academic success in Japanese schools has served as a model for America for the past forty years. However, by the turn of the twentieth century Japanese education has been marred by an increased rate of *ijime* or bullying, high rate of suicides, adolescents killing adults, and several other life threatening problems. The causes of this may be found in the increasing academic pressure and lack of support given to children.[7] Since the late 1970s and early 1980s children have been divided according to the standard deviation test, which has become a label for the child. This may well lead many children to feel isolated from their peer group.

At the same time there has been an increasing lack of communication between parents and children. Though the government policies have been advocating education in the home, school and community, it seems to have been ineffective. One of the measures to combat this has been made in the initial stages by The Extraordinary Educational Council (EEC) which was formed by the government in August 1984. This council saw modern scientific and technological civilisation as the main reason for the cause of educational devastation and proposed through moral education "to emphasize the cultivation of respect for the awesome by placing nature and transcendental existence face-to-face with modern scientific and technological civilization" (Kingston 2001: 119).

These and other policies have resulted in an increased number of hours for moral education, and have continued to be one of the main directives of the Ministry of Education since the 1980s. In 1983 the Ministry of Education conducted a survey of actual conditions of moral education in public elementary and junior high schools of which one of the suggestions was that number of hours for moral education should be increased. Even though the objectives of moral education since 1983 seems to be more concrete as compared to the previous ones, there is no clear 'means' by which it expects to achieve its aim of "enhancing pupils ability to make moral judgement," except by "supplementing, intensifying, and integrating" some moral values arbitrarily through "systematic and developmental instruction" (Mombusho 1983: 111–117).

There are now thirty four Moral Hour sessions in the first grade and thirty five hours each from the second to the sixth grade. In junior high schools, each grade has no less than thirty five hours per year. In private elementary and junior high schools, an average of one hour per week is assigned for the Moral Hour. In parochial schools, religious education may be substituted. What does not seem to concern the *Mombusho* is that more moral hours means more time subtracted from the school day and therefore more time is to be spent in the *juku* or cramming school in preparation for the intensified competition on the entrance examination. Increased tuition also results in creating a greater financial burden for parents. To cover the increasing educational costs means spending less time with the children which again adds to the isolation of children. In this situation how then do the new policies think of bringing together the home, school and community for the child's education? With home schools and alternative learning increasing at the rate of 20 per cent in USA, today Japanese schools may in turn need to look at America. However, what needs to be considered in any educational reform is the life pattern, modes of living, culture and values which are akin to the Japanese society.

For instance the value of *nintai* or tolerance has been taught from one generation to the other in Japan. With the increasing pressure of modern society and education it may well be difficult for the children to tolerate school bullying without adequate support from parents and the society. It may not be an exaggeration to state that the result of the undue emphasis on *nintai* has been an increasing rate of suicide and juvenile delinquency.

To conclude, although there have been considerable changes in the policies, curriculum and structure of Japanese schools, the aims and values of the dominant power groups have continued to influence the direction of society and education. Such as, Khan in his comparative research on the post-war moral textbook of *dotoku* with the pre-war moral textbook of *shushin* shows that in many ways contemporary Japanese moral education is an extension of prewar moral education. Japanese scholars such as Shumon Miura have also revealed that morality in Japan is still inconspicuously related to the emperor who continues to be the main symbol or representation of Japan (Miura 2001).

The Fate of Makiguchi in 21st Century Japan

In the twenty-first century Makiguchi is not well known within the educational circles of Japan. As Kumagaya finds, he is not even mentioned in the 1971 'Modern Educational History of Japan Dictionary,' which attests to the fact that although several scholars and eminent persons during Makiguchi's time admired his work, just forty years after the publication of his educational pedagogy he was virtually unknown in the educational circles of modern Japan (Kumagaya 2000). Numerous reasons can be stated for the continued lack of knowledge of Makiguchi and his values in Japan. Hisao Harima, author of *Yoku Wakaru Soka Kyoiku* (Harima 1997),[8] points out some of the main factors that have deterred the application of Makiguchi's ideas even today.[9] Chief amongst them is the tendency within the Japanese educators to be easily influenced by foreigners even at the cost of overlooking the ideas of Japanese thinkers.

Harima also finds that by and large the Japanese polity lacks the ability to challenge authority, which he claims can be attributed to their culture, namely the undue allegiance that had been given to the emperor system and caste system. This lack of initiative to understand and when necessary challenge politics and business continues to exist even today, and can be stated as a reason why the general public has not seriously engaged with the Soka Gakkai, and therefore its leader Makiguchi. The Soka Gakkai is the successor of the organisation Soka Kyoiku Gakkai established by Makiguchi in 1930, and presently includes roughly one tenth of Japan's population, as well as providing political endorsement to the ruling Komeito political party. As a growing body politic it has been of much interest to both the Japanese politicians and the media. Takesato Watanabe concludes through his research that the latter has gone on to generate a wrong image of *Gakkai* in Japanese society, through "distortions generated in the reportage of the Soka Gakkai" (Watanabe 2000: 213).[10]

Notwithstanding this, Makiguchi's ideas have gained popularity in some parts of Japan and abroad in spite of the fact that during his lifetime the practical application of his value creating theory had taken place only within his own classrooms and in Toda's[11] *Jishu Gakkan* (the results of which are not available at present). However, due to the post-war reconstruction of the Soka Gakkai by Toda, and his successor the current president, Daisaku Ikeda,[12] Makiguchi is now known by Soka Gakkai members in 190 countries, and research (by members and non-members) is being carried out on the Theory of Value Creation (as pointed out in the previous chapter). The Soka Gakkai is also registered as a Non Government Organisation with the United Nations, and in the World Summit on Sustainable Development (WSSD) held in Johannesburg in 2002, the Soka Gakkai's proposal for establishing a 'Decade of Education for Sustainable Development' beginning 2005 was accepted as a part of the 'Global Implementation Document.'

The members of the Soka Research Centre in Japan, taking from the pragmatic view of Makiguchi are encouraged to develop their own teaching methods through classroom practice (Sharma 1999: 117). These methods have not yet filtered into the wider academic community of Japan primarily because along with the ideas of Makiguchi, Buddhist philosophy informs the group's research and teaching. In order not to digress from the main subject of this section, let me summarise by saying that although Makiguchi is gaining attention within Japan, the application of his ideas is mainly restricted to the experiments carried out by research associations related to the Soka Gakkai.[13]

Based on my observations in the Soka Schools, two factors can be attributed to the successful application of Makiguchi's values in these schools. Firstly, there is a willingness among the teachers to experiment with the 'value creating theory' of their original founder Makiguchi. Secondly, and equally important is the function of Daisaku Ikeda, the person who founded these schools. Toda serves as the link between Makiguchi and Ikeda because Ikeda joined the Soka Gakkai after Makiguchi's death.[14] Bethel states that, "Ikeda, as Makiguchi, sees education as the most important factor in changing the present reality" (Bethel 1973: 121). Further, he adds that Ikeda and Makiguchi both laid emphasis on the "need for a harmonious balance within every person's life between the pursuit of values of personal gain and the pursuit of values of social good. One cannot, in other words, be a complete, happy, value-creating person by himself" (Bethel 1973: 121). This philosophy enthuses both teachers and students of the Soka Schools to be active participants in their local communities, as well as engaging in international exchanges.[15]

The factors are, however, unique to the Soka institutions. The question that follows from this is whether the values of Makiguchi are relevant for the wider Japanese educational system, which will be discussed in chapter six. This study is not a hagiography of Makiguchi's values, nor is it a despondent critique that dismisses Makiguchi's values as being inapplicable for the twenty-first century. Rather, it is an attempt to appraise the fate of Makiguchi, that is, the use and influence of his ideas within present day Japan.

A critical analysis of the restricted application of Makiguchi can be attributed to the difficulties faced by both Makiguchi and Ikeda in their endeavour to transform their respective societies both intellectually and morally through the use of both religion and politics. As Bethel analyses in his work *Makiguchi the Value Creator,*

> In Soka Gakkai, under Ikeda's leadership, intellect is not pressed into the service of the movement, but rather is aimed at transforming the quality of mind of the entire population, equipping that population to judge the movement and to hold both it and its competitors accountable . . . Soka Gakkai may well be breaking open new frontiers in this respect. (Bethel 1973: 143)

As I will argue in the conclusion chapter of this book, Makiguchi must have established the *Soka Kyoiku Gakkai* because he realised that education on its own could not compensate for society. Makiguchi's speeches within the *Gakkai* on the existing socio-political events can be seen as his efforts for enabling the members to become more politically aware. Similarly today, Ikeda and the Soka Gakkai in Japan claim that their religion is not an 'Opiate,' and therefore they have actively engaged in Japanese education, culture and politics. As will be argued in chapter six, the socio-political involvement of the Soka Gakkai in Japan has been both rewarding, as well as having created significant dilemmas for both the members as well as the larger Japanese community. Let us for now turn to an exposition of the changing values within Indian society and education, and the fate of Gandhi in the twenty-first century.

GANDHI AND THE CHANGING VALUES
IN INDIA 50 YEARS ONWARDS

Changing Values in the Indian Society

This section is an exposition of the changing values in India as it has transformed from a colonial subject to an independent democratic country in approximately the last fifty years. It is an analysis of the creation, development and sustenance of values under the changes that have taken place in Indian

politics, economics, religious affairs, media and India's international relations. It traces the dominance of power structures and the values postulated
within them by politicians, religious leaders, and contenders of economic and
technological growth. The limitations posed in such analysis are the inadequate research on the comprehensive view of changing values. Though much
work has been published on values in India, what is most often discussed
within this subject are traditional values in Indian life such as the values of
the ancient Indian religious texts like the Vedas, and their relevance in our
present day (Chattopadhyaya 1961). Studies, conferences and seminars
(ICCR 1969) have taken place on Indian values that originate from philosophers and religious thinkers such as Aurobindo, Tagore, Vivekananda and
others. There is also a lack of material available on the changing image of India as a nation.

Therefore, in order to write this section, I have perused the works of historians, social activists, political commentators and the likes to analyse the
main trends in the Indian society in the last five decades. The primary challenge that I have faced in this study has been the task of commenting on the
diverse religious beliefs, traditions, cultures, languages, caste, and class of the
heterogeneous Indian polity. This section will therefore be delimited to
analysing the main changes that have impacted the nation and the national
system of education.

Diversity in India had been used as a political tool by the British to foster
the 'divide-and-rule' policy. Likewise, the contenders of communalism,
casteism, and regional exclusiveness use it in present day India. Although, after independence (1947), the diverse values represented in the constitution
were celebrated within the Nehruvian policies. In 1950, the Indian Constitution recognised fourteen major languages, besides hundreds others, many of
which were spoken by just a million persons. The 1961 Census listed 1549
languages as mother tongues. The tribal constituting over six per cent of the
population was dispersed all over India. Each group had its own multiple
identities, which were national, state, cultural, caste and religious. In spite of
these disparities, the Indian national movement had motivated the Indian populace towards the singular cause of liberation and had been successful in its
approach.

On the eve of Indian independence Prime Minister Nehru's foremost task
in office was therefore to ensure the work of "national integration or the integration of Indian people as a political community" (Chandra *et al.* 1999:
83). This could only be possible on one hand by respecting the values of individual groups, communities and states of the nation, and at the same time,
it can also be argued, it necessitated the formulation of a singular goal that
stemmed from a popular ideology. The ideology of India as an active pacifist

had been enacted on the world stage in the years before 1947. What followed soon after was the Korean War of 1950 and American and Chinese intervention. Along with this there emerged a new reaction to colonialism spreading across the globe.

Under Nehru, India assumed the foreign policy of non-alignment[16] and anti-colonialism which were major unifying sources for the country as well as the different political parties. Also, the invasion of India by China in 1962 and the Indo-Pakistan war for possession of Kashmir were fruitful in maintaining India's focus on unity. Nehru had a two-fold strategy for securing India's unity. One, as suggested above, was the creation and strengthening of India's image as an arbitrator in international conflict, and the other was India's drive for social and economic reforms. The Nehruvian policies for social reforms included the abolishment of landlordism, redistribution of land and untouchability as a crime. Impetus was given to science and technology, which Nehru saw as hope to removing the poverty that faced the millions and as a prominent role in India's defence.

Under the Nehruvian government, the values of the nationalist movement were still remembered and celebrated in Indian social life and the media. As analysed by Akbar S. Ahmed, "In the early years the ideas and values of Nehru were used and parodied by Bombay. Heroes of Bollywood[17] self-consciously, bravely spoke of *naia zamana*, new era and new light. They spoke of *pyar*, love, the struggle against *zulm*, oppression, injustice, *satyagraha*, non-violence, *shanti*, peace and *dharma*, duty" (Ahmed 1992: 292). Nehru, too, publicly encouraged and supported the stars attending award-giving ceremonies and photographic sessions.

The value-system of the Indian society after Nehru, and particularly since the 1960s was to change dramatically. This was primarily due to changing party ideologies at the centre; new forms of dominance by those in power—politicians, bureaucrats and police; globalisation and its effect; India's changing international relations, the communalisation of Indian politics and increasing violence in the Indian society. If one were to comment on the changing values in the Indian society, the roughly two decades after independence would constitute one phase and the years until now as the other. The changes that have occurred in the latter phase were so dramatic that it would be like viewing an altogether different nation. From a pacifist country that actively pursued international conflict resolution, India came to represent one of violent ideology, communal conflicts, nuclear weapons and civil unrests. Agrarian struggles were replaced by rapid technological growth and industrialisation under the Multi-National Companies (MNC). This will be discussed here onwards.

The political leaders that emerged after Indira Gandhi in the 1970s were of a different quality and skill from those who came earlier. Commenting on this, the eminent historians Bipan Chandra, Aditya Mukherjee and Mridula Mukherjee state:

> Most political leaders increasingly appealed to a region or a religion or a caste, or a conglomerate of castes. The outcome of this has been that while many Indians have looked for wider, all-India leadership to the descendants of Nehru and Indira Gandhi, others have given allegiance to leaders and parties following populist or opportunist or communal and casteist politics. (Chandra *et al.* 1999: 6)

On one hand, the democratic political system in the last 50 years has surprisingly, for both Indian as well as international critics, been able to survive inadequacy of land reforms and the existence of large-scale landlessness in the rural areas, the slow rate of growth in industry and the national income, the failure to check the high rate of population growth, persistence of gross inequalities, caste oppression, discrimination against women, a dysfunctional education system, environmental degradation, growing chaotic party situation, growing political unrest, secessionist demands and high levels of corruption and brutality, and criminalisation of politics. Democracy in India has been able to take roots in spite of the innumerable problems:

> Democratic values have become entrenched among intellectual elites and institutions vital to the consolidation of democracy. Investigative reporting in national newspapers has exposed corruption and forced political accountability; meticulous planning by the Election Commission has assured fair and free general elections . . . the Supreme Court's activism led to the prosecution of the highest elected politicians when evidence surfaced of their wrongdoing in office. (Frankel *et al.* 2000: 3)

On the other hand, the trend in Indian politics has moved from democratisation to rule by opportunists who have used religion or caste to formulate values that are particularistic to the party leaders and supporters. Political contenders of religion such as the Rashtriya Swayamsevak Sangh (RSS), Muslim League, Akali Dal, and various Christian communal groups in Kerala have continuously enacted violence such as the communal holocaust of 1947, assassination of Prime Minister Indira Gandhi, Hindu-Sikh riots in north India in the 1980s, and numerous Hindu-Muslim killings. Contenders of caste and untouchability have carved out reservations in government offices and universities for the under-privileged, which has been more a struggle for power than one for social justice.

However, more than the politics of caste, it is religious communalism that has gained much attention in recent years. Communalism in India has been well described as:

> . . . an ideology based on the belief that the Indian society is divided into religious communities, whose economic, political, social and cultural interests diverge and are even hostile to each other because of their religious differences. Communalism is, above all, a belief system through which a society, economy and polity are viewed and explained and around which effort is made to organise politics. As an ideology it is akin to racialism, anti-Semitism and fascism. In fact, it can be considered the Indian form of fascism. (Chandra *et al.* 1999: 433)

Some have attributed the rise in communal politics to illiteracy and poverty. Others comment that it is an effect of the rapid social transition experienced by the Indians, in which the old, traditional, social institutions, and support systems—of caste, joint family, village and urban neighbourhood— have been rapidly breaking down. Old values and social mores which cemented together different segments of society have been disappearing under the hammer blows of the profit motive, capitalist competitiveness and careerism, the result of which has been a moral and cultural vacuum which is highly conducive to ideologies based on fear and hate (Ibid.: 437).

It can be argued that the breakdown of social institutions has not been a solitary factor in affecting the cohesiveness in the Indian society. Perhaps the success of political parties to wield communal values among the Indian polity for its sustained existence can be viewed in terms of the support given by the media, international terrorism and bullying, and the existence of a culture that supports war and violence. Alongside this there has been in India an increasing sense of powerlessness due to corruption, economic competitiveness, and the presence of vicious social factors that perpetuate poverty, illiteracy and the inadequacy of basic needs.

Whereas on one hand the media in India have contributed to bringing together the different sections of the society, on the other hand they have immensely contributed to conflict and violence. The government's broadcasting corporation, Doordarshan,[18] for instance, undertook the serialization of the *Ramayana*[19] in the last decade, which helped the BJP (Bharatiya Janata Party) to advance its Hindutva agenda. Misuse of Doordarshan had taken place even earlier by ruling parties, for instance in the 1989 general elections it was found to publicise Congress (I) party leaders at the expense of their opponents (Frankel *et al.* 2000: 254–287). On the other hand the Indian film industry Bollywood has produced movies that mainly impart values of violence, sex and glamour. Bollywood produces more than 750 films a year and is viewed by an audience exceeding 70 million. Political life and cinema mirror each other. Many film stars go on to become politicians, and the villain in Indian movies has often been associated with 'certain hostile, foreign powers,' which for India usually means Pakistan, and for Pakistan it means India (Ahmed 1992: 311). More recently, however, movies such as *Veer Zaara* have tried to show commonality between the two nation states.

India's changing image in recent years from a nation, which actively pursued a pacifist policy to one of violent ideology, is also a result of the changing world scenario. Support given to Pakistan by the United States during India's friendship with the Soviet Union, the international pressure to ban nuclear testing in India in spite of the 'Big Five'[20] countries refusal from abstinence, the rise in international Islamic fundamentalism, and India's reaction to these international developments have culminated in India's image as a nuclear threat and a violent country. India's continued wars with Pakistan, its refusal to sign the Non-Proliferation Treaty (NPT) and the Comprehensive Test Ban Treaty (CTBT), the testing of nuclear power at Pokhran, are events that are widely celebrated by political groups, media and the general public.

If India has created an image of a violent, nuclear weapons country, paradoxically it is also seen as a potential for foreign investment and technological development. The opening of India's economy to foreign investment in the 1990s has witnessed a widespread transformation in the value structures of the society. Globalisation has come with aspirations, particularly in the youth, for Western life-styles. It has witnessed a wide spread mobilisation of the rural poor to the cities, the 'brain-drain' of a younger generation migrating to foreign countries, and increased opportunities for women. It has also affected the values that maintained caste distinctions and occupations, particularly for the 60 per cent of the population which lives in the 600,000 villages of the country. As observed by Gould,

> The technological achievement upon which the modern economic order is based necessitated, from a sociological standpoint, the removal of occupations central to the operation of the new economy from the context of kin group and their relocation in productive groups based upon bureaucratic principles. As and to the degree this occurred, the cultural significance of these occupations ceased to be determined by ritual principles derived from orthodox Hinduism. (Gould 1988: 9–10)

At the same time critics in India such as Paranjpe have argued that the recent economic liberalisation has only impoverished India further, and that it is a part of the IMF-World Bank strategy to globalise poverty and ensure the economic domination of the West (Paranjpe 1993). Grassroots activists such as Vandana Shiva on the other hand contend that the rapid technological change has come with a price tag, such as the impoverishment of the soil during the 'Green Revolution' of Punjab (Shiva 1997).

On an optimistic note one could conclude from the above observations of the Indian society that notwithstanding the corruption, illiteracy, communalisation, and so on, the values of democracy are still present in India. One would have to commend that in spite of the changes in its images and value systems "India is," as Bipan Chandra's remarks, "virtually the only post-colonial nation to sustain a system of parliamentary government for over fifty years after independence" (Chandra *et al.*1999: 185).

Changing Values in Indian Education

Given the various systems of education in India, the separate curriculum of schools and universities, the differences in the medium of instruction and so on, I have delimited my analysis to the changing values in the national educational policies and commissions that serve as the common foundation for all schools and universities. Here I will also explore the factors outside schools which have influenced children in recent years, such as the increased impact of the Western culture on Indian society; the role of media—in particular Bollywood—in shaping the notion of values and human rights for children; the communalisation in Indian politics, and its recent involvement in the national curriculum. These factors are common to those who have the privilege to receive education as well as those who do not. For more than 50 years since its independence, India has still not been able to comply in full with the expression of Article 45 of the Indian Constitution as a Directive Principle of State Policy, which aims at education for all. In August 2002 the human resources development ministry had finally begun to work on a law to implement the Constitution Amendment Bill, which will make education a fundamental right (Tikku 11 August 2002), although it still needs to be enacted and implemented.

The values in Indian education before independence can be traced to those laid down in Macaulay's Minute of 1835 which was to bring about through English education a class of persons Indian in blood and colour but English in tastes, in opinions, in morals and in intellect. Even today greatest value lies in receiving an English-medium education. This type of education is ill afforded by the poor and marginalised section of the society. Inequality in the Indian society is clearly reflected as inequality in the education system. Summarising the inequalities, comments Sinha,

> Sources of inequality in Indian education are many and varied and viewed in this context, formal, and to some extent non-formal, education works for the *perpetuation* of status and privilege and precipitates inequality through social stratification.

This is clearly reflected in a number of ways: *First,* inequality in education is accentuated and sharpened by the people at the helm of affairs of decision-making and who maneuver educational policies to sub-serve the interest of the elites . . . ; *Second,* from the above it follows that in the pursuit of creating an egalitarian educational system, intervention by the bureaucracy and the State has in actuality introduced two separate and independent educational edifices—one for the oppressed and downtrodden and another for the affluent sections of the Indian society . . . ; *Third,* concomitant with the State and bureaucratic interference is the framing of objectives of education which augment inequality in education . . . ; *Fourth,* (this trend occurs) not only in the formal education, (but) even in the domain of non-formal education . . . ; *Fifth,* . . . admission in higher education . . . rarely has any meaningful relationship to dependable projections of manpower needs. This is clearly reflected in the mad rush for admission which one encounters very often to the newly-introduced, highly-westernised courses like management, computer applications, genetic engineering, etc . . . ; *Sixth,* language as a vital means of communication and dissemination of knowledge is yet another source of inequality in Indian education. (Sinha 1997: xxi-xxii)

Not only are there inequalities in Indian education, but also little value is given to education by the Indian government. A UNICEF publication, entitled *The State of the World's Children 1992*, shows that in India, whereas between 60 and 70 children can be given primary education for the cost of training one university student, approximately half of the nation's children fail to finish primary school while the country as a whole produces more graduates than it can productively employ. On the other hand, the increased role of the United Nations in providing EFA (Education for All) and UEE (Universalisation of Elementary Education) have been looked at skeptically by educationists who claim that imparting merely basic training and skills is in effect providing for the labour to work in factories of multi and trans-national companies. Whatever the case may be the efforts for basic education have not been largely successful. *School Education After Independence* (1988), a publication of NCERT (National Council of Educational Research and Training), points out that, at that time, out of every 100 children enrolled in class I, only about 40 reach class V and only about 25 reach class VIII.

The aim of education in India, like most countries, has been chiefly to boost science and technology. The report of the Kothari Commission (1964–66), the most significant document in Indian education, begins with the words, "The destiny of India is now being shaped in our classrooms. This, we believe, is no more rhetoric. In a world based on science and technology, it is education that determines the level of prosperity, welfare and security of the people" (Kothari 1966: 1).

Another educational agenda found in all the policies and commissions irrespective of the changes in central government has been the inclusion of spiritual values in education. Whereas the Indian constitution deems that the state and its education are secular in principle, it can be argued that this constitution gives pertinence to spiritual values. This was first reflected in the Radhakrishanan Commission (1948) which strongly recommended 'spiritual training' in educational institutions. The following commission—Secondary Education Commission (1952–53)—perhaps due to the increasing tension between India and Pakistan was more specific in its recommendation. It viewed India as a secular state and hence specified that 'religious instruction cannot be given in school hours,' recommending, that all unhealthy trends of disunity, rancour, religious hatred and bigotry should be discouraged in schools.

The Sri Prakasa Committee on Religious and Moral Instruction (1959–60) that followed afterwards was more forthright in suggesting that every effort must, therefore, be made to teach students true moral values from the earliest stages of their educational life. The Kothari Commission (1964–66) reiterated this stating: "A serious defect in the school system is the absence of provision for education in social, moral and spiritual values" (Ibid: 4). The National Policy on Education (1986) re-emphasised the cultivation of social and moral values. In the 1990s due to the existing communal politics the Programme of Action NPE (National Policy of Education) 1992 was careful in separating education from the influence of any religion or politics. The framework of the policy emphasised values in education as an integral part of the school curriculum. It highlighted the values drawn from national goals, as well as universal perception, ethical considerations and character building. It stressed the role of education in combating obscurantism, religious fanaticism, exploitation and injustice.

Certain glimpses of the aims of Congress can be found by the continued emphasis given to national integration in the 1960s and citizenship values in 1976. The Emotional Integration Committee (1961), National Integration Council (1962), and Recommendations of the Education Commission (1964–66) were some steps taken under the Congress towards national integration. Article 51A of the Constitution of India was added by a constitutional amendment in 1976, emphasising the obligations of Indian citizenship.[21]

Politicisation in education at the same time has continued to take place at various levels in the nation. For instance, "in U.P. (Uttar Pradesh), a state with relatively low levels of economic development and governmental performance, decision making in schools, colleges, and universities is closely linked to intramural and extramural political connections and conflicts" (Rudolph 1972: 8).

Communalisation of education can be traced back to 1977 when the Jana Sangh merged with the Janata Party and came to share power in the Indian government. The Jana Sangh was one of the former incarnations of the BJP (Bharatiya Janata Party), and a Hindu communal force. An attempt was made to ban school textbooks written for the NCERT. The movement failed due a countrywide protest on this issue.

In 2001 the BJP cleverly sought to introduce Hinduism in the schools that follow the State curriculum, without a direct violation of the constitutional provisions. It sought amongst its allies the NCERT and CABE (Central Board of Education), the main governmental bodies that undertake the publication of model textbooks. Lines were deleted from history textbooks for middle-school children and the curriculum for Social Science and Language was changed in accordance to the directives given by the BJP. One of the lines deleted stated that Hindus ate beef at a certain period in history. Parallel to this the RSS (Rashtriya Swayamsevak Sangh) continues to run 14,000 'communal' schools. States *Asiaweek,* "Many (RSS schools) are located in areas where poor tribes people and low-caste Hindus live" (Singh 12 December 2001). While the BJP communalise education at the national level, the RSS seeks to operate at the grassroots level.

The values that emerge from the national policies and commissions, and communal politics have a direct influence on only around 52 per cent of the educated Indian population. For the uneducated, as well as educated, the values of the changing Indian society probably bear a greater impact than the changes in educational values. For instance, a recent report of the United Nations team which was entrusted with the task of investigating the many dimensions of violence in a media-controlled society, with particular reference to portrayal of violence and their effect on young minds finds that aggressive behaviour, typified in the larger-than-life performances of screen heroes in decimating and demolishing the 'bad guys,' provides the role model for a large proportion of pre-teen and teenaged boys (Guha 1998). Bollywood in particular has been found to shape the notion of human rights and justice for the average Indian youth. Whereas Bollywood has been so influential on the youth, in the twenty-first century India the aspiration to become like Gandhi is virtually absent. Today it is familiar to hear a defiant youth claim: "I am not a Gandhi!"

The Fate of Gandhi in 21st Century India

Internationally Gandhi and his *Satyagraha* movement have been the source of inspiration for the anti-apartheid movement and have influenced several other peoples and movements. James Gould shows the numerous ways in which Gandhian methods have been applied in India and abroad, such as in the 1950s in Europe, in 1952 in Italy by Danilo Dolci who was using the principle to liberate the poor in Mafia-bound Sicily, and in 1953 Lanza del Vasto used a Gandhian fast to protest against the French war in Algeria. Gould notes,

> By the 1970s there was not a country in Europe that did not have some nonviolent movement, whether the drive for environmental protection, which spread rapidly, or against conscription and nuclear war in Western Europe, or human rights assertions in Eastern Europe. . . . In the United States religious societies such as the Quakers who had both inspired Gandhi and supported him continued their quiet protests and vigils and associations promoting the spiritual basis of non-violence preached by Gandhi, such as the Fellowship of Reconciliation (1917), and secular groups like the War Resisters League (1923). (Gould 1989: 8–9)

In the mid-1950s the nonviolent protest campaigns of King, and later Mandela, came with increasing frequency and support. However, there was a poignant difference between these two successors. Both gave non-violence the character and publicity of a mass movement as Gandhi had done: however, it can be argued that although Mandela was inspired by the normative dimensions of Gandhi's values, he also used non-violence as a 'tactic' and 'strategy' that was invoked and discarded as required (see Mandela 1995: 147, 315). King, on the other hand, had a better understanding of the philosophical basis of *ahimsa* through his Christian faith (Hardiman 2003: 272).[22] This will be further analysed in chapter eight.

In contrast to this, within the post-independent Indian society the values that Gandhi postulated for a colonised, agrarian, largely rural country seem to have been hardly effective in a nation that is independent, economically progressing, rapidly urbanising, and a nuclear power. The issues of untouchability, caste and poverty are being replaced by new-found problems of globalisation, class and income disparity, environmental pollution, communal and caste politics, new role of women, new forms of dominance by Western economies and its effect on education. Whereas some scholars contend that Gandhi is still relevant in modern India, critics find him as merely a picture hanging on the walls of government, police, and court buildings.

Gandhian and Gandhism are terms that have continued to be used extensively by the various sections of the Indian society—academia, politics, media, civil servants and the general public. References to these concepts have often suited the context of those who speak of Gandhi—in speeches made at public gatherings or in printed material for the readership of the educated few. Though there have been some practitioners of Gandhi's views, in general one finds that Gandhi is more often than not used by those in positions of power to suit their own end.

Speaking on the subject of Gandhian and Gandhism, Gandhi himself is known to remark,

> I do not know myself who is a Gandhian. Gandhism is a meaningless word for me. As ism follows the propounder of a system. I am not one, hence I cannot be the cause of an ism. If an ism is built up it will not endure and if it does it will not be Gandhism. (Iyer 1991 ed.: 62)

Nevertheless, there continues to be a steady surge of Gandhians and Gandhian institutions and much talk of Gandhism. Radhakrishnan, former Director of Gandhi Smriti in New Delhi, points out that Gandhian scholars and admirers of Gandhi look at Gandhi as a god and think that all he did or said and formulated was beyond questioning and that he is infallible (Radhakrishnan 1998: 4). At the same time, as Gill mentions, in more than half a century after Gandhi's passing away, "there has been no revival of Gandhian precepts or practices in any form or place in India" (Gill 2001: 212). Continuing he says,

> In fact the moment the country became free and Gandhi's closest associates came to power, they hastened to create a polity which did not even remotely reflect the master's values and aspirations. Of course even today we have Harijan Sewak Sangh, Khadi and Village Industries Board, Gandhi Smarak Nidhi and such other crumbling memorials as symbols of our lip-service to his memory, but that is about all. (Ibid.)

Thomas Weber remarks that Gandhi, it is often said, has been forgotten in most parts of India, and more often than not is imported from the West where the names of Attenborough and Schumacher loom large. Of course one occasionally finds in India examples such as the Chipko movement.[23] However, as Weber has gathered through his interviews with leading Gandhians who were involved in Gandhian movements of the 1960s and 1970s in India, the Gandhians do not necessarily speak with one voice. Weber says,

> The differences, over and above those of individual characteristics, often depend on the ideology of the individual, whether his or her world view has been coloured more by Vinoba Bhave or Jayaprakash Narayan, and whether they believe that the political situation in the country is detoriating so rapidly that the "need of the hour" forces them to compromise on ideals if not their fundamental principles in the way that Gandhi often did . . . During the mid 1970s, as a result of the Bihar agitation and JP's (Jayaprakash's) campaign of Total Revolution which followed, the Gandhian movement split over fundamental philosophical issues. The two leaders of the Gandhian movement, JP and Vinoba, eventually came to differ in their interpretation of the use of *satyagraha*, in the

methods to be employed to bring about societal change, the speed at which useful change was possible to achieve, the degree to which Gandhians should be involved in power politics, and the importance of spiritual versus humanist reasons for acting. (Weber 1997: 19)

As will be argued through this book, today Gandhi is conveniently used as
and when required. The two main reasons for this is that, firstly, there has
been a split between Gandhians, and secondly, as argued in the previous chapter, sometimes there was a lack of consistency in Gandhi's own statements
and actions. As he himself wrote,

People say I have changed my views, that I say today something different from
what I said yesterday. The fact of the matter is that conditions have changed. I
am the same. My work and deeds are dictated by prevailing conditions. There
has been a gradual evolution in my environment and I react to it as a *satyagrahi*.
(Gill 2001: x)

Citing this Gill remarks, "It is, therefore, quite easy to prove anything
about Gandhi by selecting a set of his quotes which best serve your purpose"
(Ibid.). Gill himself has tried to "overcome this temptation" by applying two
tests to his selections: "one, how aptly a particular quote or event faithfully
reflects the mood of the moment and is true to its context; and two, to what
extent it is in consonance with Gandhi's overall thinking" (Ibid.: xi-xii). This
may, however, not necessarily overcome the challenge of not interpreting
Gandhi according to one's own argument.

Let us take a look at Gandhi and some of his political usages. Louis
Fischer points out that on 30 January 1969—the anniversary of Gandhi's
assassination—Jayaprakash Narayan stated that the Congress Party presented itself for propaganda purposes as the Gandhi party but it completely
neglected his teachings (Fischer 1968: 84). Fischer makes this comment in
the book *Mahatma Gandhi 100 Years*, which was published to commemo-
rate Gandhi's birth centenary. Interestingly, this writing is followed by an
article by Indira Gandhi, who of course oblivious to these remarks, elaborates upon the affection that existed in the Nehru family for Gandhi, and
that how they were all under the fold of Gandhi. She specifies that together
Gandhi and Nehru were the makers of the nation. This is one such example of the ways in which the Congress has time and again identified itself
with Gandhi to sustain its image in spite of the fact that almost immediately after Indian independence Gandhi was discarded in many of its policies and plans.

Professor Sukhamoy Chakravarty, who was involved in the technical and
theoretical work of economic planning and also directed the implementation
of India's Five Year Plans, writes:

When the planning process was initiated in India, there was a legacy of pre-independence debate on India's developmental problems. This debate centred on the Gandhian approach, at one pole, and the 'modernising' approach of Nehru at the other. The Gandhian approach has never been seriously discussed by either mainstream economists or by its left-wing critics. (Pinto 1998: 21)

This is not to negate the merit of the policies laid down under Nehru and Rajeev Gandhi, which was a reflection of the Gandhian influence. As Daisaku Ikeda notes, "Nehru's peace diplomacy based on the "Panchsheel," which includes nonaligned neutrality and peaceful co-existence, as well as his call for nuclear disarmament, were expressions on a global scale of Gandhi's philosophy of peace" (Ikeda 1995: 118). Ikeda adds,

Heir to the spirit of Nehru, Rajiv Gandhi developed a plan for a new world order as a means of rebuilding human civilization on a basis of non-violence. This plan, centred on the three pillars of peaceful coexistence, North-South economic cooperation, and global environment security, offered concrete suggestions for strengthening the capacities of the United Nations in each of these areas. (Ibid.)

Here the *Panchayati Raj* can be discussed as a case in example. One of the main examples which prove the disregard of Gandhi's ideas while he was still alive and associated with the Congress is the case of decentralisation or *Panchayati Raj*. In spite of it being a main tenet of Gandhi's thinking, there was initially no mention of *Panchayati Raj* in the new constitution of independent India. It only found a place for self-government at the village level in the directive principles of the constitution. Sadiq Ali states that, "This was no effective substitute for the comprehensive self-government which Gandhi aimed at, but it was some acknowledgement of its importance" (Ali 1997: 265). Elaborating upon this Dilip Chatterjee finds that,

. . . the Indian constitution, as it finally emerged, was a long way from Gandhian ideas. Members of the Constituent Assembly had two alternatives before them as models for the constitution of India; the Gandhian plan of a constitution based on the village and the *panchayats*, erecting upon them a superstructure of indirect decentralised government; and the Western type of constitution based on Anglo-Saxon principles and having a directly elected parliamentary type of government with a federal structure. Forces and factors were active in favouring a Euro-American type of constitution. A compromise was achieved by incorporating some Gandhian ideas and principles, within the framework of a Western type of parliamentary government. These ideas find expression in the provisions of fundamental rights and the Directive Principles of State Policy which constitute Part III and Part IV of the present Constitution. (Chatterjee 1990: 228)

This was in spite of the fact that at the outset of framing the constitution, while moving the resolution on 'aims and objects' Nehru characterised Gandhi on the floor of the Assembly as the 'leader of the people,' 'father of the nation,' 'architect of the Assembly,' and Alladi Krishnaswami Aiyar described him as the 'architect of India's political destiny' (Ibid.). In December 1947 when the Constitution of India was being drafted S.N. Aggarwal had drawn Gandhi's attention to the fact that there was, till then, no mention of village *panchayats* in the draft constitution. Commenting on this point Gandhi observed in the *Harijan* (21 December 1947):

> It is certainly an omission calling for immediate attention if our independence is to reflect the people's voice. The greater the power of the *panchayats*, the better for the people. Moreover, for *panchayats* to be effective and efficient the level of education has to be considerably raised. I do not conceive the increase in the power of the people in military, but in moral terms.[24]

As a result of the discussions the following directive was included in Article 40, Part IV of the Constitution of India: 'The State shall take steps to organise village *panchayats* and endow them with such powers and authority as may be necessary to enable them to function as units of self-government' (Chatterjee 1990: 234–235). Notes Dilip Chatterjee,

> The reasons for the members deviating from Gandhian ideology were various. The experience of India in representative government, the obstinacy of the Congress-Socialist group, prevailing circumstances, all added to the cause. But the real reason behind this non-allegiance was Sir B.N. Rau and Dr. B.R. Ambedkar's uncompromising attitudes. The former did not incorporate any of the Gandhian principles and the latter was a severe critic of Gandhi. Another striking reason was the undercurrent of two decades, a sense of misunderstanding between Gandhi and the influential Congress leaders, which found an outlet in the Assembly. (Ibid: 236)

Similarly Ramjee Singh blames the lack of political will, 33 years of Congress monolith which has resulted in increasing encroachments into powers of the States and bureaucracy to be the main impediments in making *Panchayati Raj* a success (Singh 1988: 69).

Moving the discussion to the commemoration of 50 years of Gandhi's martyrdom, the 50th Martyrdom anniversary of Gandhi has in particular witnessed some stark examples by which Gandhi has been used in the turn of this century. Radhakrishnan describes the Freedom Fifty Special Session of Indian Parliament that debated the measures that were to be taken in connection with the 50th anniversary of Indian Independence. Radhakrishnan states,

Over three-four days our honourable elected representatives, one after another in very eloquent manner articulated their sentiments, concern and shed tears on the poor conditions of the villages, criticised corruption in high places and took vows to root out not only corruption but they also expressed their grim determination to work tirelessly to usher in a social order which will promote justice and what not?. . . . In the final document they conveniently forgot Gandhi's name and even when this serious lapse was pointed out by many well-meaning citizens, no effort was made to correct the mistake. (Radhakrishnan 1998: 26–27)

Citing another example, Radhakrishnan said in a recent lecture,

A group of senior citizens, journalists, academicians, politicians, jurists have undertaken an initiative in Delhi to start a new institution to promote a certain cause . . . One or two meetings were held at which the aims, objectives, academic contents and other details of the proposed institute were discussed and approved . . . there was another meeting of the association which was floating this institute. There were a few special invitees also. There was heated discussion at this meeting on the name of the proposed Institute and two or three very influential persons felt that Gandhi's name would keep some section away and they would not associate themselves with the proposed institute. There was general agreement and finally they dropped Gandhi's name. (Radhakrishnan 1998: 27–28)

Finally this section would be inadequate without a brief discussion of the image of Gandhi amongst sections of the educated and elite Indian society. In 1943, when Gandhi's wife was dying, she told her 74 year-old husband to take care of their orphaned young relative Manu Gandhi. "Gandhi took this role rather seriously," Erikson writes, "being concerned, for example, with the girl's physical development . . . and having her sleep on a mat and later, on occasions, "in his bed"—whatever that designation may mean in sleeping arrangements which included neither bedstead nor doors" (Erikson cited in Nanda 1985: 16). Notes Nanda, "Gandhi shared his passing thoughts and even embarrassing dreams with the readers of his weekly journals, thus making himself an easy target for malicious critics" (Nanda 1985: 17).

In a recent national youth meet of about a hundred youth representatives gathered from the country at least a dozen held the view that Gandhi did incalculable harm to India and among the 'crimes' of Gandhi were, injecting into the Indian mind a philosophy called non-violence which made India a nation of 'cowards and timid citizens.' Further, promoting someone like Jawaharlal Nehru as his successor fortified a new Brahmanical hierarchy in Independent India (Radhakrishnan 1998: 28).

As the book *Gandhi—His Relevance for Our Time* discusses, " . . . misrepresentations are not only made by Westerners, but commonly by educated

Indians who often assume, because they are Indians, have read newspaper reports and repeatedly discussed Gandhi, that they know what they are talking about" (Mahadevan 1967: 139). Gandhi is often heard in drawing-room discussions, in parties among the educated elite of the society. Incidents such as his 'sleeping' with Manu Gandhi as cited above, his 'timid' approach in subduing Hindus are common subjects, which are talked about by people who would have not even read a chapter out of Gandhi's *Autobiography*.

Baseless conversations and citations of Gandhi have created a situation in which today political parties such as the Rashtriya Swayamsevak Sangh (RSS) attempts to do away with Gandhi in the history syllabus of the Indian education system. Historian Bipan Chandra notes that

> There is a not-so-subtle attempt to downgrade the mainstream Gandhi-led national movement and to exalt armed movements, though the former was a massive mass movement while the latter were local movements with narrow reach. The effort is to downplay non-violent and overplay armed movements. For example, for class XII, Semester III, Modern India, the Gandhi-led mass movements have been given one unit, constitutional development one unit and 19th century armed movements and revolutionary movements two units! (Delhi Historians' Group 2001: 24)

The changing image of Gandhi in the Indian society and its education system, has not just to do with Gandhi per se, but is also a reflection of the changing image of India from a protector of non-violence to one that is beset with violent ideologies. It is probably the effect of a greater change that has been produced by modernisation, economic growth and globalisation. The sense of alienation, consumerism, cut-throat competition, widening gap between the rich and the poor, communalisation in politics, environmental damage and dominance by the Western economy, politics and media seems to have created a major shift in the perception and value that one attaches to Gandhi and all that he symbolised. The few remaining Gandhian loyalists have adopted Gandhian symbols of the spinning-wheel, the cow, education through a craft, the Gandhi cap and *khadi* in their daily lives without understanding the deeper implications these had in India's boycott of the foreign power.[25] Those that are optimistic about Gandhi have not left much evidence as to how to deal with the complex situations in which Gandhi's ideas find themselves in twenty-first century India as will be explored through the study of a selected Gandhian institution in India in chapter seven.

Gandhi and Indian Education

In July 1937 Gandhi wrote in the *Harijan*:

By education I mean an all-round drawing out of the best in child and man—body, mind and spirit. Literacy itself is no education. I would, therefore, begin the child's education by teaching it a useful handicraft and enabling it to produce from the moment it begins its training. Thus every school can be made self-supporting, the condition being that the state takes over the manufacture of these schools.

Gandhi's experiments in education within his *ashrams* or communities in South Africa and India had led him to develop a model of education based on craft which he titled as *Nai Talim* (new education) or Basic Education (see Sharma 1999: 29–48). In October 1937, in a Conference of National Workers held at Wardha under the presidentship of Gandhi, these ideas on education were considered and the following resolutions were passed:

  (i) That in the opinion of the Conference, free and compulsory education be provided for seven years on a nation-wide scale.

 (ii) That the medium of instruction would be the mother tongue of the student.

(iii) That the Conference endorses the proposal made by Mahatma Gandhi, that the process of education throughout this period should centre around some productive form of manual work, and that all other abilities to be developed or training to be given should, as far as possible, be integrally related to the central handicraft chosen with due regard to the environment of the child.

(iv) That the Conference expects that the system of education will be gradually able to cover the remuneration of teachers.

The Wardha Conference appointed a Committee of distinguished educationists under the Chairmanship of Dr. Zakir Hussain to present a detailed curriculum and syllabi. The report of the Committee, published in 1938, came to be known as the Wardha Scheme of Education. The main outlines of the seven years course of Basic Education were as under:

1. The Basic Craft: Selection to be made by schools, out of the following—spinning and weaving, carpentry, agriculture, fruit and vegetable gardening, leather works, and any other craft for which local and geographical conditions favour.
2. Mother tongue.
3. Mathematics.
4. Social Studies.
5. General Science.
6. Drawing.
7. Music.
8. Hindustani.

The Scheme was approved by Gandhi and was placed before the Indian National Congress at its Haripura Session held in March 1938. The Congress accepted the Scheme. The Sargent Report or the Report of the Post-War Educational Development in India (1944) endorsed the Basic System of Education as contained in the Wardha Scheme, and after Indian independence an initial attempt was made to include Basic Education within the curriculum. However, it can be argued that this system of education was marginalised in the face of the need for a more scientific and modern system of education based on Western lines for the nation's economic development. As Aggarwal analyses, the main limitations that led to the marginalisation of Basic Education were: misunderstanding about the concept of Basic Education, the economic aspect of this scheme was over-emphasised, there was a lack of competent teachers, dearth of textbooks, high cost of basic education, lack of provision for individual differences, and the artistic and aesthetic aspect was neglected (Aggarwal 2001: 53–54).

The Report of the Education Commission (1964–66) believed that the essential elements of Basic Education were fundamentally sound but some modifications were needed. Consequently, however, all it asked for from basic education was 'work experience.' As Aggarwal notes, after this report, "the phrase 'work-experience' came in more frequent use than that of 'basic education'" (Aggarwal 2001: 55). The Government of India's Resolution on National Policy on Education (1968) did not make any mention of Basic Education. It however declared that work-experience should become an integral part of education. The Ishwar Bhai Patel Committee (1977) and the Adiseshiah Committee (1978) instead used the term 'Socially Useful Productive Work' (SUPW) that was given a trial within school curriculum as an additional subject. Finally, The National Institute of Basic Education set up by the Government of India, which functioned as an important department of the NCERT for the purpose of research, extension and training in basic education, was wound up.

NOTES

1. See note 5, chapter 1.

2. During the US Occupation of Japan (1945–52) this organisation was nominally a multilateral institution that governed the country and sought to realise the goals of demilitarisation, democratisation and decentralisation. However, it was the US and General Douglas MacArthur that mainly controlled SCAP (Kingston 2001).

3. For instance, the discrimination faced by the Ainu, an indigenous group in Japan, and the hundreds of thousands of third or fourth generation Koreans in Japan who have still not been awarded Japanese citizenship.

4. See note 1, chapter 1.

5. This was a growing concern during my stay in Tokyo in the 1990s, with stations such as Shinjuku being lined up by homeless people staying in cardboard boxes or *damboru*.

6. *Jieitai* in Japanese: the military forces of Japan.

7. Numerous articles and books have emphasised this, such as, see Fukuzawa & G.K. LeTendre 2001, and Yoneyama 1999.

8. This can be literally translated as—Easily Understandable Value Creating Education, and can be interpreted as—Enabling an Easy Understanding of Value Creating Education. This book is a study of Makiguchi's work, 'The System of Value Creating Education.'

9. The source of this information is a letter received from Mr. Hisao Harima on 3 November 2003. The translation has been done by me.

10. See note 3, Preface of this book. Watanabe's research shows that the " . . . matrix of influence and interests binding the media, state, and religion in Japan has impeded, within the Japanese press, the recognition that freedom of speech is the freedom to question and criticise those in the highest authority" (Watanabe 2000: 212). Watanabe argues that the "media coverage on *the reality of the activities* of the Soka Gakkai, Japan's largest religious organisation with an estimated membership of 4 million households, is virtually nonexistent" (Ibid, emphasis added). Instead, the Japanese press and LDP officials have tried to falsely represent the Soka Gakkai as a religious organisation that aims to eventually 'take over Japan and impose its belief as a state religion' through its increasing financial and political strengths (Ibid: 218).

11. Josei Toda or Toda Jyogai (1900–1958) was an educationist and the second President of the Soka Gakkai.

12. See note 6, chapter 1.

13. Outside Japan several researches as well as applications of Makiguchi's values are taking place by both members as well as non-members of the *Soka Gakkai*, such as Soka Ikeda College in Chennai that has been established by a non-member, Mr. Sethu Kumanan.

14. See Ikeda 1972–1976.

15. See the activities by the Kansai Soka Schools at http://www.kansai.soka.ed.jp/

16. The policy of non-alignment basically meant that India would not favour either the United States or the Soviet Union as they emerged as the two contending superpowers.

17. Indian films produced in Bombay (now known as Mumbai).

18. Doordarshan, the government's broadcasting corporation, is the largest source of television programming in India.

19. An ancient Hindu epic.

20. The 'Big Five' countries are USA, Soviet Union, Britain, France and China.

21. Some research in ongoing to foster the values of citizenship in India. See Shyam. *et al.* 1990 (ed.).

22. For details of King's mass movement also see Gould 1989: 9.

23. In the Chipko movement of the 1970s and 1980s, villagers whose substenance was provided by the forests, embraced trees so as to shield them from the contractors who wanted to cut them down.

24. See Aggarwal 1951.

25. For an interesting analysis of Gandhi's symbols see Parekh 1997: 8–9.

Chapter Six

Makiguchi's Values within the Soka Schools in Present Day Japan

OVERVIEW

In this chapter I will investigate the use and influence of Makiguchi and his values within the Soka Schools in Tokyo and Kansai. The reasons for the specific focus on the Soka Schools, as stated in the introduction chapter, is that Makiguchi's educational ideas were formed during his professional career as a primary school teacher and principal; secondly, amongst all the Soka educational institutions[1] his values are explicitly invoked within the Soka Schools documents; and thirdly, in the Soka Schools, unlike the universities, most of the faculty, staff and students are members of the Soka Gakkai, which bears an important impact on the analysis of how, if so, the ideals of this organisation are transmitted within the schools. As noted earlier, the Soka Gakkai is a lay Buddhist organisation that regards Makiguchi as their original founder and leader. As the school documents reflect there is a strong influence of the Soka Gakkai's ideals on the students.

It must be specified however, that in spite of the link with the Buddhist organisation, religious instruction is not given in the Soka Schools. The Soka Schools in Tokyo opened in April 1968, and were succeeded by the Kansai Soka Schools in April 1973. The Soka Schools follow the national curriculum and operate as a private educational institution. The Soka Schools in Tokyo consist of the Primary, Secondary and High Schools under the 6.3.3 system. The Soka Schools in Kansai are made up of the Secondary and High Schools only. Following the establishment of these schools, numerous kindergartens, schools and universities have been set up under the Soka system in many parts of the world.[2] The main point of distinction of these educational institutions (barring the Soka Ikeda College in India)[3] is that Daisaku Ikeda has established them, and Makiguchi is regarded as the original founder. Since the Soka Schools in Tokyo and Kansai look like any other Japanese schools, it poses the difficulty of evaluating the use and influence of Makiguchi and his values within these schools.

Therefore, in this chapter I have chosen to do a content analysis of key documents of the Soka Schools to trace and analyse the representations of Makiguchi and his ideas within these schools. Content analysis of the school documents will be done to show the ways in which Makiguchi and his ideas on 'value creation' are invoked. It will also provide information to distinguish the learning that takes place within the Soka Schools, and its resemblance and differences to mainstream education. The three key school documents have been selected for the content analysis. The first two documents contain the 'Mission Statement' and 'Ideals of Soka Education' that commonly apply to the entire network of Soka educational institutions (appendix V). The third document contains the 'Mottos and Principles' of the Soka Schools in Tokyo and Kansai (Ibid.).

To evaluate the representation of Makiguchi and his ideas in the school documents, I will also rely on my interviews with the staff of the Soka Schools, and my observations that were conducted during my visits to these institutions since 1996. The key questions that will be addressed within the investigation into the use and influence of Makiguchi in this chapter are: How are Makiguchi and his ideas represented in the Soka Schools documents? Have the Soka Schools been able to apply Makiguchi's ideas while teaching the Japanese national curriculum within the school hours? Further, does this investigation lead to any general conclusions related to the present day applicability of Makiguchi's ideas? Such as, has it become easier to apply Makiguchi's ideas in present day Japan, or are there new challenges posed by the changing values and ideals of the Japanese society and education? These questions will be critically explored in the context of my analysis of the Soka Schools in Japan.

CONTENT ANALYSIS OF THE SOKA SCHOOL DOCUMENTS

This section will elaborate the choice and use of content analysis as a method for investigating the presence of Makiguchi and his ideas within the aforementioned Soka School documents. The choice of content analysis is to identify key words and phrases in all three documents respectively. The suitability of any other method, different from the one I have undertaken cannot be ruled out, as expressed by Weber: "there is no single right way to do content analysis. Instead, investigators must judge what methods are appropriate for their substantive problems" (Weber 1990: 69).

The content analysis that I will undertake in these documents will be done in the four stages of measurement; representation; indication; and interpretation (see Weber 1990). Measurement is the first step, in which I will count the 'key' words and phrases in the original language of the documents with the aid of the computer's search engine. The first and third document is originally in Japanese, and the second in English. The measurement in all three documents will be done in a manner similar to Tufte (1978: 75), for example, who counted certain words in the 1976 Democratic and Republican party platforms, including indicators of distributional issues, such as 'inequality,' 'regressive,' 'equal,' and 'redistribution,' and indicators of concern with inflation, such as 'inflation,' 'inflationary,' 'price stability,' and 'rising prices' (for details on counting see Krippendorff 1980: 22).

In order to select the 'key' words and phrases, I will look at those words and concepts that have a high frequency, as well as those that are known to be associated with Makiguchi, such as 'value,' 'education,' 'individual,' 'social,' 'religion,' as noted in chapter 4 of this book. These words and phrases provide data for a 'pragmatic analysis' of the use of Makiguchi's ideas and values in these documents of the Soka Schools. A count of the number of times the word 'Makiguchi' or the 'founder' is mentioned will serve to provide evidence of the presence as well as the significance of Makiguchi in these documents. That is, through these representations and indications necessary data will be collected to analyse the present use and understanding of Makiguchi and his values, and whether or not they make a relevant contribution within these schools.

This content analysis has to deal with three main issues or concerns. The first and primary concern is with the translation of documents one and three which were originally in Japanese. The translation of these documents (from Japanese to English) was done in a way that was considered both valid for an English reading of the documents as well as that conveyed the original meaning of the Japanese texts. For instance, the word 'soka' in Japanese conveys a specific understanding of the ideas on 'value creation' of Makiguchi. In my English translation the word 'soka' will be mostly used as it appears in the Japanese version. However, at times, the term 'value' or 'creation' will be used instead, depending on the emphasis and meaning that is given in the usage of 'soka.' Bearing this in mind, the measurement of the word 'soka' will be done based on the Japanese reading.

The second concern is to do with the issue of reliability. In order to provide a better reliability in the selection of the unit of analysis, I will avoid coding paragraphs or whole texts, and for reasons stated above, will limit the content analysis to the selection of key words and phrases (for issues on reliability see Kaplan & Goldsen 1965: 83–84).

The third concern is to do with my interpretation of these documents as I answer specific questions related to these documents, such as: what is the main argument made by the producers of these documents; to whom are these documents addressed, and how, in identifiable ways [if any], potential influence is generated through these documents. Diagram 6.1 (adapted from Lindkvist 1981) gives the multiple dimensions that will be taken into account in my interpretation of each text or document.

I will argue that central to the discussion on both the intent of the producer (the Soka Schools), as well as the influence of these texts on the consumers (students and staff of the Soka Schools and the larger Japanese society) is the interpretation that is given to these documents. As stated by Slater (1966), the language of interpretation is the language of the theory or debate that is generated through an analysis. Therefore, the translation and interpretation is the prime relationship (highlighted in the above diagram). The level of authorship is therefore not only what the producers of the text have said, but also what the interpreter (in this case myself) is saying. As Weber notes, "Those who naively believe that data or texts speak for themselves (the doctrine of radical empiricism) are mistaken. The content analyst contributes factual and theoretical knowledge to the interpretation" (Weber 1990: 62).[4] I must however add here that the interpretation is not the only goal of this content analysis. Krippendorff (1980) rightly stresses that the content of texts, however interpreted, must be related either to the context that produced them or to some consequent state of affairs.

Producer (Soka Schools)→**Text**(Documents)→**Audience**(Students, Staff, Japanese society)

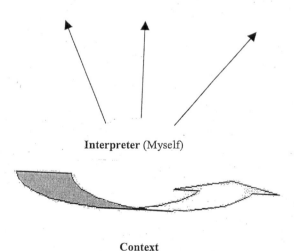

Interpreter (Myself)

Context

Diagram 6.1.   Interpretation of the selected documents of the Soka Schools.

Measurement, representation and indication of the selected documents of the Soka Schools are in appendix VI. Here onwards I will draw upon the data gathered through the process of measurement, representation and indication, and thereby interpret the use of Makiguchi in these documents. To begin with let us summarise the data. First, the table on the pragmatic analysis of Makiguchi's values (Table AVI.1 in appendixes) reveals that emphasis is given to the words 'education' and 'soka' (value creation), as well as key aspects of Makiguchi's educational theory being represented here. Similarly the representations of key words and phrases reveal some concepts of Makiguchi which I will discuss further on in this chapter: 'the learner's life-long happiness,' and 'fostering creative individuals who create value for self and others.'

At the same time certain words repeated in all documents are not from Makiguchi's work (or the 'Fundamental Law of Education' which pertains to all Japanese schools). These are—in order of their ascending frequency— 'dignity of life,' 'global citizen,' and 'humanism.' Therefore, while elaborating on the aims within Makiguchi's 'Value Creating Pedagogy,' the schools have developed new values and ideals, which need to be considered.

In regard to the analysis of Makiguchi the person, the above study shows that a specific image of Makiguchi has been created by the Soka Schools (see Table AVI.2 in appendixes). It can be argued that since two out of three key documents are in Japanese, this image is directed to the Japanese audience, to whom Makiguchi is portrayed as a pioneer in educational experiments who had voiced his concern for the improvement of education and the happiness of humanity in spite of the severe circumstances in which he was placed. It makes a brief comment on the 'recognition' that Makiguchi is now gaining (internationally). These schools emphasise their aim as fostering 'global citizens,' who 'pursue justice and truth,' towards the creation of 'peace' and towards contributing to the Japanese society and the world at large.

Arguably, it can be implied that in doing so the schools take a stance that implicitly denounces the actions of the 'narrow-minded Japanese nationalists' who 'unjustly and falsely' accused and imprisoned Makiguchi while he stood upon his beliefs to defend human happiness and peace. The next section further explores the reconstruction of Makiguchi's history by his successors.

THE SHIFT FROM MAKIGUCHI'S *SOKA EDUCATION PEDAGOGY* TO IKEDA'S 'SOKA EDUCATION'

The Reconstruction of Makiguchi's History by Successors

In the above documents Makiguchi is introduced not only as an educator but also as the first president of the Soka Gakkai, which shows that the school's understanding of Makiguchi is inextricably linked with that of the Soka Gakkai. As analysed earlier, contending opinions exist between educationists with regard to the 'history' of Makiguchi. To briefly recapitulate, certain educationists such as Brannen (1964) and Bethel (1973) who are not particularly sympathetic to Makiguchi's Buddhist conversion, regard his turning to faith as a consequence of the abrupt end of his career within the given social scenario of his time. However, some others, such as Ikeda (2001b) and Furukawa (2001), are amongst those that view Makiguchi's 'martyrdom' as a Buddhist leader to be of great significance to the history of his religious as well as educational movement. It is to the latter way of thinking to which the Soka Schools lend their support.

In these documents as stated earlier, both Josei Toda and Daisaku Ikeda are introduced as the second and third presidents of the Soka Gakkai respectively, and as the founders of the Soka Schools. All three presidents, Makiguchi, Toda and Ikeda are referred to as *sensei* which is the Japanese word for teacher or mentor which appears in my English translation of these documents. The usage of the word *sensei* is a popular expression in the Japanese religious and academic world. Toda and Ikeda are viewed not only as religious leaders but also as educationists, and the schools documents show the influence of Ikeda's educational ideas which I will analyse further on in this chapter.

The Soka Schools place an unequivocal emphasis on the mentor and disciple relationship typified by Makiguchi, Toda and Ikeda. The normative standard is established by the example of Makiguchi who died a 'martyr' opposing authoritarianism. The schools establish themselves as value creating schools working for peace with their global network of the Soka Schools and Universities. The normative standards that are usually present in the manifestos of other Japanese schools perhaps fall short of the unique disposition of the Soka Schools in which the transmission of values and ideals is not limited to the schools but also takes place in the broader community of the Soka Gakkai. These values and ideals originate from both Makiguchi's and Ikeda's ideas. I will analyse this in the next section.

The Shift from 'Value Creating Education Pedagogy' to 'Value Creating Education' in 21st Century Japan

Drawing inference from the measurement table representing the pragmatic account of Makiguchi's ideas it can be noted that the word *soka* is mentioned 23 times in the first document, 10 in the second and twice in the third.[5] In sum, it is the most popular expression within these documents. This concept is related to the 'creation of value' and 'happiness' as expressed in Makiguchi's pedagogy. As I had discussed in chapter four, Makiguchi regarded happiness to be the aim of life and education. Happiness, according to Makiguchi, comes from the ability to create value for the benefit of the self as well as the good of the other, that is, to harmonise one's own interest with that of the other. All the Soka Schools documents emphasise this, for instance, the motto of the Soka Schools in Kansai states, 'Do not build your happiness on the unhappiness of others.'

At the same time, the key documents of the Soka Schools show the influence of the broader national education within which they operate. To summarise my analysis of document three (in appendix V), the 'school principles' contain words and phrases that can be found in the *kyoikukihonho* or the 'Fundamental Law of Education.' The Fundamental Law of Education is the basic tenet of Japanese education, drafted and enacted since 1947, which it is now proposed to amend. The key words and phrases from the Fundamental Law of Education that can be found in the Soka Schools principles include tackling issues such as directing students to take responsibility; for them to be kind, polite, and courteous; and to become people who can contribute to Japan and world peace. It also includes tackling problems that are common to Japanese education, such as bullying. Further, it aims to strengthen good relations between junior (*kohai*) and senior (*senpai*) students.

Apart from this, the word 'peace' is mentioned in all the Soka Schools documents, which is also central to the *Constitution of Japan* (article 9, 1947) and *The Fundamental Law of Education* (1947). The *Constitution of Japan* states:

> We, the Japanese people, desire *peace* for all time and are deeply conscious of the high ideals controlling human relationships, and we have determined to preserve our security and existence, trusting in the justice and faith of the *peace-loving* people of the world. We desire to occupy an honoured place in an international society striving for the preservation of *peace*, and the banishment of tyranny and slavery, oppression and tolerance for all time from the earth. We recognise that all peoples of the world have the right to live in *peace*, free from fear and want.
>
> Article 9: Aspiring sincerely to an international *peace* [we] renounce war as a sovereign right of the nation and the threat or use of force as a means of settling international disputes. (Beauchamp & Vardaman 1994: 96, emphasis added)

The *Fundamental Law of Education* states:

> Having established the Constitution of Japan, we have shown our resolution to contribute to the *peace* of the world and welfare of humanity by building a democratic and cultural state.[6] (Ibid: 109, emphasis added)

In addition, article one of the educational law states that one of the aims of Japanese education is the 'rearing of the people' as 'builders of a *peaceful* state and society' (Ibid.).

It must be argued, however, that whereas the Soka Schools invoke the value of 'peace' as in the above documents, here there is a specific understanding of this term. Document one (sixth paragraph) states that the aim to bring about peace is based on the concept of an education that 'fosters global citizens,' which is 'people of talent who possess courage, wisdom, and compassion,' and can 'contribute to the world.' Details of this can be found in Ikeda's speech delivered in Columbia University that engages with the concept of 'global citizens' at length and identifies it with the Buddhist term *Bodhisattva* (Ikeda 2001b: 102).[7] In spite of *zero mention* of 'religion' or 'spirituality' in the schools documents (table AVI.1), arguably, the aims of the schools are not separate from the faith that unites all those that are involved in these schools. However, the aims of the school are free from any religious myopia. Such as, all the schools documents advocate a 'humanistic education' that is based on respecting the 'dignity of life.' The documents also refer to this 'humanistic education' as *Soka Education* or Value Creating Education and link it to Ikeda's ideas. As I had explored in another article, the term *Bodhisattva* is key to Ikeda's Soka education system and suggests the description of a global citizen to be "a human being endowed with courage, compassion and wisdom who, as an active citizen, concentrates on the positive transformation of one's own life, and therefore transforms one's nation and humanity" (Sharma June 2007).

Consequently from the above reading of the documents it can be stated that there is a mixture of aims and values within these schools that stems from the national educational aims, as well as Makiguchi's 'Value Creating Pedagogy,' along with which certain Buddhist ideals, that are all incorporated under the new title of 'Value Creating Education.'

The above analysis of the representation of Makiguchi's ideas within the Soka Schools documents shows that Makiguchi's ideas tend to be incorporated according to the philosophy and life-style of this institution, which is influenced by the aims of the national education, as well as by Ikeda and the Soka Gakkai. As the school's *Mission Statement* specifies, one of the main influence on its ideals and directives has been from Daisaku Ikeda:

> The entire network of Soka education constitutes a group of people who have come together as students and staff due to their common understanding of the ideas of Daisaku Ikeda *Sensei*. (Document one, appendix V)

Also, as my content analysis shows, the influence of the values and ideals of the Soka Gakkai is apparent within all the documents of the Soka Schools. In particular, there is an emphasis on the words 'humanism,' 'dignity of life' and 'global citizens' in the school documents, which are words that can also be found within the ideals of the Soka Gakkai (see Ikeda 1976b: 238, SGI 1996). The basic tenet of Makiguchi's Value Creating Pedagogy, which is to create value for the self and others, is repeatedly linked to these concepts in the schools documents. However, as the next section shows, the documents do not practically define these concepts, nor do they give enough evidence of how the schools proceed to apply these concepts under the 'Value Creating Education' carried out by these institutions.

THE PRESENCE OF MAKIGUCHI AND HIS VALUES IN THE SOKA SCHOOLS—A CRITICAL STUDY

In this section I will critically analyse the use of Makiguchi and his ideas within the Soka Schools. Based on my interviews with the staff of the Soka Schools and my reading of the school documents, it must be argued that the only evidence which suggests that Makiguchi's ideas are being applied within the school curriculum is in the 'character writing' class. To explain briefly, Makiguchi had developed his own methods of enabling students to write Chinese characters. The first method known as the '*honegaki shugi*' can be literally translated as the 'Principle of Applied Frame Writing.' To explain simply, by using this method students learn the Chinese characters by tracing each character through a transparent paper from a 'model' sheet into a separate sheet, and then practice writing over the traced character. In the second method known as '*kagokaki*,' that can be translated as 'Principle of Outline Writing,' the students learn to write the Chinese characters by copying the outline of each character (for details see Gakuen Tosho 2005, and Mizuhata 2002). Both these methods were effectively used by Makiguchi in his classroom as the methods improved student's handwriting, and enabled even those students to write the Chinese characters who had previously found it difficult to do so (Sharma 1999: 13). These methods have been further developed by the teachers of the Soka Schools and are now being used not only within the Soka primary school, but since 1996 they have been published as a teaching aid for other schools in Japan (Gakuen Tosho 2005).

The Soka Schools however argue that apart from the above example, the implementation of Makiguchi's ideas also takes place in these schools within the 'integrated learning' period. In my correspondence with a senior teacher of the Soka Schools I questioned the applicability of Makiguchi's ideas within the schools, and was given the following response:

> The educational curriculum (in Japan) is divided into two parts—the curriculum (*kyouka*) and 'outside curriculum study' (*kyoukagai*).[8] In the 'outside curriculum study,' an 'integrated learning' or '*sogotekigakushu*' takes place, which is left to the independence of each school.
>
> Private schools, such as the Soka Schools, use these school hours to emphasise the philosophy and principles of the founder of the institution.[9]

The school's endeavour to apply Makiguchi outside the curriculum needs to be critically questioned. Let us take an example of the activity carried out by the school within the 'integrated learning.' As mentioned earlier, the schools aim at fostering 'global citizens' who they regard as 'people of talent that can contribute to the world.' In order to do so, the schools argue that they have invited over the past years more than 3,000 visitors from abroad, most of whom are dignitaries, presidents of countries, scholars, peace activists and so on.[10] This activity seems to be influenced by Makiguchi's suggestion that in order to cultivate character, students should interact with people who 'embody the value creation life-style' (Bethel 1989 ed.: 90). This proposal of Makiguchi was in itself idealistic and problematic in its orientation. It is also highly questionable as to how this limited means of interacting with foreign visitors can enable the Soka Schools students to become 'global citizens.' To emphasize, the point I have tried to raise here is not one of challenging the fact that Soka Schools students seem to be better aware and feel more responsible towards contributing to global peace. This fact is noticeable to any visitor of Soka Schools. However, it is crucial to get clarity, for the wider Japanese and international audience, of how global citizens can be fostered *within* the given Japanese education and curriculum (the next section will discuss this further).

Returning to my analysis of the presence of Makiguchi and his ideas in these schools, it can be argued that one of the main influences of Makiguchi in these schools is through the normative aspect established by his death as a 'martyr' who died for peace, and through the emphasis that is laid on individual students to contribute to world peace. In recent years researchers such as Patricia White have argued that whereas some schools give the undesirable message to students such as "this institution doesn't trust you, respect you, and so on . . . it is a sociological truism that the culture of institutions, to a large degree, shapes, for good or ill, the aspirations, habits, and dispositions of those who work in them" (White 1996: 5). One of the outcomes of the sense of mission for peace that is imparted within the Soka Schools has been the absence of *ijime* (bullying) and *futoko* (school phobia) in these schools, which are otherwise key problems for schools in Japan.

Since its establishment in the 1970s there have been approximately 20,000 graduates of the Soka Schools amongst who have become doctors (310 people), lawyers (88), accountants (105), scholars and PhDs (193), teachers (more than 1,000), university lecturers and researchers (146), pilots (7) and others (156).[11]

Alongside, the students of the Soka Schools have organised activities for environmental protection within their local community. In his work *The Geography of Human Life*, Makiguchi had emphasised the inter-relationship between the person and his/her natural environment (see chapter four). Influenced by this view, the students of Kansai Soka Schools have been able to successfully engage in conservation activities in their neighbourhood, such as conserving the fireflies in the school's neighbouring area.[12]

To summarise my critical analysis of the Soka Schools indicates that although Makiguchi is represented in all the key documents of these schools, and there has been some implementation of his ideas, it can be argued that these schools have not effectively engaged with the several ideas and proposals that were key to Makiguchi's educational theory (such as analysed in chapter four). Further, by placing Makiguchi's ideas and proposals outside the main curriculum,[13] the schools have not addressed the basic question which should have concerned all those who are involved with this institution, which is, are the principles of 'soka' applicable within the present day Japan?

THE PRESENCE OF MAKIGUCHI AND HIS VALUES IN JAPAN—AN ANALYTICAL STUDY

The above discussion on the specific use of Makiguchi and his ideas in the Soka Schools suggests that the present day context in which Makiguchi's ideas are being used is different from the one in which Makiguchi wrote his Value Creating Pedagogy. It then necessitates an analytical study that broadly discusses the present applicability of Makiguchi's ideas and proposals in Japan.

Many of the aims and aspirations of Makiguchi for a free and democratic society and education system were realised at the end of the Second World War through the Potsdam Proclamation of 26 July 1945, and the ensuing military, economic, political and educational changes brought under the American occupation (see chapter two). Whereas the Meiji Constitution had given certain rights to the subjects, the new constitution of 1947 gave the citizens freedom of religion, thought, and speech. The nation moved from emperor-centrism to representative democracy, in which women were given the right to vote.

Within education the Imperial Rescript was removed and its place was taken by the Fundamental Law of Education which, like the Japanese Constitution, gave utmost importance to building a peaceful nation. Japan's adoption of the Peace Constitution and its abstinence from maintaining an army were particularly relevant since it has been the only country to face the large scale disaster of the atomic bomb and the consequent injury to the identity and morale of her people. As the Supreme Commander for the Allied Powers (SCAP), Douglas MacArthur noted in the New York Times of 18 March 1947, "Her spiritual revolution has been probably the greatest the world has ever known." The aftermath of the world war, the emerging United Nations and the global rethinking of basic principles of government and law of the times, as well had been a significant influence in framing Japan's Peace Constitution (Beer & Maki 2002).

Tragically Japan's 'spiritual revolution' was realised only a few years after Makiguchi's death under authoritarianism for protesting against the inequalities and injustices of his society and education. Given the historical context of the early twentieth century Japan, Makiguchi's call for an equal opportunity for poor students, his proclamation that the emperor was a common man, and other such dissident acts had robbed him of his career as a school principal, disbanded his religious organisation, and made the authorities lock him up in prison. In the democratic conditions that followed shortly after his death, a new context emerged, in which values of peace and dignity of life were espoused by almost everyone. Also, as chapter 5 showed, very soon after its independence Japan strategically began to use the peace constitution for its economic growth.

Such as, while declining to join America in its war with Korea, Japan used the same war to build its industrial plants and technology. Also, all this was done while building economic alliances in East Asian countries. Noted in the same chapter was the excessive modernisation of Japan especially in the 1980s and its negative impact on educational aims and policies. At the same time, it can be pointed out that the focus on science, technology and industry within education has also made Japan into an economic power. It can be argued that the Soka Schools that follow the national curriculum on one hand, and experiment with Makiguchi's ideas on the other, should critically evaluate the broader applicability of Makiguchi's educational proposals for the twenty-first century through contextualising his ideas and values within the present day Japanese education.

For instance, let us consider one of the key proposals made by Makiguchi, which is that education of the learner should take place within the home, school and community. In recent years the *Mombusho* or MEXT (Ministry of Education, Culture, Sports, Science and Technology) has introduced a similar proposal that aims at:

> letting the children spend more time free from pressure at home and in the communities, and engage in social contribution activities and nature-oriented experiences to nurture "Ikiru Chikara" (the zest for living) in their daily lives including the abilities to learn and think by themselves, and the existence of a rich humanity, and healthy development and physical strength to lead vigorous lives.
>
> This system should be realized only with mutual cooperation among schools, families and communities with their respective skills in education. (MEXT 2005)

To achieve this:

> MEXT promotes some measures to support education in the home, including
> production and distribution of handbooks and pamphlets of education for the
> home, and development of the counseling system to answer the parents' worries
> about their children.
>
> MEXT carried out the measures through the National Children's Plan (Three-
> Year Strategy) from FY1999 to provide an environment for communities' in-
> volvement in raising children and promote the programmes for parents and chil-
> dren. According to the achievements of this Plan, MEXT is implementing a
> "New Children's Plan" to comprehensively promote social services and experi-
> ence activities including volunteer activities and some other programmes after
> school or on weekends in cooperation with the people in the communities.
>
> By effectively and steadily implementing these measures, MEXT asks for the
> cooperation of schools and homes, and thus strives to nurture children's "Ikiru
> Chikara" (the zest for living). (Ibid)

To briefly comment on these aspirations, it must be stated that even though
MEXT's aims seem noble, the feasibility of their plans seems doubtful mainly
due to the simplicity and naivety of their proposals. For example, in Japanese
education, the school week has been reduced to five days and roughly one-
third of the curriculum has been eliminated in one of the major educational
reforms. However, even though school hours are reduced, the policies for
higher economic growth and national solidarity have put an increased academic pressure on students. As I had argued earlier, by the end of the last century Japanese education had been marred by an increased rate of *ijime* or bullying, high rate of suicides, killing of adults, and several other life threatening
problems. To deal with this the number of hours given for moral lessons has
increased since the 1980s, but more moral hours means further academic
pressure on students which has a counter effect on the *Mombusho's* desired
aim of education in home and community.

This is one example of the several challenges posed in applying
Makiguchi's ideas today. In twenty-first century Japan, contending social, political and economic changes have created a context which is far more complex than the one in which Makiguchi was situated in his own time. My argument here is not to show whether the twenty-first century context has been
good or bad for Japan, but to critically question the use and relevance of
Makiguchi's ideas and values within this context. As demonstrated through
the preceding analysis, the democracy that came after Makiguchi's death has
brought with it after-effects such as the unresolved attitudes of the Japanese
government towards Asian countries—especially China and Korea. Here I
would also like to point out that if the prospect of democracy is largely de-

termined by the struggle between the dominant and subordinate classes over the right to rule,[14] then in Japan's case the dominance of power wielded by the LDP, big business, and *yakuza* (organised crime syndicates) has not allowed for much impact to be made by subordinate groups until the recent involvement of the Komeito and the Soka Gakkai in politics. In the following sections I will investigate this further.

The earlier example (in the previous section) of the common invocation of the value of peace by both the national documents and by the Soka Gakkai has been continuously challenged in the past one year with the support given by the Japanese government to the United States military operations. Fisker-Nielsen's recent research shows that in providing political endorsement to the ruling Komeito party, the Soka Gakkai has landed in a contradictory position (Fisker-Nielsen 2005). The issue itself is complex, but for our analysis it can be said that not only for the members of this organisation but for the Japanese polity in general the disregard for article 9 of the Constitution by political parties reveals paradoxes that lie within modern societies. For example, on the one hand aspirations such as 'peace' have been advocated by the Japanese Constitution as well as the Soka Gakkai and the Soka Schools that are in the lineage of Makiguchi, while on the other hand there has been the political reality in which nation states and institutions use such values.

Though 'peace' is the same word that is endorsed by all aforementioned groups, its interpretation and use varies. The national documents do not have the Buddhist interpretation of peace suggested by the schools (discussed above). The above case of values and ideals versus politics demonstrates that the political argument remains close to the socio-political affairs rather than to the issue of values. Such events as Japan's recent participation in America's war against terrorism has reinforced the power of transnational politics, and exposed the fragility and vulnerability of such values that can even be invoked to justify war for the sake of peace. Values such as 'peace' are allowed in, taken out, or suppressed depending on how politically viable or strategic they are.

At the same time this critical appraisal of the use of such values within the Japanese politics does not attempt to overlook the necessity and importance of the citizen's engagement in political transformation as shown in the above case of the Soka Gakkai's involvement as a civil society in direct alignment with the state power. As Held suggests, we do not have the option of 'no politics':

> Whether one explicitly acknowledges adherence to a political perspective or not, our activities presuppose a particular framework of state and society which does direct us. The actions of the apathetic do not escape politics; they merely leave things as they are. (Held 1987: 267–268)

It can be argued that what Fiscker refers to as 'idealism' is not misplaced because, even though the aim to achieve social transformation embedded in the Japanese constitution and the Soka Schools seems idealistic or naïve in the face of the given political and educational realities, the benefit of such ideals is not as much in the realisation of the goal (because society moves according to the dictates of other factors), but that in the process of working on their ideals the body politic obtain political awareness, that is, they are 'educated' in the broader sense of the term, as was noted in the case of Gandhi's *Satyagraha* in chapters four and five, and the Soka Gakkai members engagement in Japanese society and politics.

Dobblelaere and Wilson's study (1994) on similar lines suggests that the members of the Soka Gakkai International in UK show a greater degree of involvement in socio-political affairs than the sample taken from the general UK population. The former tend to be oriented towards the left, and as the study finds, "SGI members are, on average, better educated than the public at large, and this may encourage a more critical posture towards agencies and institutions which, for many people, are apathetically taken for granted as they are" (Dobbelaere & Wilson 1994: 142).

On the one hand democracy has lead to the freedom of expression, especially in the case of Japan in which, as a survey[15] reveals, the political rights of the people are not compromised in ways in which they are affected in other democratic countries: 'people are not imprisoned for their views, and torture is rare or exceptional' (see Potter 1993: 368). Whereas values and ideals of the constitution have inspired large sections of the Japanese to protest against the Iraq war, at the same time these values (such as peace) have continued to be exploited alongside by dominant groups. In this context the influence of Makiguchi's ideas and values ends up being negotiated in the Japanese society. In contrast to this, the example of Makiguchi and his values in an authoritarian age make a stronger impact through his imprisonment and subsequent death. I am in no way suggesting that we revert to authoritarianism, but am trying to highlight through these examples that today there are new challenges in the use of Makiguchi's ideas.

To summarise the argument in this section, whereas often people tend to look at the core of what Makiguchi has said to seek its relevance, a study of his values should not be limited to a scholastic approach of discerning and teaching his ideas, but an informed citizenry should be made to understand the ways in which his use and influence has been heavily context dependent. Such as, in the case of the Soka Schools his ideas have been used according to the philosophy and life-style of this institution. Alongside, within the Japanese political context and the recent 'global war against terrorism,' Makiguchi's ideas, and values such as 'peace' have been altered. At the same time, the Komeito, in the lineage of Makiguchi, has implemented varied welfare policies in Japan. As Fisker finds,

> Komeito politicians, Soka Gakkai officials and the daily reading of the Komei newspaper reveal that Komeito sees itself as a "brake" on the LDP, and that there are many issues on which they differ both philosophically as well as practically. Thus the justification for being in a coalition with an ideologically different party is to get their own policies passed. Such policies have been largely concerned with welfare: securing a continuation of the pension system, increased allowance for parents with young children, finding ways to help young people find work, voting rights for ethnic minorities such as Korean residents etc. In terms of Iraq, they say they did what they could,[16] but were regrettably unable to find a diplomatic solution. They acknowledge that at the current juncture everything plays out against this US-Japan Security alliance, something which they would like to see becoming more balanced but are not optimistic about happening in the near future. (Fisker-Nielsen 2005: 15)

Through such examples, it can also be argued that in the wider Japanese society many may not have read Makiguchi, but his ideas have permeated into the society in given time. Therefore, even though sometimes there is no direct reading or relation with Makiguchi, it is noteworthy that through activities such as the Soka Gakkai and Komeito's welfare policies, the aspirations of Makiguchi are influencing Japan.

CONCLUSION

There are a number of positioned arguments that can be taken to view the use and influence of Makiguchi, and the present applicability of his ideas. It would be unfair to suggest that Makiguchi remains only within the walls of the Soka Schools. In the Japanese society his values have not been cast aside, and as the above examples show, there are negotiations taking place with respect to the use of values such as 'peace.'

Prior to this analysis my question was directed at investigating the degree of influence Makiguchi has had in Japan, that is, whether or not he has been used significantly in the present day society and education. Based on this study it is now argued that the influence of Makiguchi depends on the context in which his values are used which differs in all aforementioned cases—of the Soka Schools, national policies, educational aspirations and the Japanese political context.

To conclude with an analogy, the values and aspirations of Makiguchi can be likened to strands of threads within the Japanese social tapestry of values and ideologies that appear and fade away depending on how and where we shed light on them. If we turn our focus on the Soka Schools, Makiguchi's values are clearly noticeable. While on the other hand if we shift our attention to the other agendas that govern democratic societies, these strands become hazier and at some point we can completely lose sight of them. The impact of Makiguchi and his values may vary in these contexts but certainly his influence lies undiminished in twenty-first century Japan.

NOTES

1. See document one in appendix V for all the Soka educational institutions.

2. See www.soka.edu.

3. Soka Ikeda College of Arts & Science was established in 2002 in Madhanankuppam, in the city of Chennai in the southern Indian State of Tamil Nadu, by the current chairman Dr. Sethu Kumanan, with the financial support of Mr. Sethu Bhaskaran. Dr. Daisaku Ikeda is the honorary founder of this institution.

4. See Weber & Namenwirth 1987.

5. See measurement table (AVI.1).

6. For the Japanese version see http://www.houko.com/00/01/S22/025.htm

7. In Mahayana Buddhism, practiced by the Soka Gakkai, the term *Bodhisattva* depicts a state of life that lies within every human being. It emphasises an ideal of human behaviour. It is a state of wisdom, compassion and courage by which one can overcome the restraints of egoism and work for the welfare of self and others (see www.sgi.org).

8. This is not exactly the same as 'extra-curricular activity' and therefore I have translated 'kyokagai' literally as 'outside curriculum study.' Each school makes its independent decision as to how they want to use the school hours that comprises the 'outside curriculum study.' It is not graded, that is, no marks or credit is given, but the report card comments on the activity done by each student during these hours. This is apart from the hours used to teach the national curriculum.

9. The source of this information is an email received from one of the senior teachers of the Soka Schools, Mr. Toshiaki Mizuhata, who is also the head of the 'Humanistic Education Research Committee' that is one of the key educational research institutions linked to the Soka Schools and the Soka Gakkai. Email in Japanese dated 18 November 2005, translated by me.

10. Such as the former Soviet Union President Gorbachev (in November 1997); writer Chingiz Aitmatov (in November 1998); and Dean of Morehouse College Lawrence Edward Carter (in September 2002) (note 9 above).

11. Refer to note 9 above.

12. See www.soka.edu for further details.

13. By which I mean the hours used to teach the national curriculum.

14. See Potter 1993.

15. The survey was based on reports by Amnesty International and US State Department (*PIOOM Newsletter and Progress Report*, 2:2, 1990, pp. 18–20).

16. Fisker through her interviews conducted in Japan notes in the same paper that some of the Komeito leaders such as Toyama and Hamayotsu, had tried to find a diplomatic solution to the Iraq war even before it began, such as, their attempt to initiate various Middle Eastern neighbouring countries to do something to stop the war (Fisker-Nielson: 11).

Chapter Seven

Gandhi's Values in a Selected Gandhian Institution in Present Day India

OVERVIEW

This chapter will investigate the use and influence of Gandhi in India in the present twenty-first century. To begin with, I will investigate the representation of Gandhi and his ideas within the documents of the 'Ikeda Centre for Value Creation' (ICVC). The documents I have chosen for my analysis are the 'Mission Statement' and 'activities' carried out by the ICVC. The choice of selection of this institute is based on the fact that this educational institution is interested in both the ideas of Gandhi as well as the principle of *soka* or 'value creation.' My study of these documents of ICVC will critically access the 'dialogue' that takes place in this institution between *soka* and Gandhi's *ahimsa* (non-violence).

The key questions that will be addressed within my investigation into the use and influence of Gandhi in this chapter are: How are Gandhi and his ideas represented in the ICVC documents? Has this educational institution been able to apply any of Gandhi's ideas, and Makiguchi's ideas on 'value creation'? Further, does my investigation lead to any general conclusions related to the present day applicability of Gandhi's ideas? Such as, has it become more or less appropriate to apply Gandhi's ideas in present day India or are there new challenges posed by the Indian society and education in the twenty-first century? These questions will be critically explored in the context of my analysis of the ICVC.

The Mission Statement of ICVC

The Ikeda Centre for Value Creation (ICVC) established in 2002 is a part of 'The Mahatma Gandhi Centre for Non-violence and Development' (MGCND) in the State of Kerala, south of India. The aim of the centre is to "recognize the importance of Value Creation in the emerging scenario and in honour of the great value creator Dr. Daisaku Ikeda."[1] The Mission Statement of the ICVC is as follows:

> Ikeda Centre for Value Creation is an initiative launched by Gandhian scholar and peace activist Prof. Neelakanta Radhakrishnan and a few others who have been inspired by the work and teachings of Gandhi, Martin Luther King and Daisaku Ikeda to promote and foster nonviolent outlook in various segments of people in different parts of the world.
>
> The principal aims of the Ikeda Centre for Value Creation are (1) to promote inter-cultural dialogues, (2) arrange regular training for value creators, (3) propagate the complementarities in the teachings of Gandhi, King and Ikeda by encouraging students, teachers, researchers, scholars, and peace activists and socially committed individuals to undertake extensive research and study issues connected with the focus of the Centre, and to (4) strive to form a consortium or networking of institutions and centres which are in the field particularly such as Soka University, Institute of Oriental Philosophy, Boston Research Centre for the 21st Century, Toda Institute, Pacific Basin Research Centre, etc.
>
> The Ikeda Centre fosters values both at the individual, collective and global scale by arranging interactive conferences (both micro and macro level), dialogues of various types, training programmes in non-violence, continuing education programmes, carnivals for children, teachers and community to evolve a new outlook and approach both in individual and community life.
>
> The ICVC is an independent, nonpartisan, and nonprofit organization committed to the pursuit of values and nonviolent leadership with children, youth, and women as principal foci of a new endeavour towards nonviolent value creation.

The Activities of the ICVC

The ICVC has held panel discussions, workshops, exhibitions, seminars and so on. Overall the programmes of the ICVC are:[2]

1. To foster training in Shanti Sena[3] on a regular basis.
2. Three-month Certificate Course in Non-violence (jointly with Jain Viswabharti).
3. Self Employment Training Programmes in Toilet and Washing Soap, Book Binding and Book Making, Candle Making, Chalk Making, etc. (jointly with Centre for Gandhian Studies, University of Kerala).
4. P.G. Diploma Course in Gandhian Strategies in Management (jointly with SN Institute of Management of Ranchi University).
5. Ph.D. Programmes in Gandhian Studies, Non-violence, Human Rights and Environmental Studies, Kingian and Ikeda Studies (in association with various universities).

Associated with the ICVC is the Rangaprabhat experiment that has been ongoing for around 25 years in Kerala. This experiment by a group of artists and educators aims towards 'value creation in children and to prevent school drop-out through children's drama and a host of other activities' (ICVC 2003: 18). The document on this experiment claims that in the past few decades it has created a significant change in the participating students and the community in which it exists

> by the integration of nonformal education and formal education through a liberal and creative use of the vast opportunities offered by children's drama and by offering opportunities to selected children to spend their leisure time in such activities that would enhance in them a spirit of co-operative endeavour, involvement in craft activities, story telling, improvisations, creative dances and folk music. The aim was to offer facilities and opportunities to children to supplement and augment their classroom learning in an atmosphere of relaxed freedom which would promote creative involvement in the children. (Ibid. See appendix VIII)

The document states that the experiment has lead to successful results such as: no drop-out in the schools among those who were coming to Rangaprabhat, students scored better grades in their schools, exhibited more confidence in their ability to express, and displayed better hygienic and personal habits (ICVC 2003: 19). The document gives us a string of positive results from this experiment, but leaves us to do the challenging task of studying the representation and implementation of any *Soka* or Gandhian ideas that takes place within this experiment.[4] The 'Mission Statement' of the ICVC states two of its 'principal aims' to be 'the promotion of inter-cultural dialogues,' and 'arranging regular training for value creators.' There has however been no clear explanation in any of its documents as to what is meant by, and how it proposes to undertake the task of 'training for value creators.' I will return to it later, but in the meantime let us turn to the two issues raised in this section, that is, the institutionalisation of Gandhi and his ideas, and the dialogue between *Soka* and Gandhi.

Common to the ICVC's 'mission statement' and 'activities,' and the Rangaprabhat experiment is the use of the term 'non-violent value creation.' Arguably this phrase has been coined through Gandhi's 'non-violence' and the *Soka* principle of 'value creation.' It seems to represent an endeavour to institutionalise these values, and also to show a dialogue between *Soka* and Gandhi.

THE INSTITUTIONALISATION OF GANDHIAN AND *SOKA* VALUES

There are several ways of engaging with this 'dialogue,' but the question that I will now address based on the above description is whether this dialogue indicates some form of *development* of ideas that gives relevance to them. The word 'development,' as I have used here, can be seen as a process of, what John Cobb suggests as 'creative transformation' (Kung 1991: 103–104). What Cobb refers to, is, that instead of adding to our old faith, or ideals in this case, the institution that is in the process of development transforms itself through dialogue in a way that it allows itself to be reformed by what is learnt, so that its ideals are not destroyed, but enriched. In light of this understanding let us now analyse the exposition of the term 'nonviolent value creation' by the ICVC and its allied experiment.

First let us consider the term 'value creation' as used here. Even though Ikeda has been mentioned in the Mission Statement of the ICVC, there is no indication in any document that either Ikeda or Makiguchi's ideas have been implemented. For example, the term 'value creation' is used extensively in a document titled 'Values in a Changing World,' that is a record of the proceedings of a 'dialogue' organised by the ICVC in May 2002, (ICVC 2002) in which participants discuss their understanding of what this term signifies, but no one except one, has even mentioned Makiguchi's name.

On the other hand, the use of the term 'value' within the Rangaprabhat experiment seems to be closest to the work of Peter McPhail (1972, 1982), which Elwyn Thomas explains as:

> The essence of moral behaviour is consideration, care and mutual respect. McPhail works on the assumption that moral behaviour is a direct consequence of what we take from our environment and the people that make up this environment. The message the consideration model delivers is that human values are essentially *caught rather than taught*. (Thomas 2000: 258)

The attempt of the Rangaprabhat experiment has been to give utmost importance to creating an 'atmosphere' in which learning takes place. As the document implies, students are not instructed through lessons on values, morality, character building, hygiene and participatory living that are the aims of the experiment, but are provided with an educational environment in which to bring forth their creative skills that in turn leads them to develop confidence building, community consciousness and so on (appendix VIII, points 1–10).

However, it is questionable as to how the experiment strives to do this or enhance the creativity of the students through art education. There is no clearcut understanding of the use of art in education such as has been dealt with by Herbert Read in his work *Education through Art* (1958). Through his work Read argues that education is a process by which individual uniqueness can be reconciled with social unity through integration. He elaborates upon the scope and function that aesthetic education can play for the preservation of the natural intensity of all modes of perception and sensation; the co-ordination of the various modes of perception and sensation with one another and in relation to the environment; the expression of feeling in communicable form; the expression in communicable form of modes of mental experience which would otherwise remain partially or wholly unconscious; and the expression of thought in required form (Read 1958: 8–9).

Interestingly the understanding of values as portrayed by the ICVC and its allied experiment is similar to the 'values education' proposals and programmes being carried out within mainstream Indian education.

The NCERT[5] has been identified by the MHRD (Department of Education),[6] Government of India as the nodal centre for strengthening value education in the country at school level. Subsequently, a National Resource Centre for Value Education (NRCVE) has been set up in the Department of Educational Psychology and Foundations of Education. The NRCVE was inaugurated on 14th September, 2000.[7] (NCERT 2005)

Under the 'training' programmes of the NRCVE the focus is to promote communal harmony, provide opportunities for Learning to Live Together, for children to learn and sing patriotic songs of various Indian languages, and develop the feeling of national and emotional integration.[8] Camps have been organised for teachers and teacher-educators in which singing community songs in various Indian languages is encouraged. These activities, however, seem naïve and fall terribly short when compared for instance to the kind of research that has been carried out in England on the integration of values within the curriculum, particularly in relation to prime subjects such as language, mathematics and science.[9] At the same time an analysis is required of the meaning and implication of 'values education' in the Indian context, where values have been associated with religious and cultural values. As the 'preamble' of the NRCVE states:

Value education to prevent erosion of values in public life has been a matter of concern, since independence. The values embedded in the Indian philosophy, cultural heritage and literature need to be nurtured in schools. A number of legendary books have highlighted the desirable values and the procedures for inculcation of values . . . The Preamble to the Constitution, the Fundamental Duties enshrined in the Constitution and National Policy of Education 1986/1992 highlighted the need to nurture core universal values like truth, peace, love, righteous conduct, and non-violence in students. These universal values have been emphasised by all religions.[10]

It seems that preventing the 'erosion of values' in public life is a coded appeal to times gone by when, presumably, values were generally agreed and desirable. This document also presupposes that 'Indian philosophy' is some kind of unitary category, or at least that its 'Indianness' is of key significance.

It can be argued that the issue of values in the Indian context has however been a complex one, which has not been adequately dealt with either by the NRCVE or the Rangaprabhat experiment. As analysed in chapter five of this book, although several commissions and policies have expressed the need for social, moral and spiritual values, in terms of its implementation very little has been done because of the increasing communal politics and its interference in mainstream education. In the face of these political realities the above programmes of the NRCVE can be critically viewed as an attempt to create isolated atmospheres of religiosity and patriotism in which participants are encouraged to emulate values through vocational activities.

As the NRCVE incorporates the values of different religious and cultural groups, it can be argued that the Rangaprabhat experiment as well has incorporated the values of non-violence and value creation, and does not give rise to the sort of creative transformation that Cobb asks for. In fact, the incorporation of values within the Rangaprabhat experiment leads to what Kung argues as the 'strategy of embrace' that he finds as a means by which religions try and reach a resolution on the question of truth. What Kung suggests is that if a religion adopts the 'strategy of embrace' towards the 'truth' of other religions, it may seem as the most convincing strategy, but his analysis shows that "what looks like toleration in practice proves to be a kind of conquest through embrace, a matter of allowing validity through domestication, an integration through a loss of identity" (Kung 1991: 81). Arguably, the ICVC, which has been established primarily by Gandhians, has embraced the principle of value creation but has not practically engaged with this principle.

Contrary to the way in which Makiguchi's and Gandhi's values are used here, *soka* and *ahimsa* were concepts that were rooted in an understanding of the interdependence of the individual and society, that in practice lead both thinkers to actively engage with their respective societies (this has implications for citizenship education which will be dealt with in the next chapter).

To recapitulate the analysis of Makiguchi's and Gandhi's values in chapter four, Gandhi's primary value of *ahimsa* as he used it meant non-violence inextricably linked with *dharma* or the universal law. Living based on *ahimsa* and *dharma* implied carrying out one's duties for the betterment of oneself and others. As Gandhi claimed, being a 'good' Hindu did not lead him to the Himalayas, but forced him to contend with the issues within the Indian society and politics. Similarly, value creation or *soka* is a neology formed from the two words *sozo* (creation) and *kachi* (value),[11] and the theory of value creation aims at the process by which value can be created for the benefit of the self and the good of society. Creating value for self and society is a creative notion that requires an individual to harmonise personal interest with public duties. This is similar to what Gandhi suggested, that is, individual rights should come from fulfilling one's social responsibility as an active citizen.

The understanding of values for both thinkers was not limited to ascribing value to a fixed object, for instance a national flag or the spinning-wheel, such as was done within the programmes of the NRCVE and the ICVC. It can be argued, that primarily what Makiguchi's and Gandhi's notion of values implied was taking action in one's life based on one's ideas and values. The implications of taking action based on their ideas meant that both Makiguchi and Gandhi actively protested against, and hence were also persecuted by the authoritarianism of their respective societies.

Contrary to this, Gandhi's ideas have been applied within the ICVC and its programmes such as 'candle making and book binding,' but they do not make the same impact which was generated by Gandhi in his 'education through a craft.' Whereas Gandhi's *charkha* or spinning-wheel like his Salt March symbolised an alternative socio-economic strategy for India,[12] the Gandhians in the present day have taken up spinning and weaving as a vocation, which has no significant bearing on the larger political and economic issues faced by the nation. In several lectures addressing students across the country, Gandhi specified that the '*khadi*[13] movement'[14] was a step toward rectifying the economic imbalance within India in which the colonisers and Indian elite were profiting at the expense of the poor section of society. The *charkha* and *khadi* that had enthused millions of youth during the nationalistic struggle is now marginalised in its use by those for whom spinning and weaving is a means of obtaining economic substance. In twenty-first century India, while Gandhi's will for political engagement is abandoned, the use of his arts and crafts is romanticised. What one hopes for instead is a creative use of values to achieve equity, equality and justice at a social level as exemplified by Gandhi.

This analysis identifies some of the rhetoric in the Gandhian institutions, but also makes a second point. That is, Gandhi tends to be interpreted and incorporated into the lifestyle, philosophies, social, political and educational reality of the institution in which he is invoked. Even though the ICVC invokes Gandhi and his values, nowhere is there a specific engagement with the theoretical underpinnings of his ideas. The view of values education found here has been influenced less by what Gandhi suggested, and more by the philosophy of the founders of the Rangaprabhat experiment, as well as by the mainstream Indian education. I do not intend to overlook the fact that the Mahatma Gandhi Centre for Non-violence and Development (MGCND) is one of the few surviving institutions in India that at least attempts to give a trial to Gandhi's ideas. The helplessness of these institutions to provide any substantial evidence of the use of Gandhi's ideas has also to do with the general lack of understanding of Gandhi and how his proposals might be actualised within the broader societal and educational changes in India, which is analysed in the next section.

THE PRESENCE OF GANDHI AND HIS
VALUES IN INDIA—AN ANALYTICAL STUDY

Gandhi, the Present Indian Political Structure and Education

As noted in chapter five, under the political changes in post-independent India the new constitution that was framed was based on Anglo-Saxon principles having a directly elected parliamentary government with a federal structure. This was in contrast to the Gandhian plan of decentralisation or *Panchayati Raj,* which under the new constitution was put under directive principles. By not seriously considering Gandhi's proposed socio-political structure the framers of the constitution also avoided the pertinence given to education by Gandhi who had insisted that " . . . for *panchayats* to be effective and efficient the level of education has to be considerably raised" (*Harijan* 21 December 1947). Education as envisaged by Gandhi was to educate the polity towards carrying out a broader role and responsibility of self governance starting from the local level.

Post-independent India is still struggling with Education for All (EFA). Also, the only real engagement of education with politics has been limited to 'civic education' in which the youth can scarcely receive an education that allows for the political involvement that Gandhi had wanted. Part of the problem has been the lack of initiative to develop Gandhi's proposals, but another problematic issue is that Gandhi's proposals for *Nai Talim* (new education) or Basic Education that he forwarded under the 'Wardha Scheme' in 1937 were oriented towards achieving an educational and social revolution. Gandhi proposed that education should be imparted through some craft or productive work, and suggested that the craft should be able to pay for the teaching staff. If this could be successfully implemented, Gandhi argued, the State would be able to introduce free and compulsory education. What Gandhi was asking for is a change in education geared towards a social revolution.

Contrary to this, if we view Gandhi's writings in the *Harijan* and *Young India* addressed to the youth during the nationalistic struggle, we find that at every stage of the struggle for freedom, Gandhi was giving clear direction to the students, whether to boycott the national universities, or to stay away from politics. When students were not actively involved in the political struggle, they were asked to spend their time studying in schools, to use their vacations to contribute to the social welfare programmes of health, sanitation and hygiene within the villages, and to work with the All India Spinners Association. Gandhi was therefore educating the youth, both politically and socially.

The difference between the above broad-based education and the Wardha Scheme is that in the former case education was not asked to compensate for society, and the educational revolution was taking place through a social and structural revolution. An example would be the experiments in education which Gandhi conducted in the communities or *ashrams* established by him, on the intellectual, moral and physical development of the adult and youth residents. This kind of education was pertinent to the time and social structure in which it was placed. However, Gandhi's subsequent proposal for a formal system of education based on craft was a challenging proposition in the face of modernisation and without the necessary decentralised socio-political structure to support it in the independent India.

Since 1947 Indian educational policies and aims have moved away significantly from Gandhi's education. Instead, Western education and research have been highly influential in Indian education. Now that citizenship education is becoming a prominent issue in the educational debates across the world, in India as well attempts have been made (without relevant success) to include citizenship education within the diverse school curriculums. A review of the *Consultation Paper on Effectuation of Fundamental Duties of Citizens* by *The National Commission to Review the Working of the Constitution* (Advisory Panel 2001)[15] published in 2003 shows that the discussion on citizenship values is part of the all too often lack of scholarly use of concepts from ancient Hindu, Jain and Buddhist texts that are given no translation or practical use within the existing political structure or the educational systems.

Interestingly the above document on citizenship education highlights the need for Gandhi's ideas and values. It is the only relevant discussion in education on 'redeeming' Gandhi. However, the socio-political structure in which the attempt is made to bring back Gandhi is different from that suggested by him. The key Gandhian concept invoked in this document is 'duty bound rights,' that is, rights must evolve from carrying out one's duty. The Indian constitution however views duties and rights separately—article 51A deals with the fundamental duties and articles 12 to 35 of part III of the preamble to the constitution of India contain the fundamental rights of an Indian citizen.[16]

The consequence of this paradoxical situation, it can be hypothesised, will end up with one of the following options being exercised in the ongoing discussions on citizenship: the futile attempt to invoke Gandhi will be abandoned, or an attempt will be made to address his ideas and values through citizenship education (as within Gandhian institutions in which these values are largely estranged), or as has been till now, discussions and debates on citizenship education will take place outside the curriculum, while instead schools continue to run classes on 'civic education' in which students are provided a general and theoretical understanding of the constitution and political structure of India. Arguably however, what is *required* is to take a look again at the socio-political structures that Gandhi envisaged (such as the *Panchay-*

ati Raj), and an insight into how it might be possible for his aspirations for the education of the Indian polity to find relevant meaning within the curriculum.

Notwithstanding this argument, I do not intend to dismiss the fact that the thrust of Gandhi and his ideas has not disappeared within modern India even though the Indian state functions in a somewhat paradoxical way. The past 60 odd years of democracy have seen the realisation of Gandhi's aspiration for an active civil society, while at the same time there has been a failure to meet its basic needs of poverty, illiteracy and overpopulation.

Gandhi in Democratic India

The Indian democracy has grown and developed since 1947 but is beset with paradoxes as Alam notes:

> The paradox lies in the persistence of widespread poverty and mass illiteracy, along with consistency of democratic commitments on the part of the poor. That democracy functions without the adequate spread of the foundations of civil society is another paradox. (Alam 2004: 130)

Even though the change of bureaucracy in independent India gave way to a narrowly conceived, Western capitalist inspired modernisation which was far from the Gandhian vision of decentralisation and the political education of the polity, as Alam's recent study reveals, the large majority of Indians, in particular the depressed and marginalised sections, have participated in growing numbers within the electoral process, and assertively affirmed their faith in democracy. On the other hand, the upper classes appear to be more apathetic. This has been proved through the state election of 2004 that has come as one of the biggest political surprises in which a government that was not beneficial to the marginalised sections, the BJP coalition, was voted out and the Congress that bore a promising future for these sections was elected. The surprising element here is that it is the *illiterate* section of the Indian polity that has shown an increasing awareness of the meaning of franchise and the efficacy of the vote (see Alam 2004).

The clamour and din of the Indian political scenario has often been negatively associated with chaos and disruption. Arguably however, the Indian example of democracy has proved to be a unique one. The Indian state like the society is a diverse and complex composition of groups[17] that are bound by caste, religion, sex and so on, in which people view their power-holding (in an otherwise powerlessness situation of corruption, poverty, etc.) in their rights, particularly the right to vote. This has been underestimated until now

by those such as Moore, who a few years ago had predicted that "The danger
for Indian democracy is that the Indian state nationally and locally is gradually losing its autonomy in relation to dominant classes while becoming too
impervious to democratic demands to form increasingly restless political
movements grounded in subordinate classes" (in Potter 1993: 369–370).

As Gandhi had identified, and as the recent political affairs have revealed,[18]
in the Indian context what binds the diverse communities of people within the
broader Indian community is their respective moral and cultural outlooks. As
argued in chapter four, Gandhi's own understanding of politics was not a
purely Western one, but had strong indigenous elements. The new political
vocabulary he used constitutes terms that cannot be comprehended within a
Western understanding of politics. Gandhi's socio-political understanding
was based on the concept of law that was understood by the Indian polity.
Whereas he used civil laws such as writing petitions, he was also invoking the
'common brotherhood' of the disparate multicultural Indian community
through appealing to their shared understanding of a 'causal law,' that is even
now expressed in popular terms such as fate, destiny, or the will of God
(Bhagvan or Allah). Thereby Gandhi made use of both the notion of law that
had come in from the West but also created an indigenous political understanding that took the causal law or *satya* as a peg, to which were added terms
borrowed from the diverse communities, such as *ahimsa* from Jainism,
dharma from Hinduism, love from Christianity, and notions of equality from
the Buddhist *sangha*.

At the same time there have been a great deal of Indian and foreign commentators on the Indian social and political chaos that has acted as a mock-
ery in the face of democracy, with communal violence, nuclear power, technological progress that benefits a few, lack of education for all, poverty of the
millions, and policies wielded for political purposes. In this situation the
looming presence of Gandhi and the values of nationalism are found within
the high aspirations embellished in the constitutional and educational laws, to
which, more often than not, lip-service is paid by power-holders. This is the
kind of argument that Varma makes in his recent work on *Being Indian* (2004)
where he portrays a rather bleak picture of the Indians who he sees as being
largely hypocritical, individualistic in their desire for material and spiritual
progress (*artha* and *moksha*), and more entrepreneurially aggressive than the
outside world has realized.[19]

Though there is an extremity in Varma's views, what is certainly true in his
argument is, as he himself expressed to me in our meeting[20] in 2004, that in
India there is a tendency to focus on an untenable 'ought' and less on the un-
deniable 'is.' Varma extends the same logic to Gandhi who is suffused with
idealism and distanced from reality. He finds that the only reason why Gand-

hian values such as non-violence have worked in India is not so much because of their moral relevance but rather because they are considered as effective strategies. However, as I will argue in the next chapter, this is an oversimplified statement on the pertinence of values such as non-violence.

Returning to the analysis of Gandhi in India, it can be argued that the reason why Gandhians and Gandhian institutions are largely fork-tongued is because they reflect the highest ideals and often do not adequately take into account the socio-political and economic realities of a complex society. This can be seen in the preceding excerpt from the Rangraprabhat experiment that decries the aspirations of the parents for their children's individual progress and expects them to be motivated by the 'altruistic goals' of the founders of the institution (appendix VIII; ICVC 2003: 20). Of course parents can be idealistic as well, but the point I am trying to make is that institutions like these, that seek the relevance of high moral ideals of Gandhi must take into account the personal interests and utility value they have within society, the latter being as tangible as the ideals and aspirations that are expressed in the school mottos.

CONCLUSION

This critical study of Gandhians and Gandhian institutions does not overlook the fact that whether Gandhi is directly espoused or not, his influence remains within the experiments that are carried out on his ideas and values. In the broader national context as well, Gandhi's relevance has not diminished. The change in independent India's political and educational structures did not reflect the Gandhian aspiration for education of the polity. Nevertheless Gandhi and his ideas maintain a thrust within the debates on citizenship education. At the same time, amidst the chaos and corruption of Indian democracy, Gandhi's desire for the political participation of the civil society has gained momentum through the active engagement of groups that are bound together with their respective moral and cultural values.

Gandhi and his ideas continue to be negotiated within different contexts in the Indian Diaspora. Such as under the influence of Hindutva Gandhi is represented as a weak person and the non-violence movement of Indian nationalism is shown as a degeneration of the Hindu society in the light of the 'martial heritage of the Hindus' symbolised by heroes such as Shivaji and the battle of *kurukshetra*.[21] While at the same time Gandhi is celebrated as the Father of the Nation and exists as an icon of the values of Indian nationalism.

The view presented by Varma of the Indian Diaspora on the other hand is a fairly restricted one. His simplification of the 'Indian mentality' and society finds a comfortable solution for a more equitable society through the promotion of economic growth and entrepreneurship. However, as I have tried to show through my analysis in this chapter, the issue is more complex. There is a gamut of socio-political and educational contexts in which the degree of influence of Gandhi depends on the context in which his ideas and values are used, which differs in all the aforementioned contexts—of Gandhian institutions, aspirations of the state, and the Indian society and politics.

The analysis of the relevance of both the thinkers, Gandhi and Makiguchi, in their own societies today shows that in spite of the political and educational paradoxes of our modern societies,[22] the positive potential for creative transformation does not vanish. In Gandhi's time this was proved by the 'Aundh experiment' in 1938 when the Raja of Aundh, acting on Gandhian lines, not only gave away his kingdom to the people, but also initiated the first successful case of an independent state (Rothermund 1983). The next chapter brings together the different strands of arguments that have been made within this book to evaluate the ideas, use and influence of Makiguchi and Gandhi.

NOTES

1. The source of this and the Mission Statement below is an unpublished booklet by the Ikeda Centre for Value Creation. The series title is 'Nonviolent Leadership and Empowerment' and has been printed in the city of Thiruvanathapuram.

2. Ibid.

3. Can be directly translated as 'Peace Corps'.

4. My discussion does not mention how the Ikeda Centre for Value Creation proposes to apply the ideas of Martin Luther King, as stated in the Mission Statement, as this study concerns itself with Gandhi and soka. Also, no other reference to King was found in the materials of ICVC.

5. National Council of Educational Research and Training.

6. Ministry of Human Resource Development.

7. http://www.ncert.nic.in/sites/valueeducation/recent-initiatives.htm

8. See http://www.ncert.nic.in/sites/valueeducation/training/htm

9. See Lawton *et al.* 1999; Cairns 2000.

10. http://www.ncert.nic.in/sites/valueeducation/valueeducation.htm

11. Josei Toda had coined the neology.

12. In March 1930 Gandhi and the other *satyagrahis* marched to the ocean to gather salt in a campaign to boycott the British. See note 38 in chapter four.

13. Hand-spun and hand-woven cloth.

14. See Hingorani ed. 1945: 307–308 for details of how Gandhi boycotted the British goods by making their own cloth, etc. and thereby gave an impetus to small scale industries that were lagging behind.

15. On 6 July 2001, the Advisory Panel on the 'Effectuation of Fundamental Duties of Citizens' presented a consultation paper (vol. 2003) in New Delhi that has been published by the National Commission to Review the Working of the Constitution.

16. Both the Gandhian concept of 'duty bound rights,' and the views on duties and rights in the Indian constitution may have their own respective merits that need further investigation.

17. See Parekh 1993: 170.

18. See Alam 2004: 122–123.

19. Also see BBC Radio 4 (Marr 2005).

20. In a meeting on 7 July 2004 at the Nehru Centre in London.

21. See Neufeldt 2003; also see note 25 in chapter 4 of this book.

22. I have used the term 'our modern societies' in chapter 8 as well, by which I am referring to societies such as Japan and India that have moved towards modernisation, industrialisation and democraticisation in the past several decades.

Chapter Eight

Conclusion

OVERVIEW OF PRECEDING CHAPTERS

Central to this study has been the investigation of the 'relevance of Makiguchi and Gandhi for the twenty-first century context.' The aim of this research has therefore been to critically evaluate whether or not there has been any influence of Makiguchi and Gandhi within their respective national educational systems, as well as within selected educational institutions linked to these thinkers.

Let me recapitulate the main arguments made within this study to examine the ideas, use and relevance of Makiguchi and Gandhi in their respective countries. The broader phenomena that I have sought to describe and explain are the use and relevance of Makiguchi and Gandhi within their respective countries in the twenty-first century. In order to show the absences and presences of these two thinkers I have engaged with the factors that have lead to a small or great influence of these dissidents in their present society and education. Chapters two, three and four were therefore an exposition of their values that were formulated in the early part of the twentieth century. Chapter five analysed the changes that have taken place within Japan and India in the past fifty years so as to perceive the shift in the context in which these values were formed, to the present day context in which they operate.

Whereas some changes were seen to work as facilitators in the application of these ideas and values, it was also argued that some of the changes that have taken place (in both Japan and India) have served to work as impediments in the use of Makiguchi's and Gandhi's ideas and values in present day society and education. Chapter five also provided a backdrop to show the degree to which the present state education system has not been receptive to these thinkers. At the same time, chapters six and seven have shown that in spite of these constraints certain groups of people have attempted to apply the ideas and values of Makiguchi and Gandhi, such as the Soka Schools in Japan and the ICVC in India.

To summarise some of the main reasons for the presence and absence of Makiguchi and Gandhi today, three main aspects were considered—the difficulty in adopting what they said, the limitations of the present state education system that has not been receptive to these ideas, and why some people have been inspired by their educational ideas.

As pointed out in chapter four, although both Makiguchi and Gandhi had made certain creative proposals for the education system of their own time, there are challenges in applying their ideas today. Such as, in the case of Makiguchi the main impediment is the unsystematic compilation of his thoughts. In the case of Gandhi, the contradictions in his writings as well as the different interpretations between Gandhi and his contemporaries, such as Nehru and Ambedkar, have alienated the Father of the Nation from the major social and political decisions that were made in modern India. As argued in chapter five, within mainstream Indian education as well, although Gandhi is invoked within national policies and documents, his presence often serves only as a symbol of the values of *Satyagraha* and Indian nationalism. In practice Gandhi's ideas like 'spinning the wheel'[1] have become out of context in modern India in which the determining influence has been cast by Nehruvian policies of modernisation, industrialisation and economic growth. These policies have better suited the centralised socio-political structures of democratic India. The bottom-up decentralised approach that Gandhi had envisaged for India, in which decision making originated from the local *panchayats*, could not have an adequate impetus within this new structure. Along with this there has been division between leading Gandhians in the Indian political scenario, chiefly between Vinoba Bhave and Jayaprakash Narayan.

In the case of Makiguchi, chapter five argued that in the present day Japanese society there is a tendency for Japanese educators to be easily influenced by foreigners at the cost of overlooking the ideas of Japanese thinkers (Harima 1997). Further, most people in Japan perceive Makiguchi as the leader of the Soka Gakkai, which is suspiciously and incorrectly (Watanabe 2000) viewed as a threat because it is a religious organisation providing political endorsement to the ruling Komeito party. As I have earlier argued, most of the methods developed by the teachers of the 'Soka Research Centre' have not directly filtered into mainstream Japanese education primarily because along with the ideas of Makiguchi, Buddhist philosophy informs the group's research and teaching.

Further, the investigation into the use and influence of Makiguchi's and Gandhi's ideas in the selected educational institutions in chapters six and seven have shown that the fate of both the thinkers has been that their ideas are interpreted and incorporated into the lifestyle, philosophies, social, political and educational reality of the institution in which they are invoked. The Soka Schools in Japan have adopted their founder, Makiguchi's ideas on *soka* (value creation) in light of his Buddhist beliefs. Whereas in India, the Ikeda Centre for Value Creation as an independent educational institution in a suburban part of South India focuses on vocational activities—borrowing from Gandhi's proposal for 'education through a craft.'

Chapters six and seven of this book also argued that a different discourse emerges when we investigate the use and influence of thinkers like Makiguchi and Gandhi, as compared to a research that examines their ideas and proposals. Although several researches have been carried out on their life and action (as pointed out in chapter four), there has been no research conducted on the fate of these thinkers. This study shows that in the case of Makiguchi as well as Gandhi, their fate does not necessarily emerge from what they said, or by the action that they took within their own lives. Most of Makiguchi's and Gandhi's ideas that were discussed in chapter four do not appear in the documentary analysis of the Soka and Gandhian institutions in chapters six and seven. The reason for this, as pointed out earlier, is that their use is contextual in the institutions that use them, as well as in the national context. Further, there tends to be rhetoric in their use, particularly in the case of Gandhi, whose ideas are found to be not as confrontational as they were in his own time.

During the course of my investigation I have had to reinterpret my question on the 'relevance' of these thinkers. Based on my previous research (Sharma 1999) I had started this study with the disposition (like many Soka educationists and Gandhians), that the ideas and proposals of Makiguchi and Gandhi need to be identified and used for the twenty-first century education. My study of the institutional and national documents reveals that their use has been heavily context dependent. Therefore, I have studied the representation of Makiguchi and Gandhi within their respective institutions, and critically questioned the application and applicability of their ideas within the educational and national context of Japan and India respectively.

Chapters five to seven have demonstrated that the fates of Makiguchi and Gandhi have had similarities as well as dissimilarities. (I will engage further with their dissimilar fates in the next section.) To summarise some of the similarities in their use:

(i) Their ideas tend to be interpreted according to the philosophy and lifestyle of the institution in which they are invoked.

(ii) Their ideas tend to be invoked utilising a great deal of rhetoric without practice or strategic implications.

(iii) Their ideas are not as confrontational as they had been within their own time.

(iv) The application of their ideas is dependent on the educational as well as national context in which they are used.

It is possible that such patterns and tendencies may be generalised as applicable to other dissident or creative thinkers, who had been confrontational within his or her own society. A unique characteristic that both Makiguchi and Gandhi however face as educators is that their ideas tend to be used in a more significant way by individuals rather than by institutions. Unlike some of their contemporaries like John Dewey, Makiguchi and Gandhi are not taught in any teacher's training institutions. Some of the significant research that has been done on Makiguchi's life and education is by researchers who became interested in his work through reading his book[2] at a local bookstore. This includes Dayle Bethel (1973) and Kazunori Kumagaya (1994a), with both of whom I have worked in the past decade. For instance, Bethel's research in recent years has been related to alternative learning, for which he finds Makiguchi's ideas to be highly relevant (1994, 2000).

Whereas, in the case of the Soka Schools, the main influence has been from their present founder Daisaku Ikeda, who in turn was influenced by Josei Toda—a teacher and a leading member of Makiguchi's educational organisation. Ikeda has taken certain radical steps within the Japanese society by directing the establishment of schools and political institutions that are linked to the Buddhist organisation, the Soka Gakkai (as discussed in chapters five and six).

These are some points that emerge from studying the relevance of Makiguchi and Gandhi. This critical study does not attempt to judge whether their fate has been good or bad, but has tried to highlight that there is a new context in which their ideas are being used today. I will now discuss some of the other issues that have arisen through this investigation into the relevance of Makiguchi and Gandhi.

THE NEED FOR POLITICAL EDUCATION

In relation to the issues linked to the fate of dissident thinkers, the underlying concern of this study has been with citizenship or political education (as outlined in chapter one). Chapters two to four offered an exposition of the ideas and actions of Makiguchi and Gandhi in relation to their place as citizens of their respective countries. Moving on to the twenty-first century context, in chapters five to seven, I have argued that there have been civic movements in their respective countries and abroad, to which their contribution can be delineated in certain ways. In this concluding chapter I will now analyse the issue of citizenship education based on my study of the two thinkers.

This choice is based upon the perceived relevance of the ideas and practices of the two thinkers for a field of study and practice which carries considerable educational weight in the early twenty-first century. Citizenship education somehow occupies the paradoxical position of being recognised generally as of central importance whilst being treated as peripheral in many educational institutions. There is, in effect, a struggle in process over the values which should inform the development of citizenship education.

Citizenship education has been a topic of concern for education in modern nation states. Particularly in this new century of global terrorism and Islam phobia, living with the 'other' is an issue that urgently needs to be addressed.[3] *Learning to Live Together* is a recent initiative of the UNESCO that was originally forwarded by the Delor's Commission in 1996, but has been given more thrust after 9/11. The commission highlights six major paradoxes of globalisation and the challenges of education for living together.[4] Compared to this initiative by UNESCO, the conference on *Learning to Live Together* which took place in 1936 in Utrecht was centred on the need for morality underpinned by religious values, in an age in which industrial and scientific development had begun to raise concerns about the breakdown of communities and values (Rawson 1936). My previous work on Makiguchi and Gandhi was influenced by similar concerns in which I have juxtaposed the 'reductionist' Newtonian-Cartesian paradigm with the 'holistic' views of these thinkers, so as to find a more cohesive understanding of values (Sharma 2002).

However, my present research shows that in the twenty-first century there are political implications of *Learning to Live Together* which we need to consider. The task of educating students to understand the values of the 'other,' such as Gandhi suggested, has become more complex in the twenty-first century due to the increasing contextual use of values which may be politicised or depoliticised. As this study shows, today in India Gandhians writ large have de-politicised Gandhi and his values. The *re-appearance* of Gandhi in a way other than he had been is an example of the argument that Herbert Marcuse makes on the 'classics' of literature, philosophy and politics which, in becoming available in paperbacks in local bookstore

> have left the mausoleum to come to life again . . . but coming to life as classics, they come to life as other than themselves; they are deprived of their antagonistic force, of the estrangement which was the very condition of their truth. The

intent and function of these works have thus fundamentally changed. If they once stood out in contradiction to the status quo, this contradiction is now flattened out. (Marcuse 1972: 24)

Expounding on Marcuse's argument, Ferguson states, "One of the consequences of Marcuse's analysis is, he suggests, that if one tries to conceptualise the world differently, one's arguments will not be accepted as valid for consideration until they have been reduced to the terms of the existing universe of discourse" (Ferguson 1998: 25). Though there is an extremity in the analysis Marcuse makes of the closing of the universe of discourse, his claims cannot be completely dismissed. It has been seen through this study on the presence of Gandhi that though he continues to be invoked, his writings do not make the significant contribution they did within his own time. As noted earlier, Gandhi's ideas and values engaged with the then governments through many different ways, such as through his role as the political leader of the Indian National Congress, his moral influence and perceived image as the Father of the Nation, and the impact of his movement of *Satyagraha* especially after the Salt March[5] of 1930, all of which are now framed within the Indian history textbooks.

At the same time, though there has been a 'de-politicisation' of Gandhi, there has been an opposite effect in Makiguchi's case. Whereas both Gandhi and Makiguchi had opposed their respective governments, Gandhi was an activist who was seen as a growing threat by a politically astute coloniser, while Makiguchi was an educator who was perceived as an annoyance to the autocratic leaders of the government, the Nichiren temple, and the school authorities in which he taught and served as principal. However, in post Cold War Japan, with the growth of the Soka Gakkai and the active political support it has given to the Komeito Party, any discussion on Makiguchi cannot be divorced from the socio-political use of his values in the twenty-first century. Even though the Soka Gakkai can be viewed by some as a marginalised community of 'believers,' my argument made through the study of the Soka School documents is that there exists a specific discourse on Makiguchi as the founder of the body politic of the Soka Gakkai and the Soka educational institutions.

Therefore, it is argued here that in spite of the leading discourse, or let us say 'socially constructed knowledge' (Kress and Leeuwen 2001) that exists within societies, that have been formed largely by the agendas of power-holders as analysed in chapter five, there are as well new discourses that arise constantly to challenge the existing ones. Whereas, on the one hand, dissident thinkers like Gandhi are made 'safe' in India by depriving them of their antagonistic force, some like Makiguchi in Japan have assumed a role after their death that is more political and active than they themselves had been.

A vital implication of the above two examples of the politicisation and de-politicisation of thinkers is that the ideas and values of dissident thinkers tend to lose their creativity and efficacy when they are used in a way that does not contend with the existing power structures of society. On the other hand, when their ideas and values are used within the politics of the society in which they are placed, such as in the case of the Soka Gakkai and Komeito, then there are issues of power that need to be contended with (as discussed in chapter six).

As demonstrated by this study, in the twenty-first century context, values such as non-violence, peace and value creation for human happiness are often processual, and can therefore be invoked, politicised and de-politicised according to the context in which they are placed. Based on this research it is argued that in the twenty-first century, an investigation into values in education cannot be limited to an approach based on philosophy and ethics. *Learning to Live Together* with the values of the 'other' has political implications as well, in which issues of power must be taken into account from the classroom to the international level. These implications need to be further examined as will be done in this chapter. Let us first return to how these thinkers themselves addressed this issue of learning for social participation.

THE EDUCATIONAL ASPIRATIONS OF MAKIGUCHI AND GANDHI

Both Makiguchi and Gandhi aspired to transform their respective societies. Makiguchi hoped to contribute to this transformation through his education and practice, whereas Gandhi was able to make a poignant impact within Indian society through the *Satyagraha* movement. Common to both thinkers was the normative aspect of their ideas, their reliance on truth as the law of the universe and their perceived interdependence of human life. Makiguchi's *value creating theory* and Gandhi's political philosophy aimed to develop methods by which the individual could be made socially responsible.

To recapitulate, Makiguchi's concept of *Soka* was formulated with the understanding that it is in the creation of value for self and others that the purpose of human life and hence education lies. *Soka Kyoikugaku Taikei* or 'The System of Value Creating Education' is a pragmatic theory of knowledge that for Makiguchi had implications for revitalising teaching strategies and education as a whole. Addressing this key concern Makiguchi states:

Education consists of finding value within the living environment, thereby discovering physical and psychological principles that govern our lives and eventually applying these newfound principles in real life to create new value. In sum, it is the guided acquisition of skills of observation, comprehension, and application. (Bethel 1989 ed.: 168)

As a teacher Makiguchi carried out research conducted through "the scientist's method of inducting findings from actual experience" (Bethel 1989 ed.: 8) despite the fact that the trend within educationists was to imitate foreign theories at home, and also in spite of the disadvantage Makiguchi faced in not being a highly qualified academic, but 'only a school teacher.' Social acceptance of his educational work was important to Makiguchi, and he spared no efforts to form relations with eminent people in politics and education such as Tsuyoshi Inukai, the prime minister of Japan from December 1931 to May 1932; Magoichi Tsuwara, minister of commerce and industry; and Itamu Takagi, professor of medicine at Tokyo Imperial University. Makiguchi saw his role as an educator to extend beyond the boundaries of his own classroom, and was keen to have an impact on the Japanese education system as a whole.

However, in the latter years of his educational career Makiguchi realised that education in schools, without the necessary societal and structural change, was not adequate to actualise his proposals for *value creating education*. For instance, his proposal of 'half day' learning at school and part of the day as an apprentice was not readily accepted within the educational structure and system of the modernising and industrialising Meiji era, and neither was it considered in later years under the militaristic government and its aim of indoctrinating the youth to participate in the war.[6]

Whereas Brannen and Bethel claim that Makiguchi turned to religion as a solace and therefore established the Value Creating Education Society (cited in chapter four), it can be argued that Makiguchi formed this organisation as a result of his understanding that a societal change was necessary for an educational transformation. This organisation drew educators as well as other members of society who were interested in his value creating theory as well as Nichiren Buddhism. Makiguchi's speeches to this group were not only to do with education, but also religion, society and politics. Eventually he was imprisoned because of his statements denouncing the emperor and the Japanese war.

Gandhi's role as an educator, however, was not limited to school education, and he was able to influence a much wider group of people in his role as the *Mahatma*. His education encompassed learning to use the *charkha* (wheel), wearing hand-made *khadi*, protecting the cow from being slaughtered, and other social reforms that were to transform the minds of the Indians and educate the populace to a life of values that contributed to both the individual and social welfare. To the Congress this was an effective policy, but to Gandhi it was his creed that stemmed from his commitment to *ahimsa* which he hoped would allow the Indians to see "the universal and all-pervading spirit of Truth leading to identification with everything that lives" (Gandhi 1957: 504). Unlike the Congress Gandhi saw his movement as an educational one, in which the educator (himself in this case) was also a role model. Through his own experiments Gandhi as the *Bapu* (or father) hoped to lead people to understand and practice a life of truth and non-violence.

In fact, values such as *ahimsa* were able to generate an impact not only because it was pertinent, but due to the methods of application within the context of the Indian political movement. Gandhi was constantly creating values in his engagement with politics, religion, economics, industry and education. In *Satyagraha* the values of non-violence, tolerance, love for humanity, amongst others, were constantly associated with Gandhi's personality, his symbols, and the entire movement.

Dennis Dalton borrows from Burns to attribute to Gandhi the role of an educator, and states,

> Burns gives to the conception of leadership a normative dimension that Plato stressed but that is often missing in contemporary political science analysis. Burns views the leader as essentially an educator engaged in a creative relationship with followers. Gandhi saw Satyagraha as heuristic because it employed a kind of power that encouraged reflection and reexamination of motives, needs, and interests. He believed, as Burns suggests, that this educative procedure depended on the development of an engagement of all those involved in a situation to extend awareness of human needs and the means of gratifying them. (Dalton 1993: 193)

Within each act of the *Satyagraha* was Gandhi's aim of transforming himself as the leader and those he led, in order to move his people and their country further on the path of *swaraj*.[7] Another vital purpose of Gandhi's education, as Dalton notes, was "that satyagraha must be used to gain the empowerment of those who had never been politicised" (Dalton 1993: 194). Rajagopalachari observed that the purpose of the Dandi march[8] was to manufacture not salt but civil disobedience, and Gandhi responded more precisely that it was "to use *satyagraha* to produce *swaraj*" (Ibid.).[9]

However, this two-pronged educational approach—the liberation of the individual and the independence of the country—was difficult to sustain due to several factors such as the ideological differences between Gandhi and the Congress; the regular eruption of violence within the movement that interrupted its progress; and the contradictions in Gandhi's own conduct as a *Satyagrahi* (see chapter four).

A common value that both Makiguchi and Gandhi have stressed in their educational proposals is the formation of character that stemmed from both thinkers' understanding that social transformation was possible through a change in the individual. Makiguchi arrived at his definition of character through his educational work and experience. For him, a person of character was someone whose existence centred on creating value that enhances to the fullest both personal life and the network of interdependent relationships that constitutes the individual's communal life. The means to cultivate character for Makiguchi were primarily through the influence of the teacher (Bethel 1989 ed.: 98) and "by studying the success stories of persons who embody the value-creation life-style" (Bethel 1989 ed.: 90) both of which seem quite idealistic and problematic in their method and orientation.

Gandhi arrived at a similar conclusion. Since his assumed role as a teacher in the Tolstoy Farm in South Africa, Gandhi advocated that students should have contact with men and women of 'unimpeachable moral character,' though it was not quite clear how Gandhi sought to develop character except through stories of the lives of great people. Character building was emphasised in all his schools and ashrams including Sabarmati in Gujarat (Sharma 1999: 32). Character, for Gandhi, meant "Creation of a pattern of living based on truth (*satya*) and non-violence (*ahimsa*)" (Avinashilingam 1960: 35). Addressing students in Madras soon after the establishment of his *ashram* at Sabarmati he said, "But truth, as it is conceived here, means that we have to rule our life by this law of truth at any cost" (Avinashilingam 1960: 13).

Makiguchi's and Gandhi's proposals suggest that education in schools on its own is not enough and there is a need for education of the society. As discussed through this book, one of the reasons why *Satyagraha* worked was because political education was not only taking place within the school but also in the outside society. Whereas Makiguchi was unable to 'succeed' because he did not have the adequate societal support required for his educational proposals to be implemented.

I had begun this study by questioning the limited educational application of both thinkers, with the assumption that their values were not given a fair trial within the educational systems of Japan and India respectively. However, a closer examination of their ideas shows that there are political implications in applying their ideas that need to be considered.

THE PRESENT POLITICAL IMPLICATIONS OF MAKIGUCHI'S AND GANDHI'S VALUES

Richard Falk's article *Mahatma Gandhi and the Revival of Nonviolent Politics in the Late 20th Century* makes an interesting analysis of the range of militant political movements that have to a varying degree endorsed and practiced non-violence. Falk states:

> These movements have not been self-consciously Gandhian, but have pursued a political course that appears guided by an opportunistic assessment of relative strengths and weaknesses in particular contexts of struggle. The precariousness of their commitment to non-violence is disclosed, to some extent, by the adoption of violent methods once the movement has succeeded in achieving control over the apparatus of state power and shifts roles from that of being in a posture of resistance to that of being in charge. (Falk 1998: 4)

Falk refers to this as 'tactical non-violence' and cites five recent political activities—the Iranian revolution, people power in the Philippines, Eastern Europe (especially Poland and Czechoslovakia), the intifada of the Occupied territories, and the pro-democracy movements in China and Burma. Of course, as the author points out, unlike the others, the movement articulated by Aung San Suu Kyi in Burma is clearly "a principled character resting on philosophical grounds that would not likely be discarded if the movement found itself forming a government" (Falk 1998: 7). Falk's analysis of the cited examples reveals that in all cases the means and ends were distorted, and violence and non-violence were used as a tactic when required. In comparison to this he notes, that Gandhi's ideas and values were powerful normatively and yet encouraged creative responses to particular realities.

However, in recent years Gandhi's values have been invoked to suit the context of the people and movement. At the same time some have chosen to maintain the normative standards when borrowing from the Gandhian heritage, and have been closer to the founder's ideas. However, even here the issue is complex such as the case of Mandela who is an apostle of values such as freedom and justice, and at the same time has resorted to using violence within his struggle. To explain further, during the anti-apartheid struggle Mandela and many of his compatriots viewed non-violence as a 'strategy' and 'tactic' (Mandela 1995: 147, 315). Expressing his stance Mandela states in his autobiography,

> I saw non-violence on the Gandhian model not as an inviolable principle but as a tactic to be used as the situation demanded. The principle was not so important that the strategy should be used even when it was self-defeating, as Gandhi himself believed. I called for non-violent protest for as long as it was effective. This view prevailed, despite Manilal Gandhi's[10] strong objections. (Ibid: 146–147)

Though Mandela refers to the African National Congress' 'commitment to non-violent struggles' (Ibid. 297), he acknowledges that the formation of the armed Umkhonto or MK in November 1961 (related to ANC) was justified because the ends were noble, and thereby violent means may be used in the African context, which, unlike the Indian one was faced with a brutal oppressor. Despite the philosophic and normative difference between Gandhi and Mandela, as Hardiman states, "The moral stature that he (Mandela) has as a result achieved throughout the world is one that in modern times has been equalled only by that of Gandhi himself" (Hardiman 2003: 284). The philosophic orientation of Martin Luther King Jr. on the other hand, was closer to that of Gandhi's. As Greg Moses argues, King did not find the 'Christian' concept of love and the 'Nietzschean' will to power as 'polar opposites' but were the necessary co-conception of ethical development as manifested by Gandhi (Hardiman 2003: 272).[11] Like King, Petra Kelly was also influenced by her religious (Catholic) beliefs, and drew inspiration directly from the Gandhian tradition of non-violent moral activism. Kelly, who was aware of Gandhi and King's 'lonely path to martyrdom,' was herself subject to a violent death, which as Hardiman notes "represented a profound failure for the principle of non-violence at the most personal of levels" (see Hardiman 2003: 284–293).

It is necessary to mention here that even though Gandhi has been referred to and linked with the above political actors he has also made a significant contribution to areas that are outside the narrowly defined political arena. He has had a large influence on important branches of the disciplines of ecology, peace research and economics through his profound influence on leading figures in the disciplines, such as Arne Naess, Johan Galtung and E.F. Schumacher. Weber explains that the 'one dimensional' Gandhi as a political actor, such as highlighted by Gene Sharp needs to be substituted by the 'whole Gandhi.'

> If, however, we look at the whole Gandhi, instead of just Gandhi the clean smelling politician or beyond reproach saint, we see a person struggling very publicly to discern the meaning of life, someone who not only knew that there was something more to human existence than the mundane, but had the courage to reach out for it and admit to failure. (Weber 2004: 8)

Ashis Nandy finds that Gandhi did not attempt to provide a systematised theory, ideology or utopia. Rather, he provided a vision of a society that stood in constant opposition to the oppressions, hierarchies and technologies that prevailed in the world of his day. His approach represented a state of mind rather than a clear-cut theoretical system (Hardiman 2003: 10),[12] and as Gundara analyses, the influence of Gandhi on successors and movements in recent decades "are an acknowledgement of the political creativity of the re-invention of his ideas and the ways in which they have continued to survive over time" (Gundara 2004: 24).

Underlying these perspectives is the shared view that Gandhi's ideas and their application need to be evaluated in the light of the creativity with which these values are engaged within the different societies and politics. As argued in the previous chapter, Gandhi's own understanding of politics was a creative attempt to weave together the disparate indigenous elements within the Indian community. The appeal this made to the Indian polity was the greatest asset to Gandhi's movement, but this can be misunderstood if we do not look into the persona of Gandhi. There can be said to be two Gandhis. The first is Gandhi the person, for whom truth and non-violence was his creed. Then there was the Gandhi who had to play the role of the Mahatma, the moral leader and a nationalist, who had to work through the problematic intercultural issues typified by religious conflicts between the Muslims and Hindus. It can be argued that whereas the former is a 'teachable Gandhi,' the latter and more complex Gandhi has been influential within the recent socio-political activities.

For education this opens up a complex number of issues. Take the first Gandhi. Teaching this Gandhi has not been easy. The history of Gandhi has been re-written under changing political powers in India. Further, in the mainstream society the use of Gandhi's values has been contextual. When teaching these values in school it is a challenge to engage with questions related to the contextual use of values in society. The question also arises as to how do we teach the second, more complex and equally relevant Gandhi? In relation to this we need to ask how we can encourage civic aspirations within classroom teaching, given the constraints of the curriculum, time, discipline and other such factors within mainstream education.

Similar issues arise in the case of Makiguchi. As shown in chapter six, by adopting the educational concept of *soka*, the Soka Gakkai in Japan has inherited the underlying philosophical understanding within it, a process that has been possible due to the common philosophy of Buddhism that both the 'founder' and the 'successors' have followed.[13] In addition, as argued earlier, the socio-political movement of the Soka Gakkai as a body politic has been an educational movement (see chapter six). Bethel, through his work *Makiguchi the Value Creator,* concludes that:

> In Soka Gakkai, under Ikeda's leadership, intellect is not pressed into the service of the movement, but rather is aimed at transforming the quality of mind of the entire population, equipping that population to judge the movement and to hold both it and its competitors accountable. (Bethel 1973: 143)

While I will not go into the detail of Bethel's argument, what is relevant for my analysis based on the preceding examples is that there are normative as well as pragmatic sides to both Makiguchi's and Gandhi's ideas and their applications within socio-political activities. Whereas the educational institutions have only invoked the normative aspect, socio-political activities have made use of tactics, methods and strategies as required. Within the socio-political activities there is creativity in their use in which the political education of the entire community takes place. I am not suggesting that as educators we are expected to go around transforming our society, but what I have argued is that, as this research shows, there is a paradox between the educational aspiration for civic engagement and the political reality that needs to be considered.

THE PARADOX OF EDUCATIONAL ASPIRATIONS AND POLITICAL ENGAGEMENT

The socio-political movements borrowed from the heritage of the thinkers, Makiguchi and Gandhi, have exhibited political creativity and arguably are able to generate civic propensity through the use of creative methods. On the other hand, the education within the schools related to both thinkers has invoked the normative standards of truth and humanity, but finds it problematic to respond to the heuristic aspect of these values that asks for 'those educated' to be self-reflective and play an active role in social transformation.

Here, however, I would also like to point out that the use of these values within society and politics is complex and requires further analysis through future research. For instance, it is sometimes difficult to distinguish between the use of value as a method or tactic such as King and Mandela have done within their respective political contexts and the abuse of these values that Falk describes as 'tactical non-violence.' Arguably of course, common to all the well-known political successors of Gandhi—like Mandela—has been the strong normative basis of their values, and the use of violence only as the last resort.

Within the education of modern nation states, citizenship education acts as the only space within the curriculum that in recent years has allowed for some development of civic propensity.

THE IMPLICATIONS FOR CITIZENSHIP EDUCATION

The previous chapter had argued that in India the discussions on citizenship have invoked the values of Gandhi but have not been able to apply them in practice due to the limitations set by its post independence centralised socio-political structure. Gandhi's emphasis on a decentralised political community resonates with the proposals of Makiguchi as well as some radical postmodernists who have argued for our re-engagement with the issue of community and values.

Some radical postmodernists have shown that in general postmodernists in their critique against modernity have ended up casting aside the merits of political and ethical solidarities that can be gained through community and values (for example see Cohen 1985, MacCannell 1992, Marquand 1988, Squires 1993).

At the same time, as Bauman warns, there are complications that accompany our engagement with community and values:

> People collecting together, giving their loyalties to communities may separate communities and the people more than before. Also, in the world of alienation, these communities act as a secure 'burglar-proof' house in an otherwise insecure neighbourhood. (Ibid.: 276–277)

Further, Bauman notes that communities start to dictate the definition of moral conduct.

> The paramount concern of their moral legislation is to keep the division between 'us' and 'them' watertight; not so much the promotion of moral standards, as the installation of *double* standards . . . (Ibid: 277)

This is characteristic of the communal politics in India, especially since 1970, that has affected education in several ways as highlighted in chapter five. The worst example of which is the Rashtriya Swayamsevak Sangh (RSS) schools that have targeted poor tribe people and low caste Hindus to indoctrinate Hindutva values.

As Bauman notes, the 'compulsive modernisation' within modernity has lead to what Ulrich Beck calls, the *Risikogesellschaft* or risk society, and Bauman further states that, " . . . ours is a kind of society in which the order-making urge results in the generation of a new series of disorders, imbuing all order-making endeavours with risks which can perhaps be roughly calculated in probability terms, but are never avoidable" (Bauman 1989: 230).

Fear, anxiety and personal security have become matters of greatest concern in our societies and much of the political capital is lodged in the present-day obsession with safety. In this situation one finds political players eager to deploy that capital in the power game. In the early part of the twentieth century Makiguchi had addressed this pattern within his society. The way out of this for Makiguchi was to construct a more cohesive society that allows for individual self-reflection to enhance 'a sympathetic communion with others.'

> Self-reflection allows us to discover the principles that govern our existence, and by bringing our actions in line with knowledge through these principles we can achieve a life of sympathetic communion with others. We uncover the basic commonalities of spirit and thought that underscore our sense of fairness, ex-

change value, self-gain, and the benefit of other—the foundation of our political and economic livelihood—though as yet self and others are blind to goals higher than those involving security. (Bethel 1989 ed.: 48)

Makiguchi's and Gandhi's notion of community and values as analysed earlier through this study rejects the alienation within our modern societies that strengthens the self-other bifurcation. There is cohesiveness in the notion of community suggested by both thinkers who arrived at it through their own spiritual understanding. At the same time as they had specified, their spiritual interests did not allow them to disengage from socio-political and educational affairs. Gandhi was adamant that his spirituality did not mean that he should shut himself in the Himalayan caves, and Makiguchi stressed that in his theory of value creation there was no need for a separate 'sanctity' value (see chapter four for details). Their notion of interdependency was embedded in their political and educational activism. However, they were not just activists but also thinkers who used their creative imagination to build an intimate connection between the autonomous, morally self-sustained and self-governed citizen and a fully fledged, self-reflective and self-correcting socio-political and educational community.

The relevant contribution that Makiguchi's and Gandhi's ideas make within citizenship education is that values must not be prescriptive but should be creative in their engagement with society and education. There needs to be a more creative approach to values and moral education in countries like Japan and Burma, and citizenship education in India and Britain.

Crick's report in the UK engages with several vital issues related to citizenship. Sections 1.9, 5.4 and section 10 of the report draw up guidance on the discussion of controversial issues that may arise in the promotion of pupils' Spiritual, Moral, Social and Cultural (SMSC) development. But in summing up the report states:

Schools can only do so much. They could do more, and must be helped to do so; we must not ask too little of teachers, but equally we must not ask too much. Pupils' attitudes to active citizenship are influenced quite as much by values and attitudes in schools as by many factors other than schooling; by family, the immediate environment, the media and the example of those in public life. Sometimes these are positive factors, sometimes not. (Crick 2000a: 9)

Crick's report is a carefully written document that provides useful tools as guidelines for teachers engaging with controversial issues related to Personal, Social and Health Education (PSHE), SMSC, History, Geography, and English. However, it does not look at the complexities of engaging with values that arise from the personal domain that have to do with intercultural education. It advocates that students adopt "a willingness and empathy to perceive and understand the interests, beliefs and viewpoints of others" (Ibid: 57) but does not deal with the issue of challenging and if necessary developing one's own values and beliefs through such interaction that is the requirement for a heuristic education.

Citizenship education is a concern common to all modern nation states. In particular the issue of learning to live with the values of the 'other' concerns everyone today more than ever. As argued earlier, *Learning to Live Together* has political implications for the youth. Within our global 'risk society' an increased number of insular communities such as the RSS have mushroomed that serve to perpetuate double standards, and in some extreme cases even nurture terrorism. These communities attract the youth by empowering them with a sense of mission for which they are even prepared to sacrifice their own life. It can be argued that these issues, which are the macro politics of education, should be the concern of citizenship education. At present citizenship education is mostly limited to imparting civic lessons. Alongside there are the micro politics of education that need to be addressed such as the sense of alienation and disempowerment that pose as challenges for the youth.

REVIEWING VALUES FOR EDUCATION
IN THE 21ST CENTURY

Knowledge and Values—A Qualitative Approach to Learning

Recently research on values in education has pointed towards the need for more knowledge of the 'other.' Haydon for instance considers the implications of teaching issues that deal with "values as a cause of conflict" such as the abortion in the USA and the treatment of animals in Britain. He proposes "that understanding differences over values in a plural society requires a great deal of knowledge. And the only way that such knowledge is likely to be acquired by substantial numbers is through formal education" by focussing not only on the difference "in the content of moral views but in the significance of moral concepts to the people who hold them" so that it enables the learner to view things from the "perspective on the inside" (Haydon 1997: 142).

It must however be argued that knowledge on its own is not enough. Let us take for instance the case of the recent terrorist actions in UK. We now *know* that most of the suspected terrorists were British born Pakistani Muslim youth. We also *know* that there is a need to be tolerant towards the British Muslim community as the *Jehadis* have been barbaric even to those 'within.' However, is this knowledge enough to avoid racial tension and scepticism about the 'other'?

Even within the micro level politics of school education, as argued earlier, bullying and violence have more to do with issues of trust and sense of mission that the youth are lacking, rather than knowledge of the 'other.' The role of educational institutions to impart trust is even more important now. The most clear-cut contribution of both the Soka Schools as well as the Gandhian institutions is in the 'message' given to the students through its ideals and mottos as seen in chapters six and seven of this book. As pointed out in chapter six, the research carried out by Patricia White in *Civic Virtues and Public Schooling* finds that whereas some schools give the undesirable message to students such as "this institution doesn't trust you, respect you, and so on," there is a need for institutions "to give thought to their positive corporate efforts to promote and foster democratic dispositions" (White 1996: 5).

Ironically this sense of mission and trust is imparted more strongly by the fundamentalist *Madrasas* (Islamic religious schools) and extremist Hindu schools under the RSS than within mainstream education. The difficulty mainstream education also faces is that education in schools on its own cannot compensate for society. It is inadequate to 'politically' educate the learner within the closed brick walls of schools where in most cases the learner is expected to drop their 'identity, way of life, and its symbolic representations at the school gate.'[14] A radical step today would be to draw upon the values of the learner, the family and society, and allow for dialogue that leads to development (as briefly discussed in chapter seven).

One of the key underlying concerns of this study, as well as my previous works (Sharma 1999, 2002), has been to identify the role of knowledge and values in learning that enhances social participation, a theme that transpires in Makiguchi's *value creational ideas*, Gandhi's *sarvodaya*[15] and Dewey's *participatory democracy* (Sharma 2002). Through my previous research I had identified the contributions these thinkers made in their respective societies and education system, in particular, to the issue of knowledge and values. In my book *Value Creators in Education* (1999) I had highlighted Gandhi's Socratic proposal to bring together knowledge and morality through teaching students the lives of people of 'impeachable moral character,' instead of narrating stories that had a moral ending. I began this present study with a similar disposition (common to Gandhians I have met in the past decade) that Makiguchi's and Gandhi's ideas need to be taught.

However, this study on the use of Makiguchi and Gandhi has presented a fairly complex picture. Although I still agree that Makiguchi and Gandhi were fine figures who unified their thoughts and actions, based on the preceding studies of the Soka and Gandhian educational institutions it can no longer be simply assumed that teaching about them would result in their values being transmitted within the institutions. As viewed in chapters six and seven, along with the ideas of these thinkers, there are other influences that affect values in these institutions, which may exert a more powerful impact than the thinkers themselves.

The task of teaching values has become more complex in the twenty-first century. Within the present socio-political structures decision-making is increasingly taken away from the learner. Although there needs to be more focus on enabling teachers to deal with sensitive issues within the classroom such as human rights, the task is not easy. Knowledge imparted in schools is not adequately equipped to allow the learner to engage with the contextual meaning of values that take place in the outside society, where values such as peace and justice are negotiable in society and politics. Unlike what Durkheim suggests, our task through knowledge to identify fixed laws (or values in this case) so as to predict how societies will operate is not feasible. In rapidly globalising modern nation states macro and micro level politics are contextually defining the meaning and use of values.

To re-state, a quantitative approach, such as imparting values through more knowledge or teaching values through a list, is not enough. Further emphasis needs to be placed on the qualitative approach to knowledge and values so that values can be practiced within the institution.

Suggestions for Future Research

For future research, this study has shown that methodological studies on the present relevance of such thinkers need to take an inter-disciplinary approach. This historical-comparative study of the two thinkers has been concerned to address sociological, pedagogical and political issues.

The research questions of this study, as stated in chapter one (last section) were:

1. What are the key contradictions and paradoxes which can be identified in a contextual and historical analysis of the value systems of Makiguchi and Gandhi?
2. How have the 'values' systems or values and beliefs of both thinkers impacted upon contemporary Japan and India?
3. Is there any way in which the findings of this analysis may have generalisable use for future research?

Based on this study, I have pointed out (above) certain patterns and tendencies that may be generalisable as applicable to the fate of thinkers like Makiguchi and Gandhi. Even though these thinkers were embroiled in their own socio-political and educational history, within the twenty-first century their ideas end up being interpreted according to the institution and national context in which they are invoked. Since their use tends to be contextual, future research on the applicability of such thinkers should not be limited to searching for a *literal adoption* of their ideas. There is an increased tendency among 'Soka educationists' to borrow words and phrases from Makiguchi's *Education for Creative Living* to improve their classroom practices. Meanwhile there are Gandhians who have literally implemented Gandhi's suggestions in *Nai Talim* (New Education) such as 'education through a craft.' In doing this they do not respond to the demands of a technologically advancing India.

Further, by situating such thinkers within their own histories, future research should aim to identify their strategies, beliefs, and behaviours as *citizens*. Makiguchi and Gandhi did not provide a single, linear and reductive prescription for the needs of their respective societies, but instead, contended with the complexity of their respective social and educational contexts. Future research on other such thinkers, who were interested in the transformation of their own societies, should therefore question the key contradictions and paradoxes that can be identified in a grounded or 'situated' analysis of their respective ideas and value systems.

NOTES

1. See note 38, chapter 4.
2. The System of Value Creating Education or *Soka Kyoikugaku Taikei* (1965).
3. In hindsight, having written this in London just before the terrorist bombs, I cannot overstate at present the need to address this issue.
4. See Unesco 2001: 15–17.
5. See note 12, chapter 7.
6. See chapters 2 and 4 of this book.
7. Independence or liberation.
8. Salt March. See note 12, chapter 7.
9. Interview with C. Rajagopalachari in Madras on 24 May 1967.
10. The *Mahatma*'s son and editor of the newspaper *Indian Opinion.*
11. From Moses 1997.
12. From Nandy 1981: 173.
13. See documents of Soka Schools in appendix V.
14. See Bernstein 1970: 345.
15. Universal welfare; social good, public interest.

APPENDIXES

Appendix I

The Commonalities between the Theory of Value of Seyuda and Makiguchi

Kumagaya notes five commonalities in the theory of value of Makiguchi and Seyuda (Kumagaya 1994b: 114). These are:

1. Both relate value (*kachi*) to life (*jinsei*) and person (*ningen*).
2. The backbone for Seyuda theory is the values of Truth (*shin*), Goodness (*zen*), Beauty (*bi*) and Holy (*sei*). He also looks at functional values for society such as his 'economic value theory' (*keizaiteki kachiron*) and the combination of the economics value to his 'philosophy value theory' (*tetsugakuteki kachiron*).
3. Both Seyuda and Makiguchi started from an awareness that the phenomena surrounding value arises from the evaluating subject and evaluated object.
4. Seyuda's 'economics value theory' is related to subjective and objective value.
5. For both the individual value can be created subjectively.

However, the fundamentals of Seyuda and Makiguchi's value theory were different (Ibid.: 113–114). For instance, Seyuda described value that is objectively stated by society as 'cultural value' (*bunka kachi*) and value which is created subjectively by the individual as 'creator value' (*souzousha kachi*) (Ibid.: 112) (for details see Ibid.: 109–114). Makiguchi on the other hand looked at value as existing in the relation between the object and the subject (the former theory being based on an absolute perception, whereas the latter being an experiential one). Also, unlike Seyuda, Makiguchi joined the concept of value with 'creation' and 'happiness.'

Appendix II

The Commonality between Makiguchi and Durkheim as Viewed by Kumagaya

Kumagaya states that both Makiguchi and Durkeim regarded value as existing in the relationship, but unlike Durkheim Makiguchi saw value in the relationship between object and subject of life. Makiguchi's point of view, states Kumagaya, can be seen to be based on the standard of life, whereas for Durkheim it was based on a conceptual basis. Both took a relative perspective of value, but the basis for Makiguchi was a utilitarian view of the happiness of the individual as the aim, whereas for Durkheim the stability of the society was the aim (Kumagaya 1994b: 137–143).

Appendix III

Nichiren Buddhism
and Makiguchi's Values

Daisaku Ikeda finds the following aspects of Nichiren Buddhism that attracted Makiguchi: 1) an emphasis on empirical experience and congruence with the scientific method; 2) the centrality of a universal law or principle (dharma) as the focus of faith rather than an anthropomorphic being or deity; 3) an emphasis on social engagement and a stance using religion's contribution to society as the measure of its validity (Ikeda 2001c: 28).

Appendix IV

The Lotus Sutra
and Makiguchi's Values

KAZUNORI KUMAGAYA'S VIEW

Kumagaya finds three points of commonality between Makiguchi's educational pedagogy and the philosophy of the Lotus Sutra (Kumagaya 1994b: 160–166). Here I will briefly narrate the reasons why Kumagaya finds that Makiguchi embraced the Lotus Sutra. Kumagaya states that Makiguchi may have come across the following two limitations of his Value Creating theory: (1) relativism and (2) that this theory was applicable only for the inhabitants of the earth (Kumagaya 1994: 162–163). According to Kumagaya, since the Value Creating Theory is a relative theory, in which value exists between subject and object, this would result in postulating no fixed values. The Lotus Sutra, according to Kumagaya, while understanding the phenomenon of the world exists in relative relations, it also recognizes a universal 'law' that is constant. For Makiguchi absolute value could therefore be created in living a life in accordance with this law through the practice of Nichiren Buddhism (Ibid.).

ATSUSHI FURUKAWA'S VIEW

Furukawa states that the Buddhist law of Nam Myoho Renge Kyo was the absolute truth for Makiguchi (Furukawa 2001: 150). According to Furukawa, after encountering Nichiren Buddhism, Makiguchi based his faith in the causal law of the universe, 'Myoho.' Therefore, Furukawa argues that Makiguchi built his philosophy of value creating education on this absolute truth. The result of this was his publication in 1937 of the *Sokakyoikuhou no kagakuteki, chyo shukyoteki jissen shomei* or 'The rational, supreme religious actual proof of the method of value creation' (Ibid.: 151). Chapter four of this book engages with Kumagaya and Furukawa's respective analyses.

Appendix V

The Soka School Documents
Used for Analysis

Three documents of Soka Schools were studied. Document one, which contains the 'mission statement' of these schools; document two, which is a statement on 'the ideal of Soka education'; and a third document that states the school's mottos and principles.

DOCUMENT ONE: THE 'MISSION STATEMENT' OF THE SOKA SCHOOLS, DATED 13TH APRIL 2003

(The following is my translation of the mission statement of Soka educational institutions. The original document is in Japanese. http://www.soka.ed.jp/kyoiku/s030413.html accessed on 4th February 2004):

Soka education as a whole aims at the happiness of humanity and the shaping of world peace. It constitutes the Soka School Systems (established in 1967), Soka University (established in 1971), and the entire network of educational institutions from the university to the kindergarten that have been founded by Daisaku Ikeda *Sensei*.

This includes students within Soka University, Soka University Graduate School, Soka Women's College, Soka High School, Kansai Soka High School, Soka Middle School, Kansai Soka Middle School, Tokyo Soka Elementary School, Kansai Soka Elementary School, Sapporo Soka Kindergarten that has altogether around 14,000 students. In addition are 17,000 students who are enrolled in the Soka University Educational Correspondence Department, which adds up in total to 31,000 students within the entire network of Soka education. Apart from this, outside Japan, due to local initiatives, there exists a

global network of learning which is taking place in institutions such as kindergartens in Hong Kong, Singapore, Malaysia; Soka School System in Brazil;
and Soka University and Graduate School in America.

Each educational institution has been established based on the ideas forwarded for that institution by the founder Daisaku Ikeda *Sensei* that presents
basic directives to the education within each institution, and these are un-
changeable for eternity. Common to all institutions is a 'humanism that is
based on the ultimate respect for the dignity of life,' and the aim of all institutions is to enable the individual to establish oneself as well as contribute to
other people. That is, these institutions aim at the upbringing of 'people of talent who possess wisdom and character, people who are prepared to be able to
create value for both one's own life as well as that of society.'

These institutions have been established based on the ideas of the first President of the Soka Gakkai, Tsunesaburo Makiguchi *Sensei*, that are contained
within the 'Value Creating Education Pedagogy,' as well as is based on the application of this theory by the second President Josei Toda *Sensei*, and further,
the actualisation of these educational concepts by Daisaku Ikeda *Sensei.*

The entire network of Soka Education aims first of all at a 'humanistic education,' the primary aim of which is the actualisation of the 'lifelong happiness of the pupil or student.' The purpose of Soka education is the happiness
of the human being, that is, the upbringing of people who can contribute both
to the happiness of oneself and that of others. A 'humanistic education' that
respects the individual's character and personality, and allows the boundless
potential of each individual to blossom, is the need of our time. The staff and
students of the school respect each other, and the school is student-centred.

The second aim of the schools is peace, and is based on the concept of an
education that 'fosters global citizens,' which is people of talent who can contribute to the world. The aim is therefore to carry out the essential task of educating global citizens through the teaching standards and motto of each
school, which broadly aim at raising 'people of talent who possess courage,
compassion, wisdom.' The corporation and exchange with various overseas
institutions, allows these schools to gain an understanding of other cultures,
as well as build interest in 'peace,' 'human rights,' and 'environment' that
contributes to the world society. In practical terms it is the enhancement of
'language education,' 'information education,' and 'reading.' A separate programme is made for each of the various educational institutions, corresponding to the above, and depending on each one's stage of development.

Thirdly, the schools aim at the upbringing of 'creative human beings.' This
means, that they aim at the appearance of people of talent who, notwithstanding the problematic circumstances that they may encounter, can create
value that is necessary for society. Towards that the schools place their focus

on culture education that deeply recognizes the relation between nature, society and human beings. It is an education that empowers people to 'recognize' and 'solve' 'problems.'

The entire network of Soka education constitutes a group of people who have come together as students and staff due to their common understanding of the ideas of Daisaku Ikeda *Sensei*. Education that is carried out within these institutions embodies the ideas of Soka education in society. In particular, it carries out the ideas of peace, culture and education through the various educational institutions working in close cooperation with each other from the entrance to high school.

In the future, in order to develop further, the Soka educational institutions will continue to examine and keep abreast with the advancements made in different fields through the establishment of the 'Soka program,' 'school management,' 'connection education,' and so on, as well as constantly reorganize/reorient itself to be a model for meeting the standard of education in Japan and in the world.

DOCUMENT TWO: THE 'IDEAL' OF THE SOKA SCHOOLS

(The original document is in English. http://www.soka.ed.jp/kyoiku/k0004 .html Accessed on 10.3.04):

Education exists for the purpose of nurturing the boundless range of talents inherent in each individual and of cultivating character so that each person is able to take on the responsibilities called for by the future. Human beings are always at the very heart of the workings of society, whether this be in industry, economics, politics, science or art. For this reason and for the betterment of society, the improvement of education is one of the most meaningful undertakings mankind faces today.

Deeply grounded in the unchanging principle of respect for the dignity of human life, Soka (Value-creating) Education considers the cultivation of humanity to be of the utmost significance. Soka Education also aims to bring up selfmotivated people who are capable of creating value in their own lives and in society. This ideal originates in the principles of education expounded by Tsunesaburo Makiguchi, the first president of Soka Gakkai. Mr.Makiguchi devoted his entire life to the reform of education, which to him meant setting up within the educational system a methodology that would serve to create real value for humanity. Mr.Makiguchi stated the purpose of Soka's humanistic educational system in no uncertain terms: "Education is the creation of value for humanity."

In order for one to enrich one's character, it is necessary to maintain a broad and flexible mind, to nurture a strong spirit able to overcome all difficulties, and to cultivate wisdom from all the knowledge one has accumulated. To realize these goals, one must pursue the study of humanity and burn with the passion to contribute to mankind.

Daisaku Ikeda, Soka Gakkai International (SGI) president and founder of the Soka Schools, has untiringly guided young people in developing themselves towards the future, while he himself devotedly carries out activities to secure the happiness of mankind. While hoping that each person is able to live a fulfilling existence and to make lifelong efforts to develop himself, Mr.Ikeda also cherishes the desire that each person can bring forth a strong sense of his responsibility to protect people, contribute to the peace of the world and advance human culture.

Following the precedents set down by Soka Gakkai presidents Tsunesaburo Makiguchi and Josei Toda, both of whom were educators, SGI President Ikeda has assumed the task of establishing schools based on the principles of value creating education.

Always striving for excellence, the Soka Schools provide an atmosphere where young men and women are able to study hard while creating bonds of friendship. Thus, imbued with the schools' noble spirit and tradition, Soka graduates will without fail become a part of the movement to expand waves of peace around the world and to light a brilliant torch of hope for all mankind.

DOCUMENT THREE: 'SOKA EDUCATION: TO CREATE A CENTURY OF HOPE'

(This document contains the Soka School's mottos and principles. The original document is in Japanese. http://www.kansai.soka.ed.jp/guide/j03.html accessed on 24/2/04 or http:///www.tokyo.soka.ed.jp/ The following is my translation in English):

Educational Policy/Plan:

1. Principle of health and talent.
2. Principle of ability and rich human spirit.

School Teaching:

1. Pursue truth, create value, be a person of wisdom and passion.
2. Under any circumstances do not cause trouble to others. Take responsibility for own actions.
3. Be kind to others, be polite and courteous, reject/refute/deny violence, value (lay emphasis on) trust and cooperation.

4. Majestically uphold and state your beliefs. Have courage to work for justice and show actual proof.
5. Increase your enterprising spirit, be a person who can give direction to bring glory to Japan, and foster yourself to be a person who can give direction to the world.

The Five Principles of Soka Gakuen (School System):

1. Dignity of life.
2. Respect for character.
3. Deep friendship. Friendship that lasts for your entire life.
4. Refute/reject/deny violence.
5. Be persons who are intellectual and intelligent.

School Slogan:

• The senior students must pamper and treasure the junior students as younger brothers and sisters.
• The junior students must respect the senior students as their elder brothers and sisters.
• Definitely do not allow for violence or bullying.

School Badge:

• Middle is the pen and on either side is shaped as the wings of a bird.
• The pen represents wisdom and the bird represents "launching into the future."

School Colour: Blue stands for wisdom, yellow for glory, red for passion.

Appendix VI

Measurement, Representation and Indication of Selected Documents of the Soka Schools in Tokyo and Kansai

A.) Measurement: A Pragmatic Analysis of Makiguchi's Ideas and Values

Table AVI.1. Measurement: for a Pragmatic Analysis of Makiguchi's Ideas and Values

Words	Document 1	Document 2	Document 3
Education/al (*kyoiku*)	26	10	2
Value (*kachi*)	3	5	2
Soka (includes 'Soka education' and 'Soka Schools')			
(*soka*)	23	10	2
Truth (*shinri*)	Zero mention	Zero mention	1
Creative (*sozo*)	4 (Only one in the English translation)	Zero mention	2
Happiness (*kofuku*)	4	1	Zero mention
Individual, self (*ningen, jishin, jibun*)	3	1	2
Personality (*kosei*)	1	Zero mention	Zero mention
Potential (*kanousei*)	1	Zero mention	Zero mention
Passion (*jounetsu*)	Zero mention	1	2
Talent/ability (*jinzai*)	4	1	2
Society (*shakai*) (includes fostering students to contribute to society)	5	3	Zero mention

(continued)

Table AVI.1. *(continued)*

Words	Document 1	Document 2	Document 3
Other (includes fostering students to contribute to others) (*tasha*)	1	Zero mention	4
Respect (*songen, keii*)?	3	2	1
Environment (*kankyo, shizen*)	2	Zero mention	Zero mention
Global Citizen (*sekai shimin*)	2	Zero mention	Zero mention
Global/World/International/ Outside Japan (*sekai, kaigai, kokusai*)	8 (5/2/1)	2	1
Humanism, humanistic (*ningen shugi*)	8 (one appears in text. Other seven are implicit)	8 (including humanity)	1 (human)
Friendship (*yuujou*)	Zero mention	1	2
Responsibility (*sekinin*)	Zero mention	2	1
Spirituality (*seishin*)	Zero mention	Zero mention	Zero mention
Religion (*shuukyo*)	Zero mention	Zero mention	Zero mention
Dignity of life (*seimei no songen*)	1	1	1
Life, lifelong (*jinsei, shougai*)?	2	2	1
Wisdom (*eichi, chie*)	1	1	3
Intellect (*chisei*)	1	1	1
Character (*jinkaku*)	2	2	1
Culture (*bunka*)?	3	1	Zero mention
Violence (*bouryoku*)	Zero mention	Zero mention	3
Peace (*heiwa*)	4	2	Zero mention

ᵃ Zero mention means that the word does not appear in the document. The term 'zero mention' has been taken from Weber (1990) and will be used to evaluate whether or not such absences can be found to have any particular meaning.

ᵇ The counting of the words has been done in the original language of the document. However, in the case of some words I have counted based on their equivalent meaning in English. For instance, the word 'individual' is not always explicit in the Japanese text, and wherever it was implicit, I have made a count of it (for example, in document three the fifth school principle has the word 'person' implicit in the Japanese version of the text).

ᶜ Pictorial analysis has not been done in any of the documents, as they do not make any significant contribution to the analysis.

The above words can be categorized as follows to show some of the key aspects of Makiguchi's 'Value Creating Pedagogy,' which are: education, value creation, over-riding the self-other bifurcation and character:

1. Education, educational.
2. Soka, value, creative, truth, happiness (concepts that are related and central to Makiguchi's idea of 'value creation').
3. Individual/self, society, others, environment, (all words pertaining to self and others).
4. Character.

In each of the documents viewed separately, the following words and phrases have been emphasized:

Document One: The 'Mission Statement' of the Soka Schools. (The original document is in Japanese):

1. Humanistic education (*ningenkyoiku*), humanism (*ningenshugi*)
2. Learner's lifelong happiness (*shogai ni wataru kofuku*), happiness of humanity (*jinrui no kofuku*).
3. Contributing to world peace and culture (*sekai heiwa, bunka*).
4. Ultimate respect for the dignity of life (*seimei no zettaitekina songen*).
5. Fostering creative individuals (*sozotekina ningen no ikusei*).
6. Creating value for self and others (*ningen to shakai ni kachi wo sozo suru*).
7. Nurturing intellect, character, wisdom, talent (*chisei, jinkaku, chie, jinzai no ikusei*).

Document Two: The 'Ideal' of the Soka Schools. (The original document is in English):

1. Nurturing character, talent, broad and flexible mind, strong spirit to overcome all difficulties, wisdom from knowledge, and therefore the need for study and passion to achieve these.
2. Taking responsibility for self and others, to protect people.
3. Respect for the dignity of life.
4. Human-centred education, cultivation of one's own humanity is most important.
5. Basing education on the unchanging principle of the 'respect for the dignity of life.'
6. Creating value for self and others.

Document Three: 'Soka Education: To Create a Century of Hope.' (Original is in Japanese):

1. School principles contain some words and phrases that can be found in the 'Fundamental Law of Education' or *kyoikukihonho* that is the basic tenet of Japanese education, drafted and enacted since 1947 (which is now proposed to be amended). These include tackling issues such as directing students to take responsibility, to be kind, polite, courteous, and for them to become people who can contribute to Japan and world peace. It also includes tackling problems that are common to Japanese education, such as the bullying. Further, it aims to strengthen good relations between junior (*kohai*) and senior (*senpai*) students.
2. In this document there is also an emphasis on the pursuit of truth, creating value, wisdom, passion, upholding and stating one's own beliefs, working for justice and show actual proof, respecting character, and the dignity of life.

Table AVI.2.   Measurement: The Presence of Makiguchi in the School Documents

	Document 1	Document 2	Document 3
Tsunesaburo Makiguchi	1	4	Zero mention
Josei Toda	1	1	Zero mention
Daisaku Ikeda	4 (2 implicit)	3	Zero mention

B.) The Representation of Makiguchi

Table AVI.2 shows the presence of Makiguchi in the documents that deals with the Soka School's 'Mission Statement,' and the 'Ideal of Soka Education.' It also shows that the present founder Daisaku Ikeda has been equivalently mentioned.

Apart from these documents, another document specifically elaborates upon the three founders of the Soka educational institutions titled, 'The Origin of Soka Education—aiming towards peace and happiness of humanity' (the original Japanese title is '*Jinrui no heiwa to kofuku wo mezasu, soka kyoiku no genryu*').This document, produced by the Soka School, Kansai, introduces the three founders, Tsunesaburo Makiguchi, Josei Toda and Daisaku Ikeda (Kansai 2004, see appendix VII). It was not feasible to do a content analysis of this document, as it is a brief description of the three people and their work. I have summarized the key issues raised by this document in the following paragraphs.

Regarding Makiguchi, the document makes the following key comments:

1. Makiguchi's works have recently "received high recognition" (paragraph one).
2. Makiguchi had carried out "pioneering educational experiments" (paragraph two).
3. Makiguchi pointed out to "the changes that were necessary in order to open up the path of humanistic education in Japan in spite of the confusions and contradictions that existed in the educational world in his time" (paragraph two).
4. Makiguchi never gave up and consistently questioned as to how to enable human beings to lead a life of happiness (paragraph three—paraphrased).

In this document Toda is introduced as a successor of Makiguchi in the realm of education. It mentions the success of Toda's experiments in the *Jishu Gakkan* in Meguro, Tokyo, in which he carried out educational experiments on 'Soka education' and highlights his authored educational material, *Suirishiki Shidou Sanjutsu*, which was used for guidance in teaching and had become the best-seller, selling more than 100,0000 copies.

Ikeda is introduced as the successor who carried out the philosophy of Makiguchi and Toda, and has established the Soka School systems with an aim to foster people of talent. It states that, "at the opening of Soka school system in 1968 (Showa 43), he (Ikeda) expressed the ideal of these schools to raise capable people who will 'shoulder the future of Japan' and 'contribute to the world culture.' Following this, he has established one educational institution after another based on his belief that "education is the greatest human task" and "the Soka school students are my life" (paragraph two).

The document refers to him as the Soka Gakkai honorary president, the president of the Soka Gakkai International (SGI), and the founder of the Min-On Concert Association, Tokyo Fuji Art Museum, Institute of Oriental Philosophy, Toda Institute for Global Peace and Policy Research (paragraph four). Further, it elaborates upon the dialogues he has held with world leaders, and the peace awards he has been given by various international peace, culture and educational organizations (last paragraph).

C.) Indication

Words that have a high frequency in the three documents are: soka, world, and humanism. Low frequency words include happiness, violence, peace, dignity of life, and world citizen. Words that have a 'zero mention' are 'spirituality' and 'religion' although it can be hypothesized that a pragmatic analysis of Makiguchi's values should reveal some mention of these terms. One reason for this is that the Japanese 'Fundamental Law of Education' forbids any preference given to a specific religion by a school.

To explain briefly, even though a private school may have a religious orientation and undertake activities such as prayer during school hours, it cannot state its preference to a particular religion or discriminate against any other religion. In light of this the Soka Schools may have abstained from expressing their views on religion or spirituality. However, their founder Ikeda has expressed his concerns about compulsory religious education in Japan and states that religious doctrine is not taught in the Soka Schools, that their aim is to develop students' abilities to ponder on the meaning and purpose of life, and the school's mission is to foster a rich humanism and spirituality that will enable students to enjoy personal growth and contribute to society (Ikeda 2001b: 49).

Appendix VII

Soka School Documents on Three Founding Presidents Titled 'The Origin of Soka Education

Aiming Towards Peace and Happiness of Humanity.' The Original Japanese Title is *'Jinrui no heiwa to kofuku wo mezasu, soka kyoiku no genryuu'* (see Kansai 2004)

Tsunesaburo Makiguchi *Sensei* diligently carried out research since the Meiji era, based on his experiments in the field of education. Makiguchi sensei's *Geography of Human Life* was his research on the principles that work within nature and the activities of human life. Along with this is the monumental collection of his educational records that deals with the formation of human beings, published together as *The System of Value Creating Education Pedagogy*. These works have received high recognition in the field of education in the world.

Makiguchi sensei carried out his pioneering educational experiments starting from his position as an instructor in the Elementary School attached to Hokkaido Teachers Training College, to his role as a school principal in Shirogane Elementary School. He pointed out the numerous changes that were necessary in order to open up the path of humanistic education in Japan in spite of the confusions and contradictions that existed in the educational world in his time.

Throughout his life Makiguchi sensei pursued the question that, 'what can be done to enable human beings to lead a life of happiness?' and held on to this in spite of the different circumstances that he met with.

The educational reformations that Makiguchi sensei had stressed on were expressed to the world by Josei Toda. In the *Jishu Gakkan* in Meguro, Tokyo, Toda sensei carried out the educational experiments on Soka education, fostering many capable people. Apart from this, he compiled his everyday educational material for guidance in teaching in his work *Suirishiki Shidou Sanju*, which was the best-seller, selling more than 100,0000 copies.

Toda *sensei* succeeded the will of Makiguchi *sensei* and for the people's happiness and peace laid down a great foundation for the future generation.

'Education is life's ultimate sacred work.'

'Soka School students are my life.'

Ikeda sensei has carried out the philosophy and educational work of Makiguchi and Toda sensei, and has established the Soka school systems with an aim to foster people of talent. At the opening of Soka school system in 1968 (Showa 43), he expressed the ideal of these schools to raise capable people who 'shoulder the future of Japan' and 'contribute to world culture.' Following this, he has established one educational institution after another based on his belief that "education is the greatest human task," and "the Soka school students are my life." He was born on 2nd January 1928 in Tokyo and graduated from Fuji University. He became the Soka Gakkai honorary president, and the president of Soka Gakkai International (SGI). Apart from the Soka educational institutions, he has established the Min-On Concert Association, Tokyo Fuji Art Museum, Institute of Oriental Philosophy, Toda Institute for Global Peace and Policy Research, contributing to peace, culture and education. He has conducted dialogue with various people in the world. He has received peace awards from various nations and organizations including the United Nations Peace Award, and the National Order of the Southern Cross of the Republic of Brazil, as well as honorary degrees from Moscow State University, University of Glasgow, University of Denver, University of Nairobi, amongst others. His published works include The Human Revolution (12 Volumes). His published dialogues include Choose Life: A Dialogue with Arnold J. Toynbee, Dawn After Dark with Rene Huyghe, Before It Is Too Late with Aurelio Peccei, and A Lifelong Quest for Peace with Linus Pauling.

Appendix VIII

Excerpts from a Case Study on the Rangaprabhat Experiment

The following is an excerpt from a publication by the ICVC that describes one of the experiments carried out by the ICVC (ICVC 2003: 18–25). I have not amended the mistakes in the original print:

A group of artists and educators led by Prof. G. Sankara Pillai, a great artist and visionary and his disciple K. Kochunarayanapillai initiated at a place called Venjarammood, about 20 kilometers north of Trivandrum, what was at that time (around 2 decades ago) called experiments in primary education by the integration of nonformal education and formal education through a liberal and creative use of the vast opportunities offered by children's drama and by offering opportunities to selected children to spend their leisure time in such activities that would enhance in them a spirit of co-operative endeavour, involvement in craft activities, creative dramatics, story telling, improvisations, creative dances and folk music. The aim was to offer facilities and opportunities to children to supplement and augment their classroom learning in an atmosphere of relaxed freedom which would promote a creative involvement in the children. This led to the gradual development of an alternative campus or school, centred around the house and the thatched shed that was put up near the house of Sri. Kochunarayanapillai, himself a distinguished teacher of a local school.

The experiment very soon turned out to be a quite useful one and it went a few steps ahead of the popular western concept and practice of Theatre-in-education. The manner in which the programmes developed at this centre indicated that it succeeded in:

1. Creating community consciousness,
2. Exploring the moral, spiritual, and cultural dimensions of education,

3. Creating awareness among the parents of the locality of the need for letting children involve in what is euphemistically described non-academic programmes,
4. Developing leadership qualities in children,
5. Confidence building,
6. Character formation,
7. Value creation,
8. Making learning more enjoyable,
9. Creating awareness of indigenous cultural traditions, and
10. Involving children and teachers in developing a love, respect and pride on the folk arts of the country and encouraging them in its preservation.

The experiment began with story sessions through which both Prof. Sankara Pillai and Kochunarayanapillai were able to attract the attention and sustain the interest of a group of over sixty children initially. Story-telling gradually led to creative dramatics during which the feature of this experiment was the time the children spend in child games and songs. They were encouraged to develop dramatic moments and situations from their games and songs. The atmosphere was participatory and never competitive in sharp contrast to the situations that existed at the schools. On holidays the small house and shed which had by now assumed the name of "Rangaprabhat" would be swarming with children of the age group between five and sixteen involving themselves in activities of their choice under the guidance of elders. The emphasis was to encourage relaxed and participatory learning and acquisition of skills and confidence building.

What guided all those who themselves were involved in the experiment was the emphasis which Prof. G. Sankara Pillai always made, to understand children and to catch them young and lead them to an atmosphere of not under compulsion but learning through a variety of activities which are not available in the schools they are studying. There were those who could offer help in the regular academic learning so that the children did not lag behind in academic preparations also. In short, very soon the house of Sri. Kochunarayanapillai became a centre of new and bold experiments in non-formal education essentially at primary school level.

A monitoring group attached to this work indicated in the first two years of its work four important aspects related to learning which encouraged the organizers to go ahead with the experiments with confidence. They were:

1. There were no drop-outs in the school among those who were coming to Rangaprabhat and the group admirably acted like a good bridge between the school and the children.

2. The activities offered by Rangaprabhat helped the children in sustaining interest in their academic programme.
3. The children scored more marks in their annual examinations.
4. The children exhibited more confidence in their ability to express and
5. They displayed better hygienic and personal habits.

Prof. Sankara Pillai, the brain behind the experiment, was encouraged to streamline the activities of Rangaprabhat by introducing puppetry and children's drama in the experiment. He, thus, launched the revolutionary concept of Children's drama in Malayalam for education for which he himself wrote new plays and in the next 22 years he wrote several play-all for the children of Rangaprabhat to act. His aim was not to create new actors or actresses but to help children involve in activities that would enable them to imbibe values and attitudes the formal education set-up does not offer them at present. The emphasis was to help children learn through creativity and based on what Prof. Pillai would always quote, the child likes to learn but hates to be taught.

The third important stage in the development of Rangaprabhat came when with the efforts made to involve the local population in the activities of the Centre so that the centre would truly become a community centre of non-formal education for children, gradually began influencing parents in the rural area to understand their children . . .

In collaboration with the Indira Gandhi National Centre for Arts it launched a Summer, mobile awareness creation campaign through children's Plays all over Kerala during a period of 45 days in the summer of 1995. The forty-five day programme covering a distance of over 2000 kilometers in fourteen districts in Kerala was a three-tier programme of play-seminars, visit to historically important places and to expose rural children to an exciting phase of group-living . . .

The Rangaprabhat has now become a community centre of extremely important educational experiments involving not only students and teachers but also parents. It has earned the distinction of acting like a bridge between the school and the community. This does not mean that the entire surrounding village community always appreciates what is going on in this centre. It has to weather always the strident and orchestrated criticism of a community which is caught up on the web of materialistic temptation of entertaining visions of all their children becoming doctors or engineers or professor, do not want their children to waste their time in drama activities which according to the conventional opinion is not good. The apathy of ordinary citizens toward creative involvement of their children is very strong and they feel that these are diversions and certainly would affect the children in their efforts to secure more marks. And it is this which the Rangaprabhat has been fighting . . .

The centre is in its Silver Jubilee Year now and this year witnessed another landmark in its resolve to involve over forty schools in the rural areas in the Trivandrum District in creating community consciousness and stressing the importance of moral, spiritual and cultural dimensions of education . . .

The Rangaprabhat experiment attracted attention both from the State and other agencies involved in the curriculum development and experiments in education.

What sustained the experiments which would not claim to be extraordinarily significant, was the conviction of both Prof. Pillai and Sri. Kochunarayanapillai and their associates that the experiment is bound to influence the community, though recognition came only very slowly and that too gruntingly. The reluctance of a phony society to any change could be seen here also. Opposition to any creative and innovative effort would be felt strongly and anybody except Prof. Pillai and Kochunarayanapillai would have left this and taken to other more profitable areas but for their commitment to the cause.

The emphasis of the organizers over the years has been to develop an alternative programme of nonviolent value orientation to the children first and then indirectly to the parents as against the feverish attempts that are being made to inculcate values in the children by an elderly society which does not practice any of them. The Rangaprabhat experiment does not aim at teaching children any thing, rather it seeks to offer children a variety of situations for them to choose and internalize, absorb and get themselves immersed in their own world—a world of play, games, songs, dance, painting, puppetry, fantasy, creativity, etc . . .

Bibliography

Advisory Panel on 'Effectuation of Fundamental Duties of Citizens' (July 6, 2001). *A Consultation Paper on 'Effectuation of Fundamental Duties of Citizens.* New Delhi: National Commission to Review the Working of the Constitution.

Aggarwal, J. C. and Bhatt, B.D. (1969). *Educational Documents in India (1831–1968).* New Delhi: Arya Book Depot.

Aggarwal, J. C. (2001). *Modern Indian Education—History, Development and Problems.* New Delhi: Shipra.

Aggarwal, S. K. (1999). *Gandhian Vision: India, Fifty Years of Independence, 1947–97, Status, Growth and Development.* New Delhi: B.R. Publishing Corporation.

Aggarwal, S. N. (1951). 'Village Panchayats in the Indian Constitution'. *Modern Review* [n. i.], 89.

Ahmed, A. S. (1992). 'Bombay films: the cinema as metaphor for Indian society and politics'. *Modern Asian Studies,* 26 (2), 289–320.

Alam, J. (2004). *Who Wants Democracy?* New Delhi: Orient Longman.

Ali, S. (1997). 'Political and Economic Decentralisation in India,' in Antony Copley and George Paxton (eds) *Gandhi and the Contemporary World—Essays to mark the 125th anniversary of his birth*, Chennai: Indo-British Historical Society, 263–269.

Ali, S. W. (1919). 'Nationalism'. *Modern Review,* XXVI, 36–42.

Almond, G. A. (1989). 'The Intellectual History of the Civic Culture Concept,' in Sidney Verba and Gabriel A. Almond (eds) *The Civic Culture Revisited*, London: Sage Publications, 1–36.

Almond, G. A. and Verba, S. (1965). *The Civic Culture—Political Attitudes and Democracy in Five Nations.* Boston: Little, Brown and Company.

Almond, G. A. and Verba, S. (eds) (1989). *The Civic Culture Revisited.* London: Sage Publications.

Alston, L. (1910). *Education and Citizenship in India.* London: Longmans.

Anderson, B. (1991). *Imagined Communities—Reflections on the Origin and Spread of Nationalism.* London: Verso.

Anderson, B. D. (1987). *A Comparative Structural Analysis of the Contexts of Images of the Third World in American and English News Publications: The Significance of Alternative Institutional Formats in Relation to the Evaluation of Bias.* Unpublished Ph.D. Thesis, Institute of Education, University of London, London.

Annette, J. (2000). Citizenship Studies, Community Service Learning and Higher Education, in R. Gardner, D. Lawton and D. Cairns (eds), *Education for Values: Morals, Ethics and Citizenship in Contemporary Teaching*, London: Kogan Page Limited.

Arnold, D. (2001). *Gandhi: Profiles in Power.* London: Pearson Education Limited.

Atkinson, D. W. (1989). *Gandhi and Tagore: Visionaries of Modern India.* Hong Kong: Asian Research Service.

Avinashilingam, T. S. (1960). *Gandhiji's Experiments in Education.* New Delhi: Ministry of Education.

Azmi, K. (2002). 'Why Modi Must Go.' *Hindustan Times*, 15 April 2002, 5.

Baig, T. A. (1990). 'Essence of Citizenship: Social and Moral Values', in Shyam Ratna Urs Schöttli, and Jürgen Axer (eds), *Citizenship Values in India—Individualism and Social Imperatives*, Calcutta: Mandira, 3–11.

Bakshi, S. R. (1988). *Gandhi and Concept of Swaraj.* New Delhi: Criterion Publications.

Ballou, R. B. (May, 1952). 'American Education and the New Japan'. *Journal of Higher Education* 23, 229–236.

Bartolf, C. (2000) (ed.). *The Breath of My Life: the Correspondence of Mahatma Gandhi (India) and Bart de Ligt (Holland) on War and Peace.* Selbstverlag, Berlin: Gandhi-Information-Zentrum.

Bassey, M. (1999). *Case Study Research in Educational Settings.* Buckingham: Open University Press.

Basu, A. (1945). *Education in Modern India—A Brief Review.* Calcutta: Orient Book Company.

—— (1982). *Essays in the History of Indian Education.* New Delhi: Concept Publishing Company.

Bauman, Z. (1989). *Modernity and the Holocaust.* Cambridge: Polity.

—— (1992). *Intimations of Postmodernity.* London: Routledge.

Bauman, Z. (1995). *Life in Fragments: Essays in Postmodern Morality.* Oxford: Blackwell.

Baxi, U. and Parekh B. (eds) (1995). *Crises and Change in Contemporary India.* New Delhi: Sage Publications.

Beauchamp, E. R. and J. M. Vardaman, (eds) (1994). *Japanese Education since 1945–A Documentary Study.* London: M.E. Sharpe.

Beer, L. W. and J.M. Maki, (2002). *From Imperial Myth to Democracy: Japan's Two Constitutions, 1889–2002.* Colorado: University Press of Colorado.

Benhabib, S. (1992). *Situating the Self.* Cambridge: Polity.

Bernstein, B. (1970). 'Education Cannot Compensate for Society'. *New Society*, 387, 344–347.

Berube, M. R. (2000). *Eminent Educators—Studies in Intellectual Influence.* London: Greenwood Press.

Bethel, D. M. (1973). *Makiguchi the Value Creator—Revolutionary Japanese Educator and Founder of Soka Gakkai*. Tokyo: Weatherhill.

—— (ed.) (1989). *Education for Creative Living—Ideas and Proposals of Tsunesaburo Makiguchi*. Ames: Iowa State University Press.

—— (1994). *Makiguchi—the Value Creator—Revolutionary Japanese Educator and Founder of Soka Gakkai*. New York: Weatherhill Inc.

—— (1994). 'Renewing Educational Structures: Imperative for the 1990s', in D.M. Bethel (ed.) *Compulsory Schooling and Human Learning: The Moral Failure of Public Education in American and Japan*, California: Caddo Gap Press.

—— (2000). 'The Legacy of Tsunesaburo Makiguchi: Value Creating Education and Global Citizenship', in D.M. Bethel and B. Wilson (eds), *Global Citizens—The Soka Gakkai Buddhist Movement in the World*, Oxford: Oxford University Press, 42–66.

—— (2002). (ed.). *The Geography of Human Life*. San Francisco: Caddo Gap Press.

Bordia, A. (2001). 'Consensus Be Damned.' *Hindustan Times*, 24 September 2001, 4.

Bose, N. K. (1948). *Selections from Gandhi*. Ahmedabad: Navajivan Publishing House.

Brannen, N. S. (June 1964). 'Soka Gakkai's Theory of Value.' *Contemporary Religions Japan* 5, 143–154.

Brien, J. (1985). 'Eastern Spirituality and the Religious Educator', in J.M. Lee (ed.) *The Spirituality of the Religious Educator*, Birmingham: Religious Education Press.

Brooks, C. (1970). *Modern Rhetoric*. New York: Brace & World.

Brown, D. (2004). *Bullying: from Reaction to Prevention*. Surrey: Young Voice.

Brown, J.M. (1989). *Gandhi—Prisoner of Hope*. New Haven: Yale University Press.

Bullock, A. (1998). *Hitler and Stalin—Parallel Lives*. London: Fontana Press.

Bunting, M. (2004). 'Today's Youth: Anxious, Depressed and Anti-Social'. *The Guardian*, 13 September 2004, 2.

Bush, C. (1988). *Mohandas Gandhi*. London: Burke.

Cairns, J. (2000). 'Morals, Ethics and Citizenship in Contemporary Teaching', in R. Gardner, D. Lawton and J. Cairns (eds), *Education for Values: Morals, Ethics and Citizenship in Contemporary Teaching*, London: Kogan Page Limited.

Capra, F. (1983). *The Turning Point*. London: Flamingo.

Carr, E. H. (1978). *What is History*. London: Pelican.

Chakrabarti, M. (1992). *Gandhian Humanism*. New Delhi: Concept Publishing Company.

Chakravarty, S. (1987). *Development Planning: The Indian Experience*. Oxford: Clarendon Press.

Chakravartty, G. (1987). *Gandhi—A Challenge to Communalism (A Study of Gandhi and the Hindu-Muslim Problem 1919–1929)*. New Delhi: Eastern Book Centre.

Chandra, B. (2001). 'Historical Blunders'. *Hindustan Times*, 2 December 2001, 7.

—— (2002). 'Truth is God'. *Hindustan Times*, 15 April 2002, 4.

Chandra, B., A. Mukherjee, and M. Mukherjee, (1999). *India after Independence*. New Delhi: Viking.

Chandra, S. (2001). 'Guru Tegh Bahadur's Martyrdom.' *The Hindu*, 16 October 2001, 11.

Chandra, S. (2001). *Medieval India—Class XI*. New Delhi: National Council of Educational Research and Training (NCERT).

Charles, C. G. (1813). *Observations on the State of Society Among the Asiatic Subjects of Great Britain*. London: Select Committee of the House of Commons on the Affairs of the East India Company.

Chatterjee, D.K. (1984). *Gandhi and Constitution Making in India*. New Delhi: Associated Publishing House.

Chatterjee, D. K. (1990). 'Gandhi and the Directive Principles of State Policy', in V.T. Patil (ed.) *Problems and Issues in Gandhism*, New Delhi: Inter-India Publication, 225–238.

Chattopadhyaya, S. (1961). *Traditional Values in Indian Life*. New Delhi: Oriental Publishers.

Cogan, J. J. (1998). 'Citizenship Education for the 21st Century: Setting the Context', in J. Cogan and R. Derricott (eds) *Citizenship Education for the 21st Century—An International Perspective on Education*, London: Kogan Press, 1–22.

Cohen, A. P. (1985). *The Symbolic Construction of Community*. London: Ellis Horwood and Tavistock Publications.

Covey, S. R. (1994). 'The Way to a Valueless Society', in M.K. Gandhi Institute for Non-violence (ed.) *World without Violence: Can Gandhi's Vision become Reality?* Memphis: Wiley Eastern Ltd., 39–44.

Cowen, R. (1990). 'The National and International Impact of Comparative Education Infrastructures', in W.D. Halls (ed.) *Comparative Education—Contemporary Issues and Trends*, London: Jessica Kingsley Publishers, 321–352.

Crick, B. (2000a). *Citizenship for 16–19 Year Olds in Education and Training: Report of the Advisory Group to the Secretary of State for Education and Employment*. Coventry: Further Education Funding Council.

—— (2000b). *Essays on Citizenship*. London: Continuum.

Cummings, W. K. (2003). 'Why Reform Japanese Education?' in R.G.D. Phillips (ed.) *Can the Japanese Change their Education System?* 12 (1), 31–42, Oxford: Symposium Books.

Currell, M. and G. Ostergaard, (1971). *The Gentle Anarchists: A Study of the Leaders of the Sarvodaya Movement for Non-violent Revolution in India*. Oxford: Clarendon Press.

Curtis, S. J. (1967). *History of Education in Great Britain*. London: University Tutorial Press.

Dalton, D. (1993). *Mahatma Gandhi—Nonviolent Power in Action*. New York: Columbia University Press.

Das, R. (2002). *Gandhi in 21st Century*. New Delhi: Sarup & Sons.

Delhi Historians' Group, J. N. U. (2001). *Communalisation of Education—The History Textbooks Controversy*. New Delhi: Deluxe Printery.

—— (3rd March 2002). *Summary of Presentations Made at the Workshop*. New Delhi: SSS Committee Room, Jewaharlal Nehru University.

Derricott, R. and J. Cogan, (eds) (1998). *Citizenship Education for the 21st Century—An International Perspective on Education*. London: Kogan Page.

Dev, A. (2001). *Modern India—Class VIII*. New Delhi: National Council of Education and Research Training (NCERT).

Devdutt (1994). 'Gandhi's Non-violence and India Today', in M. Kumar (ed.) *Nonviolence: Contemporary Issues and Challenges*, New Delhi: Gandhi Peace Foundation, 201–214.

Dewey, J. (1908). 'Religion and our Schools'. *The Hibbert Journal* 6, 796–809.

—— (1909). *Moral Principles in Education*. Boston: Houghton Mifflin.

—— (1915). *The School and Society*. 2nd Edition. Chicago: University of Chicago.

—— (1920). *Letters from China and Japan*. New York: E.P. Dutton Company.

—— (1922). *Human Nature and Conduct: an Introduction to Social Psychology*. New York: Holt.

—— (1970). *Educational essays [by] John Dewey*. Portway: Cedric Chivers Ltd.

—— (1990). *The School and Society*. Chicago: The University of Chicago Press.

Dobbelaere, K. and B. Wilson, (1994). *A Time to Chant: The Soka Gakkai Buddhists in Britain*. Oxford: Clarendon Press.

Doyle, A. (2001). *Ethnocentrism, Nationalism and History Education*. Unpublished Master Dissertation, London: Institute of Education, University of London.

Dutta, S. C. (1988). 'Citizenship Education,' in D.N. Saxena (ed.) *Citizenship Development and Fundamental Duties*, New Delhi: Abhinav Publications, 137–145.

Easwaran, E. (1989). *The Compassionate Universe*. New Delhi: Penguin Books.

Education, Ministry of Education (1972). *The Image of the Ideal Japanese*. Tokyo: Printing Bureau of the Ministry of Finance.

—— (March 1989). *Chugakko Gakushu Shido Yoryo*. Tokyo: Ministry of Finance Printing Bureau.

Edwardes, M. (1986). *The Myth of the Mahatma—Gandhi, the British and the Raj*. London: Constable.

Eells, W. C. (1957). 'A Compact Report'. *Journal of Higher Education* 28(2), 113–114.

Embree, A. T. (1962). *Charles Grant and British Rule in India*. London: George Allen and Unwin.

Epp, R. (1969). 'Japan's Century of Change: Intellectual Aspects'. *Japan Christian Quarterly* XXXV, 2, 72–74.

Erben, M. (1999). 'The Biographic and the Educative: A Question of Values' in D. Scott (ed.) *Values and Educational Research*, London: Bedford Way Papers, Institute of Education, University of London, 77–92.

Evans, R. J. (1997). *In Defence of History*. London: Granta Books.

Falk, R. (1998). *Mahatma Gandhi and the Revival of Nonviolent Politics in the Late 20th Century*. Lund: The Transnational Foundation for Peace and Future Research (TFF).

Ferguson, R. (1998). *Representing Race—Ideology, Identity and the Media*. London: Arnold.

Ferro, M. (1984). *The Use and Abuse of History or How the Past is Taught*. London: Routledge and Kegan Paul.

Fischer, L. (ed.) (1962). *The Essential Gandhi—An Anthology*. London: George Allen & Unwin Limited.

—— (1968). 'Where is Gandhiji?' in K.S.S. Radhakrishna (ed.) *Mahatma Gandhi 100 years*, New Delhi: Gandhi Peace Foundation, 83–86.

—— (1983). *The Essential Gandhi—His Life, Word and Ideas. An Anthology.* New York: Vintage Books.

—— (1990). *The Life of Mahatma Gandhi.* Bombay: Bharatiya Vidya Bhavan.

—— (1998). *The Life of Mahatma Gandhi.* Bombay: Bharatiya Vidya Bhavan.

Fisher, R. (2000). 'Philosophy for Children: How Philosophical Enquiry Can Foster Values in Education in Schools', in R. Gardner, D. Lawton and J. Cairns (eds) *Education for Values: Morals, Ethics and Citizenship in Contemporary* Teaching, London: Kogan Page Limited.

Fisker-Nielsen, A. (2005, January 27). *Religious Idealism and Political Reality: Young Soka Gakkai members and the Komei Party.* Paper presented at the Centre for the Study of Japanese Religion of School of Oriental and African Studies, University of London.

—— (2005, July 9). *Religious Idealism and Political Reality: The Issue of the Iraq War and Soka Gakkai Member's Support for Komeito.* Lecture delivered at the Institute of Oriental Philosophy (IOP) European Centre, London.

Foundation, T. J. (2003a). 'Chugakko no Kyoshitu Kara', in Japan Foundation (ed.) *Face of Japan*, Tokyo: The Japan Foundation.

—— (2003b). 'Juken Sangyo,' in Japan Foundation (ed.) *Faces of Japan*, Tokyo: The Japan Foundation.

Fowler, R. (1986). *Linguistic Criticism.* Oxford: Oxford University Press.

—— (1996). *Linguistic Criticism.* 2nd Edition. Oxford: Oxford University Press.

Frankel, F. R. (2000). *Transforming India—Social and Political Dynamics of Democracy.* New Delhi: Oxford University Press.

Fukuzawa, R. and G.K. LeTendre (2001). *Intense Years: How Japanese Adolescents Balance School, Family, and Friends.* New York: RoutledgeFalmer.

Furukawa, A. (2001). *Kofuku ni Ikiru Tame ni—Makiguchi Tsunesaburo no Mezashita Mono.* Tokyo: Daisanbunmeisha.

Gakuen Tosho (2005). *Shogakko Shoha.* Tokyo: Gakuen Tosho.

Gandhi, G. and E.S. Reddy, (ed.) (1993). *Gandhi and South Africa 1914–1948.* Ahmedabad: Navajivan Publishing House.

Gandhi, I. (1968). 'Legacies of Gandhi', in K.S.S. Radhakrishnan (ed.) *Mahatma Gandhi 100 years*, New Delhi: Gandhi Peace Foundation, 87–92.

Gandhi, M. K. (1934). *Speeches and Writings of Mahatma Gandhi.* 2nd Edition. New Delhi: Natesan.

—— (1938a). *Educational Reconstruction.* Ahmedabad: Navajivan Publishing House.

—— (1938b). *Hind Swaraj or Indian Home Rule.* Ahmedabad: Navajivan Publishing House.

—— (1940). *An Autobiography or The Story of My Experiments with Truth.* Ahmedabad: Navajivan Publishing House.

—— (1949). *Gandhi: an Autobiography: the Story of My Experiments with Truth.* London: Phoenix Press.

—— (1951). *Basic Education.* Ahmedabad: Navajivan Publishing House.

―― (1957). *An Autobiography or The Story of My Experiments with Truth.* Boston: Beacon Press.

―― (1958). *Hind Swaraj or Indian Home Rule.* Ahmedabad: Navajivan Publishing House.

―― (1958–1994). *The Collected Works of Mahatma Gandhi.* New Delhi: Ministry of Information and Broadcasting, Government of India.

―― (1959). *All Men are Brothers—Life and Thoughts of Mahatma Gandhi as Told in His Own Words.* Paris: Orient Longmans Private Ltd.

―― (1961a). 'Ethical Religion II, Chapter II: Ideal Morality', in K. Swaminathan (ed.) *The Collected Works of Mahatma Gandhi,* Vol. VI (1906–1907), pp. 280–281, New Delhi: The Publications Division, Ministry of Information and Broadcating, Government of India.

―― (1961b). 'Ethical Religion—IV, Chapter IV: Is there a Higher Law', in K. Swaminathan (ed.) *The Collected Works of Mahatma Gandhi,* Vol. VI (1906–1907), pp. 298–300, New Delhi: The Publication Division, Ministry of Information and Broadcasting, Government of India.

―― (1961c). 'Ethical Religion-III, Chapter III: What is Moral Action', in K. Swaminathan (ed.) *The Collected Works of Mahatma Gandhi,* Vol. VI (1906–1907), pp. 284–287, New Delhi: The Publications Division, Ministry of Information and Broadcating, Government of India.

―― (1961d). 'Ethical Religion-V, Chapter V: Morality As A Religion', in K. Swaminathan (ed.) *The Collected Works of Mahatma Gandhi,* Vol. VI (1906–1907), pp. 312–313, New Delhi: The Publications Division, Ministry of Information and Broadcating, Government of India.

―― (1961e). 'Ethical Religion-VI, Chapter VI: Religious Morality or Moral Religion', K. Swaminathan (ed.) *The Collected Works of Mahatma Gandhi,* Vol. VI (1906–1907), pp. 316–318, New Delhi: The Publications Division, Ministry of Information and Broadcating, Government of India.

―― (1964a). 'Speech at Missionary Conference, Madras, on February 14, 1916', in K. Swaminathan (ed.) *The Collected Works of Mahatma Gandhi,* Vol. XIII (January 1915–October 1917), pp. 217–225, New Delhi: The Publications Division, Ministry of Information and Broadcating, Government of India.

―― (1964b). 'Speech on 'Ashram Vows' at YMCA, Madras, Feb 16, 1916', in K. Swaminathan (ed.) *The Collected Works of Mahatma Gandhi,* Vol. XIII (January 1915–October 1917), pp. 225–235, New Delhi: The Publications Division, Ministry of Information and Broadcating, Government of India.

―― (1969). *The Collected Works of Mahatma Gandhi,* Vol. XXXIII (25 September 1925–10 February 1926), New Delhi: The Publications Division, Ministry of Information and Broadcating, Government of India.

―― (1975). *The Collected Works of Mahatma Gandhi,* Vol. LXI (27 April 1933–7 October 1933), New Delhi: The Publications Division, Ministry of Information and Broadcating, Government of India.

―― (1986). *The Collected Works of Mahatma Gandhi,* Vol. LXXXXVI (7 July 1947–26 September 1947), New Delhi: The Publications Division, Ministry of Information and Broadcating, Government of India.

—— (1982). *An Autobiography or The Story of My Experiments with Truth*. London: Penguin Books.

—— (1991). 'Letter to P.G. Mathew, Yeravda Mandir, September 8, 1930.', in R. Iyer (ed.) *The Essential Writings of Mahatma Gandhi*, New Delhi: Oxford University Press.

—— (1994). 'M.K. Gandhi on Non-violence', in M.K. Gandhi Institute of Non-violence (ed.) *World Without Violence—Can Gandhi's Vision Become Reality?* New Delhi: Wiley Eastern Ltd., 18–21.

—— (1997). *Hind Swaraj and Other Writings*. Cambridge: Cambridge University Press.

Gardner, H. (1993). *Creating Minds—An Anatomy of Creativity Seen Through the Lives of Freud, Einstein, Picasso, Stravinsky, Eliot, Graham, and Gandhi*. New York: Basic Books.

—— (1997). *Leading Minds: An Anatomy of Leadership*. London: HarperCollins.

Gardner, R. (eds) (2000). *Education for Values: Morals, Ethics and Citizenship in Contemporary Teaching*. London: Kogan Page Limited.

Gaur, V. P. (1977). *Mahatma Gandhi: A Study of his Message of Non-violence*. New Delhi: Sterling Publishers Private Limited.

Giddens, A. (1990). *The Consequences of Modernity*. Cambridge: Polity Press.

Gill, S. S. (2001). *Gandhi—A Sublime Failure*. New Delhi: Rupa and Co.

Gillham, B. (2000). *Case Study Research Methods*. London: Continuum.

Gopal, S. (ed.) (1972–1979). *Selected Works of Jawaharlal Nehru*, Vol. 3. New Delhi: Jawaharlal Nehru Memorial Fund.

Gould, H. A. (1988). *The Hindu Caste System*. New Delhi: Chanakya Publications.

Gould, J. W. (1989). 'Gandhi's Relevance Today', in J. Hick and L.C. Hempel (eds) *Gandhi's Significance for Today*, London: Macmillan Press Ltd., 7–17.

Green, A. (1997). *Education, Globalization and the Nation State*. London: Macmillan Press Ltd.

Green, M. (1983). *Tolstoy and Gandhi, Men of Peace—A Biography*. New York: Basic Books Inc.

Guha, B. (1998). *Conflict and Violence in Indian Society*. New Delhi: Kanishka Publishers.

Gundara, J. (26–29 August 2000). 'Diverse Communities, Inclusiveness and Education for Intercultural Understanding', in *Commemorative International Symposium for the Opening of the Asia-Pacific Centre of Education for International Understanding*, Seoul: Ministry of Education, Republic of Korea, Korean National Commission for UNESCO, Seoul (Plaza Hotel) and Ichon (ACEIU), Republic of Korea, 61–85.

—— (2000a). *Interculturalism, Education and Inclusion*. London: Sage Publications.

—— (2000b). 'Religion, Human Rights and Intercultural Education'. *Intercultural Education*, 11, 127–136.

—— (2000c). 'Social Diversity, Inclusiveness and Citizenship Education', in Dennis Lawton (ed.) *Education for Citizenship*, London: Continuum, 14–25.

—— (2002). 'Issues of Identity: Intercultural Education, Citizenship and Social Cohesion' in *Runnymede Conference: Cohesion, Community and Citizenship*, London: The Runnymede Trust, London School of Economics, 9–23.

—— (2003). *Intercultural Education: World on the Brink?* London: Institute of Education, University of London.

—— (2004 October 2). *Mahatma Gandhi: Political Creativity and Intercultural Understandings*. Gandhi Memorial Lecture delivered at Mahatma Gandhi Institute, Moka, Mauritius.

—— (ed.) (1997). *Young People's Understanding of Human Rights: A Four Country Study*. London: International Centre for Intercultural Studies, Institute of Education, University of London on behalf of the Department for International Development (Britain), the Commonwealth Secretariat, and the Department of Education, Northern Ireland in conjuction with Minstries and agencies in Botswana, India, Northern Ireland and Zimbabwe.

Gupta, D. (2000). *Culture, Space and the Nation State—from Sentiment to Structure*. New Delhi: Sage Publications. Schöttli, and J. Axer, (eds) (1990). *Citizenship Values in India—Individualism and Social Imperatives*. Calcutta: Mandira.

Hall, R. K. (1949). *Education for a New Japan*. New Haven: Yale University Press.

Halstead, J.M. and M.J. Taylor, (eds) (1996). *Values in Education and Education in Values*. London: Falmer Press.

Hamel, J., S. Dufour and D. Fortin, (1993). *Case Study Methods*. London: Sage Publications.

Hardiman, D. (2003). *Gandhi—In His Time and Ours*. New Delhi: Permanent Black.

Harima, H. (1997). *Yokuwakaru Soka Kyoiku*. Tokyo: Daisanbunmeisha.

—— (2002) 'Soka Kyoikugaku Taikei' to 'Soka Kyoiku'. *Soka Kenkyu*, 11, 63–70.

Harriss, J. and S. Corbridge, (2001). *Reinventing India—Liberalization, Hindu Nationalism and Popular Democracy*. New Delhi: Oxford University Press.

Hartford, E. F. (1959). 'Problems of Education in Occupied Japan as seen by 69 Japanese Educators'. *Journal of Educational Sociology* 23(8), 471–481.

Hasan, M. (2001). *Legacy of a Divided Nation—India's Muslims Since Independence*. New Delhi: Oxford University Press.

Haydon, G. (1997). *Teaching About Values: A New Approach*. London: Cassell.

—— (2000). 'What Scope is There for Teaching Moral Reasoning', in R. Gardner, D. Lawton, and J. Cairns (eds) *Education for Values: Morals, Ethics and Citizenship in Contemporary Teaching*, London: Kogan Page Limited.

Held, D. (1987). *Models of Democracy*. Cambridge: Polity Press.

—— (ed.) (1993). *Prospects for Democracy—North, South, East, West*. Cambridge: Polity Press.

—— (1995). *Democracy and the Global Order: from the Modern State to Cosmopolitan Governance*. Cambridge: Polity Press.

Hicks, D. and C. Holden, (1995). *Visions of the Future—Why We Need to Teach for Tomorrow*. Stoke-on-Trent: Trentham Books.

Hingorani, A. T. (ed.) (1945). *To the Students*. Vol. 1. Allahabad: Law Journal Press.

Hobsbawm, E. (1998). *On History*. London: Abacus.

Hollinger, D. A. (2002). 'Conference Summation', in *Runnymede Conference: Cohesion, Community and Citizenship*, held at London School of Economics. London: The Runnymede Trust, London School of Economics.

Holmes, W. H. G. (1952). *The Twofold Gandhi*. London: Mowbray & Co. Ltd.

Hooja, G. (1990). 'Society and Human Resources Development', in Shyam RatnaUrs Schöttli, and Jürgen Axer (eds) *Citizenship Values in India—Individualism and Social Imperatives*, Calcutta: Mandira, 12–21.

Hori, N. (1952) (ed.). *Nichiren Daishonin Gosho Zenshu [The Complete Works of Nichiren Daishonin]*. Tokyo: Soka Gakkai.

Horio, T. (1988). *Educational Thought and Ideology in Modern Japan: State Authority and Intellectual Freedom*. Tokyo: University of Tokyo Press.

Howes, J. F. (1995). *Nitobe Inazô: Japan's Bridge Across the Pacific*. Tokyo: Westview Press.

Huckle, J. (1996). 'Globalisation, Postmodernity and Citizenship', in M. Steiner (ed.) *Developing the Global Teacher—Theory and Practice in Initial Teacher Education, Staffordshire: Trentham Books*, London: Trentham Books in Association with World Studies Trust, 29–36.

Hunter, J. (1989). *The Emergence of Modern Japan: An Introductory History since 1853*. London: Longman.

Huntington, S. P. (1998). *The Clash of Civilizations and the Remaking of a World Order*. London: Touchstone Books.

ICCR, Indian Council for Cultural Relations (1969). *Intellectual Values in Modern India*. New Delhi: Everest Press.

ICVC, Ikeda Centre for Value Creation (2002). *Values in a Changing World—a Reappraisal*. Trivandrum: Ikeda Centre for Value Creation.

—— (2003). *Experiment with Children in Nonviolent Value Creation*. Trivandrum: Ikeda Centre for Value Creation.

Ikeda, D. (1972–1976). *The Human Revolution*. New York: Weatherhill.

—— (1976a). *Buddhism: the Living Philosophy*. 2nd Edition. Tokyo: East Publications.

—— (1976b). *Speeches on Soka Gakkai*. Tokyo: International Bureau, Board of Information, Soka Gakkai.

—— (1981a). *A Lasting Peace—Collected Addresses of Daisaku Ikeda*, Vol. 1. Tokyo: John Weatherhill Inc.

—— (1981b). 'Creative Society', in *A Lasting Peace—Collected Addresses of Daisaku Ikeda*, Vol. 1, pp. 29–38. Tokyo: John Weatherhill Inc.

—— (1981c). 'Soka Gakkai, Its Ideals and Tradition', in *A Lasting Peace—Collected Addresses of Daisaku Ikeda*, Vol. 1, pp. 235–249. Tokyo: John Weatherhill Inc.

—— (1982). *Life—An Enigma, a Precious Jewel*. Tokyo: Kodansha International.

—— (1987a). *A Lasting Peace—Collected Addresses of Daisaku Ikeda*. Tokyo: Weatherhill.

—— (1987b). 'Thoughts on Aims in Education—A Proposal Commemorating the All Japan Educators Meeting of Soka Gakkai', in *A Lasting Peace—Collected Addresses of Daisaku Ikeda*, Vol. 2, pp. 206–219, Tokyo: Weatherhill.

—— (1990). 'The Environmental Problem and Buddhism'. *The Journal of Oriental Studies* 3, 6–7.

—— (1995). 'Modern Civilization and Gandhism' in B. R. Nanda (ed.) *Mahatma Gandhi 125 years-Remembering Gandhi, Understanding Gandhi, Relevance of Gandhi*, New Delhi: Indian Council for Cultural Relations and New Age International Publishers Limited.

—— (1996a). 'Education Toward Global Citizenship', in *Soka Education—A Buddhist Vision for Teachers, Students and Parents*, California: Soka Gakkai, 97–109.

—— (1996b). *A New Humanism—The University Addresses of Daisaku Ikeda*. New York: Weatherhill.

—— (1996c). 'Gandhism and the Modern World', in *A New Humanism—The University Addresses of Daisaku Ikeda*, New York: Weatherhill, 128–139.

—— (2001a). *Creating and Sustaining a Century of Life: Challenges for a New Era.* Tokyo: Soka Gakkai International.

—— (2001b). 'Education Toward Global Citizenship, Lecture Delivered at Teachers College, Columbia University on June 13, 1996' in *Soka Education—A Buddhist Vision for Teachers, Students and Parents*, pp. 97–109. California: Middleway Press.

—— (2001c). *Soka Education—A Buddhist Vision for Teachers, Students and Parents*. California: Middleway Press.

—— (2001, January 9). *Reviving Education: The Brilliance of the Inner Spirit, Further Thoughts on Education in the Twenty-first Century.* Tokyo: Soka Gakkai International.

—— (2002). *The Humanism of the Middle Way—Dawn of a Global Civilization.* Tokyo: Soka Gakkai International.

—— (2003). *A Global Ethic of Coexistence: Toward a 'Life-Sized' Paradigm for Our Age.* Tokyo: Soka Gakkai International.

—— (2004). *Write a Grand Epic of Total Victory.* Tokyo: Soka Gakkai.

—— (October 2001). 'SGI President Ikeda's Essay Series—Wonderful Encounters, Mrs. Veena Sikri—Former Director General of the Indian Council for Cultural Relations (ICCR)'. *Monthly Soka Gakkai Newsletter*, 31–44.

Ikeda, D. and A. Toynbee, (1976). *The Toynbee-Ikeda Dialogue: Man Himself Must Choose.* Tokyo: Kodansha International Ltd.

Ikeda, S. (1969). *Makiguchi Tsunesaburo.* Tokyo: Nihon Sonoshobo.

India, Tariff Board. (1932). *Report of the Indian Tariff Board Regarding the Grant of Protection to the Cotton Textile Industry.* Calcutta: India Tariff Board.

—— (1936). *Report of the Special Tariff Board on the Enquiry Regarding the Level of the Duties Necessary to Afford Adequate Protection to the Indian Cotton Textile Industry.* Bombay: India Tariff Board.

International Society for Educational Information. (1994). *Japan in Modern History—Junior High School.* Tokyo: International Society for Educational Information, Inc.

Isao, A. (1993). *Chugaku Shakai—Rekishiteki Bunya (Junior High School Studies—Field of History).* Osaka: Osaka Shoseki.

ISEI, International Society for Educational Information (1994). *Japan in Modern History—Junior High School.* Tokyo: International Society for Educational Information, Inc.

IUCN/UNEP/WWF (1991). *Caring for the Earth—A Strategy for Sustainable Living*. London: Earthscan Publications.

Iyer, R. (1973). *The Moral and Political Thought of Mahatma Gandhi*. New York: Oxford University Press.

—— (ed.) (1986). *The Moral and Political Writings of Mahatma Gandhi. Vol. 2. Truth and Non-Violence*. Oxford: Clarendon Press.

—— (ed.) (1987). *The Moral and Political Writings of Mahatma Gandhi. Vol. 3. Non-Violent Resistance and Social Transformation*. Oxford: Clarendon.

—— (ed.) (1991). *The Essential Writings of Mahatma Gandhi*. Oxford: Oxford University Press.

—— (ed.) (1994). 'Gandhi—the Political Moralist', in M.K. Gandhi Institute for Non-violence (ed.) *World without Violence: can Gandhi's Vision Become Reality?* Memphis: Wiley Eastern Ltd., 138–145.

Janis, I. L. (1965). 'The Problem of Validating Content Analysis', in H.D. Lasswell (ed.) *Language of Politics*, Cambridge: MIT Press 55–82.

Jenkins, K. (1999). *Why History—Ethics and Postmodernity*. London: Routledge.

Johnson, C. (1982). *MITI and the Japanese Miracle*. Stanford: Stanford University Press.

Johnston, J. (1884). *Abstract and Analysis of the Report of the Indian Education Commission of 1882–83*. London: Hamilton, Adams & Co.

Jois, M. R. (1988). 'Measures for Building up Good Citizenship' in D. N. Saxena (ed.) *Citizenship Development and Fundamental Duties*, New Delhi: Abhinav Publications, 15–27.

Jones, H. (1988). *The National Curriculum—Centralisation, Instrumentalism and Control*. Unpublished Masters Dissertation. Institute of Education, University of London.

Jordens, J. T. F. (1998). *Gandhi's Religion—A Homespun Shawl*. London: Macmillan Press Ltd.

Joshi, P. C. (1990). 'Radical Thought and Social Change: the Indian Dilemma', in Shyam RatnaUrs Schöttli, and Jürgen Axer (eds) *Citizenship Values in India—Individualism and Social Imperatives*, Calcutta: Mandira, 47–55. Mandira.

Kaestle, C. F. (1988). 'Research Methodology: Historical Methods', in J.P. Keeves (ed.) *Educational Research, Methodology and Measurement: An International Handbook,* Oxford: Pergamon Press, 37–42.

Kaigo, T. (1952). 'The American Influence on the Education in Japan'. *Journal of Educational Sociology* 26(1), 9–15.

Kaigo, T. (1969). *Nationalism to Kyoiku*. Tokyo: Kokudaisha.

Kale, V. G. (1915). 'The War and Its Lessons to India'. *Modern Review* XVI, 41–52.

Kamijo, M. (1985). *A Comparative Study on Internationalisation of Education in Japan: Ideal Japanese Society, Man and Knowledge*. Unpublished Ph.D. Thesis. Institute of Education, University of London, London.

Kansai, Soka School System. (2003a). *Kibo no Seiki wo Souzou Suru-Soka Kyoiku*.[Online] Kansai, Soka School System. Available at: http://www.kansai.soka.ed.jp/guide/j03.html. Last Accessed 24th February 2004.

—— (2003b). *The Ideals of Soka Education*. [Online] Kansai: Soka School System. Available at: http://www.soka.ed.jp/kyoiku/k0004.html. Last Accessed on 10th March 2004.

—— (2003c). *Soka Ikkan Kyoiku Mission Statement*.[Online] Kansai: Soka School System. Available at: http://www.soka.ed.jp/kyoiku/s030413.html. Last Accessed 4th February 2004.

—— (2004). *Jinrui no Heiwa to Kofuku wo Mezasu, Soka Kyoiku no Genryu*. [Online] Available at: http://www.tokyo.soka.ed.jp. Last Accessed: 16th March 2004.

Kaplan, A. and Goldsen, J. M. (1965), 'The Reliability of Content Analysis Categories', in H. D. Lasswell (ed.), *Language of Politics*, Cambridge: MIT Press, 83–112.

Karkaria, R. P. (1896). *India, Forty Years of Progress and Reform*. London: Henry Frowde.

Kase, T. (1950). *Journey to the Missouri*. New Haven: Yale University Press.

Kashyap, S. C. (1997). *Citizens and the Constitution—Citizenship Values under the Constitution*. New Delhi: Publications Division, Ministry of Information & Broadcasting, Government of India.

Katz A. (ed.) (2001). *Bullying in Britain—Testimonies from Teenagers*. Surrey: Young Voice.

Kawata T. (cd.) (1993). *Atarashii shakai—Rekishi (New Social Studies: History)*. Tokyo: Tokyo Shoseki.

Keenleyside, H. and A.F. Thomas, (1937). *History of Japanese Education and Present Educational System*. Tokyo: Hokuseido Press.

Khan, M. A. (1988). 'Behavioural and Attitudinal Norms of Citizenship', in D.N. Saxena (ed.) *Citizenship Development and Fundamental Duties*, New Delhi: Abhinav Publications, 76–81.

Khan, Y. (1997). *Japanese Moral Education Past and Present*. Cranbury: Associated University Press.

King, M. (1999). *Mahatma Gandhi and Martin Luther King, Jr.: the Power of Nonviolent Action*. Paris: UNESCO Publishing.

Kingston, J. (2001). *Japan in Transformation 1952–2000*. Essex: Pearson Education Limited.

Kobayashi, T. (1990). 'China, India, Japan and Korea', in W.D. Halls (ed.) *Comparative Education: Contemporary Issues and Trends*, London: Jessica Kingsley Publishers, 200–226.

Koichi, M. (2000). *Makiguchi Tsunesaburo Gokuchu no Tatakai*. Tokyo: Daisanbunmei-sha.

Kothari, D. S. (1966). *Report of the Education Commission (1964–66)—Education and National Development*. New Delhi: University Grants Commission.

Kothari, R. (1993). *Poverty*. London: Zed Books.

Kress, G. and Leeuwen T. V. (2001). *Multimodal Discourse: the Modes and Media of Contemporary Communication*. London: Arnold.

Krippendorff, K. (1980). *Content Analysis—An Introduction to its Methodology*. London: Sage Publications.

Kumagaya, K. (1994a). *Makiguchi Tsunesaburo*. Tokyo: Daisanbunmeisha.

—— (1994b). *Soka Kyoikugaku Nyumon*. Tokyo: Daisanbunmeisha.

—— (2000). *Tsunesaburo Makiguchi*. Tokyo: Daisanbunmeisha.

Kung, H. (1991). *Global Responsibility—In Search of a New World Ethic*. London: SCM Press.

Lahiry, A. (1976). *Gandhi in Indian Politics—A Critical Review*. Calcutta: Firma Klm Private Limited.

Lall, K. B. (1990). 'A Recension', in Shyam RatnaUrs Schöttli, and Jürgen Axer (eds), in *Citizenship Values in India—Individualism and Social Imperatives,* Calcutta: Mandira,137–150.

Landsheere, G. D. (1982). *Empirical Research in Education*. Paris: United Nations Educational, Scientific and Cultural Organization.

Lawton, D. (ed.) (1999). *Values and the Curriculum: the School Context*. London: Curriculum Studies Academic Group, Institute of Education, University of London.

Leewen, T.V. and Kress, G. (2001). *Multimodal Discourse: The Modes and Media of Contemporary Communication*. London: Arnold.

Lefevere, A. (ed.) (1992). *Translation/History/Culture—A Sourcebook*. London: Routledge.

Lindkvist, K. (1981). 'Approaches to Textual Analysis', in K.E. Rosengren (ed.) *Advances in Content Analysis*, Vol. 9, pp. 23–41, London: Sage Publications.

MacCannell, D. (1992). *Empty Meeting Grounds: The Tourist Papers*. London: Routledge.

Machacek, D. and D. Wilson, (2000). *Global Citizens—The Soka Gakkai Buddhist Movement in the World*. Oxford: Oxford University Press.

Mahadevan, T.K. and G. Ramachandran, (1967). *Gandhi—His Relevance for Our Times*. New Delhi: Gandhi Peace Foundation.

Maila, N. (1990). 'Gandhi's Philosophy of Education and its Relevance to Contemporary India', in V.T. Patil (ed.) *Problems and Issues in Gandhism*, New Delhi: Inter-India Publication, 214–222.

Makiguchi, T. (1964). *The Philosophy of Value*. Tokyo: Seikyo Press.

—— (1965). *Soka Kyoikugaku Taikei*. Tokyo: Tozai Tetsugaku Shoin.

—— (1972). *Soka Kyoikugaku Taikei*. Tokyo: Seikyo Shimbunsha.

—— (1980). *Jinsei Chirigaku*. Tokyo: Seikyo Shimbunsha.

—— (1981). *Makiguchi Tsunesaburo Zenshu* [The Complete Works of Tsunesaburo Makiguchi]. Volume 2. Tokyo: Daisanbunmei-sha.

—— (1982). *Makiguchi Tsunesaburo Zenshu* [The Complete Works of Tsunesaburo Makiguchi]. Volume 5. Tokyo: Daisanbunmei-sha.

—— (1984). *Makiguchi Tsunesaburo Zenshu* [The Complete Works of Tsunesaburo Makiguchi]. Volume 8. Tokyo: Daisanbunmei-sha.

—— (1987). *Makiguchi Tsunesaburo Zenshu* [The Complete Works of Tsunesaburo Makiguchi]. Volume 10. Tokyo: Daisanbunmei-sha.

—— (1995). *Soka Kyoikugaku Taikei*. Volume One. Tokyo: Seikyo Bunko.

—— (1997). *Jinsei Chirigaku*. Volume One. Tokyo: Seikyo Bunko.

—— (2002). *A Geography of Human Life (English edition)*. California: Caddo Gap Press.

Malhan, P. N. (1990). 'Cradles of Constructive Citizenship' in Shyam RatnaUrs Schöttli, and Jürgen Axer (eds), *Citizenship Values in India—Individualism and Social Imperatives*, Calcutta: Mandira, 33–36.

Mandela, N. (1995). *Long Walk to Freedom—The Autobiography of Nelson Mandela.* London: Abacus.

Marcuse, H. (1972). *One Dimensional Man.* London: Abacus.

Markovits, C. (2003). *The Un-Gandhian Gandhi—The Life and Afterlife of the Mahatma.* New Delhi: Permanent Black.

Marquand, D. (1988). *The Unprincipled Society, New Demands and Old Politics.* London: Fontana Press.

Marr, A. (2005). *Start the Week: Contemporary India with P.K. Varma.* [Online] Interview with P.K. Varma on BBC Radio 4, UK from 9–9:45 a.m. on the 28th of March 2005. Available at: http://www.bbc.co.uk/radio4/factual/starttheweek.shtml. Last accessed 29th March 2005.

Marshall, T. H. (1992). *Citizenship and Social Class.* London: Pluto.

Master, M. K. (1970). *Citizenship of India—Dual Nationality and the Constitution.* Calcutta: Eastern Law House.

Masuda, H. (1995). Kyoshoku-tuiho no Shogeki [The Impact of the Purge]. In Nakamura, Masanori, Amakawa Akira, Yun Koncha and Igawashi Takeshi (eds) *Senryo to Kaikaku [The Occupation Reforms].* 6 volumes. Volume 2, Sengo Nihon Senryo to Sengo Kaikaku [Post-war Japan: the Occupation and Post-war Reforms], Tokyo: Iwami Shoten.

McCorcle, M. (1984). 'Stories in Context: Characteristics of Useful Case Studies for Planning and Evaluation'. *Evaluation and Program Planning: An International Journal, 7.*

McCully, B. T. (1966). *English Education and the Origins of Indian Nationalism.* Glouscester: Mass. Peter Smith.

McLean, M. (1984). *International Handbook of Education Systems.* New York: John Wiley & Sons Ltd.

McPhail, P (1972). *Social and Moral Education.* Oxford: Basil Blackwell.

—— *On Other People's Shoes.* London: Longman.

Merriam, S. B. (1988). *Case Study Research in Education—A Qualitative Approach.* San Francisco: Jossey-Bass Publishers.

Metraux, D. A. (1994). *The Soka Gakkai Revolution.* London: University Press of America.

MEXT (2005). *Education Reform.* Tokyo: Ministry of Education, Culture, Sports, Science and Technology.

Miller, G. D. (2002). *Peace, Value, and Wisdom—The Educational Philosophy of Daisaku Ikeda.* New York: Value Inquiry Book Series.

Mills, S. (1997). *Discourse.* London: Routledge.

Ministry of Education. (1972). *The Image of the Ideal Japanese.* Tokyo: Printing Bureau of the Ministry of Finance.

Ministry of Education of Japan. (1972). *Gakusei Hyaku-niji-nen-shi [The School System over the Past One Hundred and Twenty Years].* Tokyo: Teikoku Chiho Gyosei Gakkai.

Mizuhata, T. (2002). *Kokoro no page*. Tokyo: Seikyo Shinbum.

Miura, S. (2001). *Tennou—Nihon no Naritachi*. Tokyo: Shogakukan.

Mombusho (1983). *Course of Study for Elementary Schools*. Tokyo: Mombusho.

Moon, P. (1968). *Gandhi and Modern India*. London: The English Universities Press Ltd.

Moses, G. (1997). *Revolution of Conscience—Martin Luther King Jr. and the Philosophy of Non-violence*. New York: The Guilford Press.

Mukerjee, R. (1923). *Democracies of the East: A Study in Comparative Politics*. London: P.S. King.

Muley, D. S. (1988). 'Fundamental Duties and Citizenship Education' in D.N. Saxena (ed.) *Citizenship Development and Fundamental Duties*, New Delhi: Abhinav Publications, 131–136.

Murao, K. (1998). *Makiguchi Tsunesaburo no 'Kachiron' o Yomu*. Tokyo: Ushio Publications.

Nakazato, N. and Hasan, M. (eds) (2001). *The Unfinished Agenda—Nation-Building in South Asia*. New Delhi: Manohar.

Nanda, B. R. (1958). *Mahatma Gandhi—A Biography*. New Delhi: Oxford University Press.

—— (1979). *Gandhi and Nehru*. New Delhi: Oxford University Press.

—— (1985). *Gandhi and his Critics*. New Delhi: Oxford University Press.

—— (1995). 'Gandhi and Religion' in B.R. Nanda (ed.) *Mahatma Gandhi 125 Years—Remembering Gandhi, Understanding Gandhi, Relevance of Gandhi*, New Delhi: Indian Council for Cultural Relations and New Age International Publishers Limited, 127–148.

Nanda, R. T. (1997). *Contemporary Approaches to Value Education in India*. New Delhi: Regency Publications.

Nandy, A. (1981). 'Outside the Imperium: Gandhi's Cultural Critique of the "West".' *Alternatives*, 7 (2), [n. p].

—— (2001). *Gandhi after Gandhi—The Fate of Dissident in Our Times*. Lund: The Transnational Foundation for Peace and Future Research (TFF).

NCERT (1988). *School Education After Independence*. New Delhi: National Council of Educational Research and Training.

—— (2003). *National Curriculum Framework for School Education*. New Delhi: National Council of Educational Research and Training.

—— (2005). *Documents on Values Education of National Resource Centre for Value Education*. [Online] New Delhi: NCERT, Available at: http://www.ncert.nic.in/sites/valueeducation/extension.htm. Last Accessed 27th April 2005.

NDTV, Correspondent (2004). *Chauri Chaura Lies in Margins of History*. [Online] New Delhi: NDTV. Available at: http://t2ndtv.m7z.net/ Last accessed 26th October 2004.

Neufeldt, R. (2003). 'The Hindu Mahasabha and Gandhi' in H. Coward (ed.) *Indian Critiques of Gandhi,* New York: State University of New York, 131–152.

Neuman, W. L. (2003). *Social Research Methods: Qualitative and Quantitative Approaches*. 5th Edition. Boston: Pearson Education, Inc.

Newsletter, Soka Gakkai (May 5, 2001). *Soka Gakkai and New Komeito Party Representatives Meet*. [Online] Available at: www.sokagakkai.info. Last accessed 16th March 2004.

—— (November 11, 2000). *Soka Gakkai and New Komeito Party Representatives Meet*. [Online] Available at: www.sokagakkai.info. Last accessed: 16th March 2000.

Nichiren (1999). *The Writings of Nichiren Daishonin*. Tokyo: Gosho translation Committee, Soka Gakkai.

Nikkyoso (1972). *How Education in Japan Ought to Be: The Idea and Problem of Reformation*. Tokyo: Nikkyoso.

—— (May 1966). *Dai Sanjuunikai Teiki Taikai Gian (Proposals of the Thirty-second National Convention)*. Tokyo: Nikkyoso.

Nobukatsu, F. (2001). *Atarashii Rekishi Kyokasho (The New History Textbook)*. Tokyo: Fusousha.

Okubo, T. (ed.) (1972). *Mori Arinori Zenshu*. Tokyo: Senbundo Shote.

Okuma, S. C. (1909). *Fifty Years of New Japan*. London: Saionji.

Okumoto, K. (2004). *Lifelong Learning Policy in England and Japan: a Comparative Analysis*. Unpublished Ph.D. Thesis. Institute of Education, University of London.

Oliver, D. (1994). *The Foundations of Citizenship*. Hemel Hempstead: Weatshef.

Oommen, T. K. (1988). 'Citizenship Education: The Context, Contents and Instruments', in D.N. Saxena (ed.) *Citizenship Development and Fundamental Duties*, New Delhi: Abhinav Publications, 95–105.

Ostergaard, G. (1989). 'The Gandhian Movement in India Since the Death of Gandhi' in J. Hick and L.C. Hempel (ed.) *Gandhi's Significance for Today*, London: Macmillan Press Ltd., London, 203–225.

Oyen, E. (ed.) (1990). *Comparative Methodology: Theory and Practice in International Social Research*. London: Sage Publications.

Padgoankar, D. (2001). 'Utter Complexity'. *Times of India*, 16 December 2001, 6..

Pantham, T. (1995). 'Gandhi, Nehru and Modernity', in Upendra Baxi and Bhikhu Parekh (eds) *Crises and Change in Contemporary India,* New Delhi: Sage Publications, 98–121.

Paranjpe, M. (1993). *Decolonisation and Development—Hind Swaraj Revisioned*. New Delhi: Sage Publications.

Parekh, B. (1986). 'Some Puzzles about Gandhi's Autobiography' in R. Roy (ed.) *Contemporary Crises and Gandhi*, New Delhi: Discovery Publishing House.

—— (1989a). *Colonialism, Tradition and Reform*. New Delhi: Sage Publications.

—— (1989b). *Gandhi's Political Philosophy—A Critical Examination*. London: Macmillan.

—— (1992). 'The Poverty of Indian Political Theory.' *History of Political Thought*, XIII (3), 535–560.

—— (1993). 'Cultural Particularity of Liberal Democracy' in D. Held (ed.) *Prospects for Democracy*, Cambridge: Polity Press, 156–176.

—— (1997). *Gandhi*. Oxford: Oxford University Press.

—— (2002). 'Common Belonging' in *Runnymede Conference: Cohesion, Community and Citizenship held at London School of Economics*. London, The Runnymede Trust, London School of Economics, 1–8.

—— (2004). 'Why Terror? Gandhi's Challenge to Bin Ladin'. *Prospect*, 20–26.

Parel, A. J. (1995). 'The Doctrine of Swaraj in Gandhi's Philosophy' in Upendra Baxi and Bhikhu Parekh (eds) *Crises and Change in Contemporary India*, New Delhi: Sage Publications, 57–81.

Passin, H. (1965). *Society and Education in Japan.* New York: Bureau of Publications, Teachers College, Columbia University: East Asian Institute, Columbia University.

Phillips, R. G. D. (ed.) (2003). *Can the Japanese Change their Education System?* Vol. 12 (1). Oxford: Symposium books.

Pingel, F. (1999). *UNESCO Guidebook on Textbook Research and Textbook Revision.* Hannover: Verlag Hahnsche Buchhandlung.

Pinto, V. (1998). *Gandhi's Vision and Values—the Moral Quest for Change in Indian Agriculture.* New Delhi: Sage Publications.

Porter, A. (1993). *Impoverished Concepts of Citizenship in the Debate on the National Curriculum.* London: Centre for Multicultural Education, Institute of Education, University of London.

Potter, D. (1993). 'Democratization in Asia', in D. Held (ed.) *Prospects for Democracy,* Cambridge: Polity Press, 355–379.

Potter, J. (2002). *Active Citizenship in Schools—a Good Practice Guide to Developing a Whole School Policy.* London: CSV.

Pradhan, R. G. (1930). *India's Struggle for Swaraj.* Madras: Low Price Publications.

Prozesky, M. and J.M. Brown, (1996). *Gandhi and South Africa: Principles and Politics.* Pietermaritzburg: University of Natal Press.

Radhakrishnan, N. (26 March 1998). 'Gandhi and the Challenges of the 21st Century', in Gandhi Smriti and Darshan Samiti (ed.) *50th Martyrdom Anniversary— Gandhi and The Challenges of the 21st Century,* New Delhi: Gandhi Smriti and Darshan Samiti, Department of Gandhian Studies, Punjab University and Gandhi Smriti and Darshan Samiti, 1–16.

—— (ed.) (1992). *Gandhian Perspective of Nation Building For World Peace.* New Delhi: Konark Publishers Pvt. Ltd in association with Gandhi Smriti and Darshan Samiti.

Rai, B. C. (1993). *History of Indian Education.* Lucknow: Prakashan Kendra.

Raivola, R. (1986). 'What is Comparison? Methodological and Philosophical Considerations', in Philip G. Altbach and Gail P. Kelly (eds) *New Approaches to Comparative Education,* Chicago: The University of Chicago Press, 261–273.

Ram, A. (1998). *Education: India, Fifty Years of Independence, 1947–97, Status, Growth and Development.* New Delhi: B.R. Publishing Corporation.

Ramakrishnan, A. K. (2002). *Mahatma Gandhi Rejected Zionism.* Lund: The Transnational Foundation for Peace and Future Research (TFF).

Rattan, R. (1972). *Gandhi's Concept of Political Obligation.* Calcutta: The Minerva Associates.

Rawat, P. L. (1965). *History of Indian Education.* Agra: Ram Prasad & Sons.

Rawnsley, R. (1998). *The Celebration Movement and the Influence of J.F. Herbart on Moral Education in England through the work of Frank Herbert Hayward (1872–1954),* Manchester: University of Manchester.

Rawson, W. (1936) (ed.). *Learning to Live Together: Report of the Dutch Regional Conference of the New Education Fellowship in Untrecht, 14 to 20 September, 1936.* London: New Education Fellowship.

Read, H. (1958). *Education through Art.* London: Faber and Faber.

Reform, Japan Society for History Textbook Reform (1998). *The Restoration of National History—Why was the Japanese Society for History Textbook Reform Established, and What Are its Goals?* Tokyo: Japanese Society for History Textbook Reform.

Richardson, W. and G. Mc Culloch, (2000). *Historical Research in Educational Settings.* Philadelphia: Open University Press.

Rosengren, K. E. (ed.) (1981). *Advances in Content Analysis*. Vol. 9. London: Sage Publications.

Ross, F. H. (1965). *Shinto: the Way of Japan.* Boston: Beacon Press.

Rothermund, I. (1983). *The Aundh Experiment.* Mumbai: Somaiya Publications.

Rouner, L. S. (1995). 'Civil Loyalty and the New India,' in Upendra Baxi and Bhikhu Parekh (eds) *Crises and Change in Contemporary India,* New Delhi: Sage Publications, 169–186.

Roy, R. (ed.) (1986). *Contemporary Crises and Gandhi*. New Delhi: Discovery Publishing House.

Roy, S. (2001). 'What is History'. *Business Standard*, 28 November 2001, 6..

Rudolph, S. H. and I. Llyod, (1972), *Education and Politics in India—Studies in Organization, Society, and Policy.* Massachusetts: Harvard University Press.

Saifullah, Z. (1988). 'Citizen's Involvement in Karnataka's Panchayati Raj Institutions' in D.N. Saxena (ed.) *Citizenship Development and Fundamental Duties,* New Delhi: Abhinav Publications, 88–92.

Saiyidain, K. G. (1957). *Problems of Educational Reconstruction*. Bombay: Asia Publishing House.

Sangal, P. S. (1988). 'Duties of a Citizen: A Legal Perspective', in D.N. Saxena (ed.) *Citizenship Development and Fundamental Duties*, New Delhi: Abhinav Publications, 50–61.

Sarma, D. S. (1949). *The Gandhi Sutras—The Basic Teachings of Mahatma Gandhi.* New York: The Devin-Adair Company.

Saxena, D. N. (1988a). 'Basic Issues and Tasks', in D.N. Saxena (ed.) *Citizenship Development and Fundamental Duties*, New Delhi Abhinav Publications, 149–161.

—— (ed.) (1988b). *Citizenship Development and Fundamental Duties*. New Delhi: Abhinav Publications.

—— (1988c). 'Education and Training for Development of Citizenship Values', in D.N. Saxena (ed.) *Citizenship Development and Fundamental Duties*, New Delhi: Abhinav Publications, 106–120.

Selden, M. and Hein, L. (2000). *Censoring History—Citizenship and Memory in Japan, Germany, and the United States*. New York: M. E. Sharpe Inc.

Sen, S. N. (1969). *Education and the Nation: An Indian Perspective*. Calcutta: Calcutta University Press.

S.G.I. (1996). *The Soka Gakkai International Charter.* [Online] Soka Gakkai International. Available at: http://www.sgi.org/english/SGI/charter.htm. Last Accessed: 27th April 2005.

Sharma, N. (1999). *Value Creators in Education—Japanese Educator Tsunesaburo Makiguchi & Mahatma Gandhi and their Relevance for Indian Education.* 2nd Edition. New Delhi: Regency Publications.

—— (2002). 'Value Creation, Sarvodaya and Participatory Democracy—Three Legacies for a Creative and Democratic World Order through the Process of Education.' *Social Change—Issues and Perspectives, Journal of the Council for Social Development* 32, 99–116.

—— (June 2007). 'Soka Education: Fostering Global Citizens'. *Art of Living—A Buddhist Magazine* 72, 8–10.

Sharma, R. S. (1980). *Ancient India—Class XI.* New Delhi: National Council of Education and Research Training (NCERT).

Sharma, S. (1998). *Culture and Politics: India, Fifty Years of Independence, 1947–97, Status, Growth and Development.* New Delhi: B. R. Publishing Corporation.

Shenoi, P. V. (1990). 'The Constitution: A Socioeconomic Perspective,' in Shyam RatnaUrs Schöttli, and Jürgen Axer (eds) *Citizenship Values in India—Individualism and Social Imperatives,* Calcutta: Mandira, pp. 22–26.

Shibata, M. (2001). *The Education Reform in Japan and Germany under the American Military Occupation after World War Two: a Comparative Study.* Unpublished Ph.D. Thesis. Institute of Education, University of London, London.

—— (2003). 'Destruction and Reconstruction: a Comparative Analysis of the Education Reform in Japan and Germany under the US military occupation after World War Two,' in R.G.D. Phillips (ed.) *Can the Japanese Change their Education System?*" Vol. 12 (1), pp. 43–71, Oxford: Symposium Books.

Shiva, V. (1997). *The Violence of the Green Revolution: Third World Agriculture, Ecology and Politics.* New Delhi: Research Foundation for Science, Technology and Ecology.

Shukla, K. S. (1990). 'Individuals and Institutional Structures,' in Shyam RatnaUrs Schöttli, and Jürgen Axer (eds) *Citizenship Values in India—Individualism and Social Imperatives,* Calcutta: Mandira, pp. 27–32.

Silberman, Bernard S. (1993). *Cages of Reason: The Rise of the Rational State in France, Japan, and the United States, and Great Britain.* Chicago: The University of Chicago Press.

Singh, A. (12 December 2001). *A Real Textbook Case—The BJP has begun to rewrite India's history.* [Online] Available at: www.asiaweek.com. Last Accessed: 15th December 2001.

Singh, R. (1988). *Gandhi and the Modern World.* New Delhi: Classical Publishing Company.

Singh, R.S. (1991). *The Constructive Programs of Mahatma Gandhi: 1920–1939.* New Delhi: Commonwealth.

Sinha, A. N. (1962). *Law of Citizenship and Aliens in India.* London: Asia Publishing House.

Sinha, R. P. (1997). *Inequality in Indian Education.* New Delhi: Vikas Publishing House Pvt. Ltd, New Delhi.

Slater, P. (1966). *Microcosm.* New York: John Wiley.

Sonti, V. R. (2004). Palestine and the Gandhian Ethic. *Essays and Commentary on Contemporary Middle Eastern Issues—An Interactive Online Forum for Scholarly Presentation, Review, and Conversation.* [Online] Available at: http://www.eccmei .net/E/E030.html. Last Accessed 14th October 2004.

Spinks, C. N. (March 1944). 'Indoctrination and Re-Education of Japan's Youth'. *Pacific Affairs* 17(1), 56–70.

Spodek, H. (1971). On the Origins of Gandhi's Political Methodology: The Heritage of Kathiawad and Gujarat. *Journal of Asian Studies* 30, 361–372.

Squires, J. (1993). *Principled Positions—Postmodernism and the Rediscovery of Value.* London: Lawrence & Wishart.

Srivastava, R. S. (1988). 'Building Good Citizenship', in D.N. Saxena (ed.) *Education and Training for Development of Citizenship Values,* New Delhi: Abhinav Publications, 121–130.

Stake, R. (1978). 'The Case Study Method in Social Enquiry'. *Educational Researcher,* 6, 8.

Stake, R. E. (1994). 'Case Studies,' in Y.S. Lincoln (ed.) *Handbook of Qualitative Research,* London: Sage Publications, 236–247.

Stearns, P. N. (1993). *Meaning Over Memory—Recasting the Teaching of Culture and History.* London: The University of North Carolina Press.

Terasaki, M. (ed.) (1999). *Kyoiku Meigen Jiten [The Analects of Education].* Tokyo: Tokyo Shoseki.

Thapar, R. (1987). *Ancient India—Class VI.* New Delhi: National Council of Education and Research Training (NCERT).

The Christian Vernacular Education Society (1889). *Papers on Indian Reform: Sanitary, Material, Social, Moral and Religious.* Verpery: S.P.C.K. Press.

Thimmaiah, G. (1988). 'Behavioural and Attitudinal Norms of Citizens,' in D.N. Saxena (ed.) *Citizenship Development and Fundamental Duties,* New Delhi: Abhinav Publications, 65–70.

Thomas, E. (2000). 'Researching Values in Cross-Cultural Contexts', in R. Gardner, D. Lawton and J. Cairns (eds), *Education for Values: Morals, Ethics and Citizenship in Contemporary Teaching,* London: Kogan Page, 257–272.

Thompson, J. B. (1990). *Ideology and Modern Culture—Critical Social Theory in the Era of Mass Communication.* Cambridge: Polity Press & Blackwell Publishers.

Thomson, M. (1993). *Gandhi and His Ashrams.* New Delhi: Sangam Books.

Tikku, A. (2002). 'Education: Back to Fundamentals?' *The Statesman,* 11 August 2002, 8.

Toda, J. (ed.) (1964). *The Philosophy of Value.* Tokyo: Seikyo Press.

—— (1992). *Toda Josei Zenshu (Collected Writings of Josei Toda).* Tokyo: Seikyo Shimbunsha.

Toffler, A. (1974). *Learning for Tomorrow—the Role of the Future in Education.* New York: Vintage Books.

Tokiomo, K. (1969). *Kindai Nihon Kyoiku Ronshu.* Tokyo: Kokudaisha.

Tolstoy, L. (1893). *The Kingdom of God is Within You-or Christianity Not as a Mystical Doctrine, but as a New Life-Conception.* London: Walter Scott.

Tufte, E. R. (1978). *Political Control of the Economy.* Princeton: Princeton University Press.

Ueda, K. (1993). *Dotoku Kyoikuron.* Tokyo: Reimeishobo.

UNESCO (1969). *Progress of Education in the Asian Region: A Statistical Review.* Bangkok: UNESCO.

UNESCO, International Bureau of Education (2001). 'Learning to Live Together: Have We Failed? A Seminar of the Ideas and Contributions Arising from the Forty-Sixth Session of UNESCO'S International Conference on Education', in *Forty-Sixth Session of UNESCO'S International Conference on Education*, 5–8 September 2001. Geneva: UNESCO, International Bureau of Education.

Unterhalter, E. (2000). 'Transnational Vision of the 1990s: Contrasting Views on Women, Education and Citizenship', in Madeleine Arnot and Jo-Anne Dillabough (eds) *Challenging Democracy: International Perspectives on Gender, Education and Citizenship*, London: Routledge Falmer, 87–102.

Vanaik, A. (1997). *The Furies of Indian Communalism.* London: Verso.

Varma, P. K. (1998). *The Great Indian Middle Class.* New Delhi: Viking.

—— (2004). *Being Indian—The Truth About Why the 21st Century Will Be India's.* New Delhi: Viking.

—— (2005). 'India, the Image of a Budding Superpower'. *The Sunday Times,* [n. d], 8–9.

Vaugier-Chatterjee, A. (ed.) (2004). *Education and Democracy in India.* New Delhi: Manohar.

Verba, S. (1989). 'On Revisiting the Civic Culture: A Personal Postscript', in Gabriel A. Almond and Sidney Verba (eds) *The Civic Culture Revisited*, London: Sage Publications, 394–410.

Vogel, E.F. (1979). *Japan as Number One: Lessons for America.* London: Harvard University Press.

Voice, Y. (2000). *Fitting in or Fighting.* Surrey: Young Voice.

Wallace, A. F. C. (1956). 'Revitalization Movements'. *American Anthropologist* 58, 264–281.

—— (1961). 'Schools in Revolutionary and Conservative Societies', in F.C. Gruber (ed.) *Anthropology and Education*, Philadelphia: University of Pennsylvania Press, 25–54.

Ward, R. (1971). *Japan's Political Systems.* Stanford: Stanford University Press.

Watanabe, T. (2000). 'The Movement and the Japanese Media', in Bryan Wilson and D. Machacek (eds) *Global Citizens—The Soka Gakkai Buddhist Movement in the World*, Oxford: Oxford University Press, 205–231.

Watson, B. (1989). *Gandhi and Nonviolent Resistance: the Non Co-operation Movement of India.* New Delhi: Anmol Publications.

Weber, R.P. and Namenwirth, J.Z. (1987), *Dynamics of Culture.* Winchester: Allen and Unwin.

Weber, R. P. (1990). *Basic Content Analysis.* 2nd Edition. London: Sage Publications.

Weber, T. (1997). 'Gandhism, Optimism and the Gandhians', in Antony Copley and George Paxton (eds) *Gandhi and the Contemporary World—Essays to Mark the 125th anniversary of his Birth*, Chennai: Indo-British Historical Society, 19–31.

—— (1998). *Gandhi is Dead. Long Live Gandhi—the Post-Gandhian Movement in India.* Lund: The Transnational Foundation for Peace and Future Research (TFF).

—— (2004). *Reading Gandhi.* Lund: The Transnational Foundation for Peace and Future Research (TFF).

Wellington, J. (2000). *Educational Research—Contemporary Issues and Practical Approaches*. London: Continnum.

White, H. (1980). 'The Value of Narrativity in the Representation of Reality', in W.T. Mitchell (ed.) *On Narrative*, Chicago: Chicago University Press.

White, P. (1996). *Civic Virtues and Public Schooling—Educating Citizens for a Democratic Society*. New York: Teachers College Press.

Whitehead, H. D. (1924). *Indian Problems in Religion, Education, Politics*. London: Constable & Co. Ltd.

Wiker, B. (2001). Darwin and the Decent of Morality. *First Things* 117, 10–13.

Wilson, B. and D. Ikeda, (1984). *Human Values in a Changing World—A Dialogue on the Social Role of Religion*. New Jersey: Lyle Stuart.

Wilson, M. (1994). *Mahatma Gandhi*. London: ALBSU.

Wolfe, A. (2002). 'The Costs of Citizenship—Assimilation and Multiculturalism in Liberal Democracies' in *Runnymede Conference: Cohesion, Community and Citizenship*, pp. 24–40, London: The Runnymede Trust, London School of Economics.

X, Malcolm. (1968). *The Autobiography of Malcolm X—With the Assistance of Alex Haley*. London: Penguin Books.

Yin, R. K. (2003). *Case Study Research—Design and Methods*. 3rd Edition. London: Sage Publications.

Yoneyama, S. (1999). *The Japanese High School: Silence and Resistance*. New York: Routledge.

Young Voice (2000). *Fitting in or Fighting*. Surrey: Young Voice.

Yoshio, O. (1993). *Dotoku Kyoiku*. Tokyo: Mineruva Shobo.

Zeller, N. (1995). 'Narrative Strategies for Case Reports', in J. Amos Hatch and Richard Wisniewski (eds) *Life History and Narrative*, Vol. 1, pp. 75–88, London: Falmer Press.

Index

211